PROFESSIONAL
SCRUM WITH TEAM FOUNDATION SERVER 2010

PROFESSIONAL

Scrum with Team Foundation
Server 2010

PROFESSIONAL

Scrum with Team Foundation Server 2010

Steve Resnick
Aaron Bjork
Michael de la Maza

WILEY

Wiley Publishing, Inc.

Professional Scrum with Team Foundation Server 2010

Published by
Wiley Publishing, Inc.
10475 Crosspoint Boulevard
Indianapolis, IN 46256
www.wiley.com

Copyright ©2011 by Wiley Publishing, Inc., Indianapolis, Indiana

Published simultaneously in Canada

ISBN: 978-0-470-94333-5
ISBN: 978-1-118-09633-8 (ebk)
ISBN: 978-1-118-09632-1 (ebk)
ISBN: 978-1-118-09631-4 (ebk)

Manufactured in the United States of America

10 9 8 7 6 5 4 3 2

For general information on our other products and services please contact our Customer Care Department within the United States at (877) 762-2974, outside the United States at (317) 572-3993 or fax (317) 572-4002.

Wiley also publishes its books in a variety of electronic formats. Some content that appears in print may not be available in electronic books.

Library of Congress Control Number: 2011924124

To my new friends and colleagues at BlueMetal Architects for your courage to dive in early, and to my old friends and colleagues at Microsoft for the great adventures we shared around the world.

—STEVE RESNICK

To the Team Foundation Server Agile team in Redmond (Phil, Gregg, John, David, Andrew, Zheng, and Kelly), whose hard work resulted in the first release of the Microsoft Visual Studio Scrum process template.

—AARON BJORK

ABOUT THE AUTHORS

 STEVE RESNICK is a founder and managing director of BlueMetal Architects, a consulting and product development firm specializing in IT strategy, architecture, design, and delivery. BlueMetal Architects uses Agile methods to deliver products on time and on budget. Prior to founding BlueMetal Architects, Steve was the chief technology officer at the Microsoft Technology Centers, where he was responsible for organizing distributed teams to develop and deploy solutions in centers around the world. He used Agile methodologies to manage and track small and large projects. Steve has worked with Microsoft technologies since the mid-1990s. He has expertise in high-scale Internet systems, transactional systems, and integration technologies. He co-authored *Essential Windows Communication Foundation* in 2008.

 AARON BJORK is a senior program manager at Microsoft, working on Agile experiences and tooling within Team Foundation Server. Prior to joining Team Foundation Server in 2008, Aaron worked as a software engineer and development lead in Visual Studio. Aaron is passionate about application life cycle management solutions and has a strong desire to see teams improve their software engineering practices. You can follow Aaron on his blog at http://blogs.msdn.com/aaronbjork.

 MICHAEL DE LA MAZA is an Agile coach and trainer whose clients include Carbonite, Intuit, EMC, and Verizon Wireless. He is the Agile practice lead at Knowledge United and developed the 19-course KnowAgile curriculum, which is taught throughout the country. Prior to becoming an Agile coach, Michael was vice president of corporate strategy at Softricity, co-founded Answerfriend (now Inquira), and was a member of the technical staff at MIT Lincoln Laboratory. He holds a Ph.D. in computer science from MIT and can be reached at michael@hearthealthyscrum.com.

ABOUT THE TECHNICAL EDITOR

PHIL DENONCOURT is a .NET consultant who has developed a wide range of .NET applications over the past 10 years. He has over 20 years of experience writing software. He is the leader of the New England C# user group and speaks at many venues in the New England area on a variety of development topics. Phil is certified in a host of .NET technologies, including Team Foundation Server, Windows Communication Foundation, SQL 2008, and ASP.NET. Phil enjoys spending time with his wife and children, and he is an avid fan of Boston sports teams.

CREDITS

EXECUTIVE EDITOR
Bob Elliott

PROJECT EDITORS
Kitty Wilson
Jeff Langr

TECHNICAL EDITOR
Phil Denoncourt

PRODUCTION EDITOR
Daniel Scribner

COPY EDITOR
Kitty Wilson

EDITORIAL DIRECTOR
Robyn B. Siesky

EDITORIAL MANAGER
Mary Beth Wakefield

FREELANCER EDITORIAL MANAGER
Rosemarie Graham

MARKETING MANAGER
Ashley Zurcher

PRODUCTION MANAGER
Tim Tate

VICE PRESIDENT AND EXECUTIVE GROUP PUBLISHER
Richard Swadley

VICE PRESIDENT AND EXECUTIVE PUBLISHER
Barry Pruett

ASSOCIATE PUBLISHER
Jim Minatel

PROJECT COORDINATOR, COVER
Katherine Crocker

PROOFREADER
Scott Klemp, Word One
New York

INDEXER
Robert Swanson

COVER DESIGNER
Ryan Sneed

COVER IMAGE
© Chris Hellyar, iStockPhoto

ACKNOWLEDGMENTS

IT TAKES MORE THAN JUST authors to put words on a page. It starts with friends and family. They encourage us, they tell us our writing is good (even when it's not), they bring us food, they keep us caffeinated. We'd like to thank them for making this book happen.

From Wiley Publishing, we'd like to thank Bob Elliott. Starting with a rough concept, he helped shape the topic to the book you now have in your hands. Special thanks to Kitty Wilson for her editing magic! It's incredible what actual writing talent can do for a book. Thanks to Jeff Langr, who edited during the dark of winter, and Rosemarie Graham, for keeping the book on track.

For technical edits, big thanks to Phil Denoncourt, who validated and challenged our ideas. Chris Bowen, Developer Evangelist at Microsoft, was the great connector who introduced the authors when he heard about the project.

We'd like to offer our appreciation to Jim McCarthy, who was Agile before Agile was cool, for an inspirational foreword and a nod to what's possible.

Special thanks to Paul Hacker and SaaS Made Easy for providing us with our TFS infrastructure in the cloud. We used their hosted TFS to write the book and test what we wrote. Never a hiccup. Three authors with Visual Studio and no infrastructure! If you use TFS and would rather not manage a server, we recommend Paul and team at www.saasmadeeasy.com.

Finally, for us: one Scrum coach, one program manager on the Visual Studio team, and one entrepreneur who's shipping software with Scrum. We learned from each other, we counted on each other, we delivered. Thank you.

CONTENTS

FOREWORD

Agile was always something you could be before it was a particular process you could do. And it was always possible for a team to line up in a tight formation and move together in mutual support toward a goal. Teams performed scrum behaviors long before there was the proper name, Scrum, and long before there were any specified Scrum roles and terminology or any particular Scrum-prescribed deeds to be done.

Just ask the Romans.

So before there was Agile, there was agility, and before there was Scrum, there were teams living and breathing scrumish essence. It is good to remember this. Beginning in 1992, I was part of just such an agile, scrumish team, the original Visual C++ team at Microsoft, a truly great software team that pioneered many of the ways a software team could show actual agility. The number and extent of this team's accomplishments are staggering and have been pretty thoroughly documented elsewhere. No real history of software development processes and/or teamwork can safely ignore a team that was surely among the most agile of all commercial software teams.

In a period of about four years, this team, using specific agility-demanding-and-exploiting techniques, coalesced almost like magic and went on — in a sequence of increasingly impressive product releases — to reduce its previously victorious competition to a memory and to set business, technical, and process standards that define key aspects of the programming and general software development environment in which we live and create today. Take this team's standard behaviors, add pair programming, a pinch of nomenclature, and voilà! You have the fundamentals of today's most desired project practices, as defined by Agile, which first appeared in the next decade.

It is natural and fitting, therefore, that such winning practices eventually become a type of orthodoxy, that their characteristics become normative, and that technology evolve to embody tools supporting these best practices. That such technology can be found in Visual Studio is doubly fitting (and personally satisfying), given its heritage. That Visual Studio should proffer such technology also provides a certain nice self-referential quality and a pleasing reminder of the larger fractal reality in which software development always takes place.

The present volume promises to elucidate for the reader the ways and means of conducting the prevailing best practices using the prevailing technology. It is time, and past time, for such a book describing such a reality. Its publication marks a particular moment in the evolution of things: when technique and technology have aligned in time.

The current moment is one wherein a technology is synergistically both created by and creates a technique. In this case, Scrum and Agile (techniques) create and henceforward co-evolve with TFS and Visual Studio (technologies).

So it shall likely be; as it is ever so.

It is commonplace to observe that things go faster and faster. Thirty-five years ago, there was essentially nothing to program except a few ungainly huge and hugely limited machines. And twenty years ago, there was no way to program all the things there were with any sort of predictable result. Today, I think it can be safely stated, if you carefully follow the advice in this book, and if you connect with the rational energy or the results-oriented spirit of the technical culture that gave rise to — and lies behind — Agile, Scrum, and TFS, you will be able to deliver software of a desired degree of stability at a desired time and at the anticipated expense.

But please notice that, historically speaking, it is only just now that we can reliably develop software. That we can now do so will have profound impact on our world. We can expect even greater technical change than heretofore, and soon — and ever sooner still as time progresses. While our burgeoning technical culture is more a nascence than a Renaissance, there is no reason to expect that it will be of any less import. There is every reason to expect that it will be global, deeply unifying, and promotional of the freedom of information and people.

Since software is basically the codification and distribution of intelligence, and we can now do more and more of it, faster and better, what happens next? Now that we can generate software at will, and, using practices like Scrum and technology like TFS, we can deliver it more or less as desired. What, then, shall we do with this brand-new, unlimited, and unimaginably great power? What civilization shall we build? What intelligence shall we distribute?

These are the questions to ask an Agile team — and to ask only an Agile team — because only such a team can reasonably even consider the questions. When they gather up, when they Scrum, when they charge downfield together toward a goal in a mutually supportive way, a goal they will therefore surely reach, just what goal is worth hitting? What world do they choose to build?

What is your vision?

Master the lessons in and around this book, and then answer that question in what you create.

Jim McCarthy
Woodinville, Washington
2011

INTRODUCTION

LET'S FACE IT: Shipping great software is difficult. Is it rewarding? Yes. Is it profitable? Yes. Does it mix art and engineering? Yes. Is it easy? No.

Yet some companies and organizations do ship great software. They deliver products that their customers love. They do it on time and on budget. They deliver solutions and services that are highly valued in the marketplace. So how do they do it?

The answer is deceptively simple: They rely on a combination of technology, talent, and process. Each of these three elements is necessary, but each by itself is insufficient to deliver a great product. If you're missing one element, you will certainly fail. If you have all three, then you have the necessary raw ingredients to succeed.

This book focuses on one element of shipping great software: the process. It offers a road map for how to use Scrum to organize teams and activities. It shows you how to use Visual Studio Team Foundation Server (TFS) to execute a Scrum project — from planning the sprints to tracking progress. By focusing on just this one ingredient in successful software, this book provides the details you need.

In this book, you'll learn best practices for running a Scrum project and for using TFS. The book even includes templates to help you get started. Even with all this help, you will still face difficult questions for which there is no standard answers. You'll need to rely on your insight and experience.

This book is a collaborative effort of three authors with three distinct perspectives. We believe that by offering multiple views, we'll better prepare you to navigate the unique situations that you'll undoubtedly face. Each of us has years of experience with Scrum and project management. We've each shipped successful products, and we all write from experience.

It is our hope that our experience in software project management can accelerate you on your path to shipping great software with Scrum and TFS.

WHO THIS BOOK IS FOR

This book is for software developers and managers who are interested in using Scrum and TFS to build and ship great software. If you're new to Scrum and haven't used TFS before, this book is a great starting point. If you have experience with Scrum but you're new to TFS, then this book can be your guide to applying what you already know with a new tool. Finally, if you have experience with Scrum and you've used the other team management templates within TFS, then reading this book is a great way to learn the new features of the Scrum 1.0 template.

We don't assume that you have great familiarity with Scrum. Chapters 1 through 4 are enough to get you started. Of course, one book isn't a substitute for training, and training is not as effective as coaching, and coaching alone is no substitute for real experience, but this book will help you at any level. We can say that because it's not a book about just Scrum and it's not a book about just TFS. Each of those topics fills entire books on its own. This book is specifically written to help you use a great tool, TFS, to implement a great process, Scrum. It's a practical guide to doing it.

Everyone on a Scrum team is responsible for shipping the product, so everyone needs to understand the process and tools. This is one of the unique characteristics of Scrum: The whole team — not just the project leads — is responsible for shipping. Because everyone needs to know the process and tools, this book can be helpful for everyone on the team.

Finally, project sponsors will find this book helpful. You may be the business executive who funded a project, the manager who hired a consulting firm to build a product, or a venture capitalist who funded a company. If your team is using Scrum, you should be grounded in its principles. You'll find the early chapters helpful and can refer your teams to the later sections.

WHAT THIS BOOK COVERS

In writing this book, we set out to cover everything you need to run a Scrum project with TFS. It's an ambitious goal but constrained enough that we believe we've delivered. We assume that you're familiar with Visual Studio but not too familiar with TFS. We assume that you've been on software development teams before, although maybe you've never run a project by yourself.

HOW THIS BOOK IS STRUCTURED

This book is organized into 11 chapters and 2 appendixes.

Chapter 1, "Shipping Software"

This introductory chapter focuses on the basics of software project management — initiating a project, allocating resources, and organizing the team. It describes three common methodologies — Scrum, MSF, and Waterfall — and compares their essential attributes. We look at how each of these methodologies organizes teams, what its process looks like, and how it tracks progress and milestones. By the time you finish the chapter, you'll be able to translate your experience in one of the other methodologies into the common terms of Scrum.

Chapter 2, "Organizing a Scrum Team"

This chapter describes the organization of a Scrum team. It introduces the roles and responsibilities of an effective team. It describes the interactions among team members on a typical project. This chapter also discusses ways to scale a team to handle larger or more complex efforts.

This chapter also reviews the typical organization of MSF and Waterfall projects. It does this for two reasons. First, if you're familiar with those methodologies but new to Scrum, this chapter will help you understand the Scrum team organization. Second, by comparing the three team organizations, you can gain insight into how similar functions are accomplished using different methods.

There are only three roles in Scrum — product owner, ScrumMaster, and team member — but there are many more within IT. Recognizing this disparity, we put the Scrum team in the context of the broader IT community. We briefly discuss how traditional IT roles, such as database administrator and architect, are handled in Scrum.

By the end of this chapter, you'll have a good understanding of how to organize a Scrum team and how to transition from one method to another.

Chapter 3, "Tracking What's Important in Team Foundation Server"

This chapter introduces you to the tracking and reporting functions of TFS. Many developers and managers are familiar with the source control, or automated build capabilities, of TFS. However, the Scrum template builds on the tracking and reporting features in TFS.

Scrum artifacts, including the product backlog, tasks, test cases, and bugs, are all stored in TFS. Rather than just describing how and where these are stored, this chapter puts them in the context of a Scrum project. The goal of this chapter is to give you a good grounding in what you should track and how to do it with the Scrum template.

Chapter 4, "Getting Started with the TFS Scrum Template"

If you're already comfortable with Scrum and have a good understanding of TFS, you might want to start with this chapter. It begins with step-by-step instructions for downloading and installing the Scrum 1.0 template. It then goes through all the high-level steps of a Scrum project.

You'll learn how to define product backlog items (PBIs) from user stories through acceptance criteria. You'll learn how to estimate PBIs using Planning Poker. You'll also learn about the burndown chart, a basic tracking tool for Scrum. In addition, you'll learn how to use TFS to initiate and track releases, sprints, and quality.

By the time you finish this chapter, you will know how to use TFS to enter and track Scrum artifacts.

Chapter 5, "Work Items, Queries, and Reports"

This chapter goes step-by-step through the major Scrum artifacts and provides guidance and insight into how to use them in TFS. It describes each Scrum artifact in terms of its intent and data fields. The chapter also provides examples of how to fill them out and what value they deliver to the Scrum process.

This chapter describes areas, tasks, releases, sprints, impediments, bugs, and test cases. It also describes the two primary ways to work with these items in TFS: by using queries and reports. TFS enables you to create sophisticated reports in Excel, and this chapter describes how in detail.

After reading this chapter, you'll know how to use the Scrum artifacts for your specific project and how to use TFS to manage them.

Chapter 6, "The Product Backlog"

The product backlog is the queue of features to be built, the user needs to be met, and the bugs to be fixed. Managed by the product owner, the product backlog represents the single stream of input to the team. It's central to Scrum.

In this chapter, you'll learn how to create PBIs and how to use the various fields that they contain. PBIs are related to other Scrum artifacts in TFS. In this chapter you'll learn how to link them to test cases, bugs, and tasks. You'll learn how to do this using Visual Studio as well as Excel.

By the end of this chapter, you will have a solid understanding of the role of PBIs and how to manage them in TFS.

Chapter 7, "Tracking Quality"

This chapter describes three aspects of tracking and managing quality: test cases, bugs, and tasks. First, you'll learn how to use TFS to enter and track test cases. You'll see how to create test plans, individual test cases, and shared steps, and you'll learn how to handle manual and automated test cases. This chapter reviews the built-in reports you can use to assess your test plan readiness.

After discussing test plans and test cases, this chapter covers how bugs are stored and tracked in TFS. Like PBIs, bugs represent work that must be estimated, scheduled, and completed. They can be linked to tasks and other elements. As with PBIs, you can work with them in Visual Studio or Excel. This chapter describes the steps involved.

Chapter 8, "Running a Release"

This chapter is where you start to see the big picture — using TFS to manage a product release with Scrum. This chapter starts by defining what a release is in TFS and then describes the PBIs for the release.

In Chapters 5 and 6, you learned how to enter PBIs. In this chapter, you work with PBIs as part of a release. This chapter offers practical advice on what makes a good user story and how to test it. It presents success patterns and failure patterns. You will learn how PBIs relate to tasks in the context of a project and how to efficiently use Excel to monitor progress.

By the end of this chapter, you will know how to define the Scrum artifacts for a release.

Chapter 9, "Running a Sprint"

Sprints are a hallmark of Scrum. A sprint is a fixed time period during which a team builds a set of product features. This chapter describes how to create and track sprint progress in TFS.

Scrum measures sprint and release progress by tracking PBIs. The rate at which PBIs are implemented is the velocity. A common way to track PBIs and the associated velocity is by using a burndown chart. In this chapter, you'll learn how to measure velocity and how to track PBIs by using a burndown chart.

Chapter 10, "The Retrospective"

One advantage of iterative development is that your team can change how it operates after each iteration. You can change the team, change the duration of a sprint, and change the pace of development. In a very real sense, this makes a team agile. Ideally, changes that you introduce between iterations will improve the quality or velocity of subsequent iterations.

Scrum formalizes this process in a meeting called a retrospective. In this chapter, you'll learn how to run a retrospective meeting and how to use TFS to capture information from the team.

Chapter 11, "Improving Scrum by Using Spikes"

A spike is a time-boxed technical investigation that is meant to produce the answer to a problem that is blocking a team. It's used when the team is facing decisions that will significantly affect subsequent sprints. The primary difference between a sprint and a spike is that sprints produce customer-valued features, while spikes answer technical or design questions that must be answered in order to move the project forward.

This chapter describes how to use spikes within a release. Should you run them earlier or later? Should you run them in parallel with sprints or as mini-sprints? When you finish reading the chapter, you'll know when and how to run spikes within a Scrum release.

Appendix A, "Working with Scrum Assessments"

TFS is the primary tool for storing and tracking Scrum artifacts and driving a project forward. To help get you started with the various meetings and ceremonies that occur in Scrum, this appendix includes some templates. It offers a template for the daily Scrum, the end-of-sprint retrospective, the sprint planning meeting, and the product demo.

We, the authors of this book, have used the templates included in this appendix in the field. Using these templates is an effective way to ensure consistency and quality across projects.

Appendix B, "References"

There are many good books and helpful websites available for Agile software project management in general and Scrum in particular. They tend to be quite readable and offer complementary and differing viewpoints on the topic. In this appendix, we list the resources we've used over the years to learn and master the topic.

WHAT YOU NEED TO USE THIS BOOK

To get the most out of this book, you need a few tools and an open mind. For tools, you need Microsoft Visual Studio 2010, Team Foundation Server, and Microsoft Office. Having an open mind will help you transition from the old way of running software projects to Scrum.

There are many versions of Visual Studio 2010. Fortunately, they all ship with access to Team Foundation Server. If you're doing high-end development, then the higher-end versions of Visual Studio 2010 are worth purchasing. The versions are listed on Microsoft's website, at www.microsoft .com/visualstudio/. With only one exception, all versions of Visual Studio 2010 will work for the features described in this book. Microsoft Test Manager, which is briefly described in Chapter 7, ships only with the Ultimate and Test Professional editions.

You need a copy of Office. We recommend Office 2010, but Office 2007 will suffice. If you're still using an old version of Office, do yourself a favor: Upgrade.

You need a copy of Team Foundation Server 2010 (TFS), which ships with Visual Studio. To install TFS, you need IIS, SQL Server, and Windows SharePoint Services. The installation is surprisingly easy if you have the underlying platform properly configured. You can install TFS directly on hardware, or you can install it in a virtual machine. As you might imagine, Hyper-V works very well for this purpose.

As an alternative to installing TFS on local hardware, you can use a hosting provider. If you sign up with a reliable provider, the experience is flawless. All the examples in this book were created using a hosted version of TFS, through the hosting company SaaS Made Easy (www.saasmadeeasy.com). SaaS Made Easy is one of the leading TFS providers in Microsoft's BizSpark program. The company provides excellent service for TFS hosting — at a reasonable price. If you don't want to install TFS locally, try using SaaS Made Easy.

As mentioned earlier, in addition to needing some software, you need an open mind. Transitioning from one way of doing things to another can be difficult. Truth be told, the best practices for software development haven't changed much since Jim McCarthy wrote *Dynamics of Software Development* nearly 20 years ago. But Scrum does codify techniques so they can be repeated and improved over time. So keep an open mind and watch for big opportunities.

CONVENTIONS

To help you get the most from the text and keep track of what's happening, we've used a number of conventions throughout the book.

> *Boxes with a warning icon like this one hold important, not-to-be forgotten information that is directly relevant to the surrounding text.*

> *The pencil icon indicates notes, tips, hints, tricks, and asides to the current discussion.*

ERRATA

We make every effort to ensure that there are no errors in the text. However, no one is perfect, and mistakes do occur. If you find an error in one of our books, we would be very grateful for your feedback. By sending in errata you may save another reader hours of frustration and at the same time you will be helping us provide even higher quality information.

To find the errata page for this book, go to www.wrox.com and locate the title using the Search box or one of the title lists. Then, on the book details page, click the Book Errata link. On this page you can view all errata that has been submitted for this book and posted by Wrox editors. A complete book list including links to each book's errata is also available at www.wrox.com/ misc-pages/booklist.shtml.

If you don't spot "your" error on the Book Errata page, go to www.wrox.com/contact/ techsupport.shtml and complete the form there to send us the error you have found. We'll check the information and, if appropriate, post a message to the book's errata page and fix the problem in subsequent editions of the book.

P2P.WROX.COM

For author and peer discussion, join the P2P forums at http://p2p.wrox.com. The forums are a Web-based system for you to post messages relating to Wrox books and related technologies and interact with other readers and technology users. The forums offer a subscription feature to e-mail you topics of interest of your choosing when new posts are made to the forums. Wrox authors, editors, other industry experts, and your fellow readers are present on these forums.

At http://p2p.wrox.com you will find a number of different forums that will help you not only as you read this book, but also as you develop your own applications. To join the forums, just follow these steps:

1. Go to http://p2p.wrox.com and click the Register link.

2. Read the terms of use and click Agree.

3. Complete the required information to join as well as any optional information you wish to provide and click Submit.

4. You will receive an e-mail with information describing how to verify your account and complete the joining process.

 You can read messages in the forums without joining P2P, but in order to post your own messages, you must join.

Once you join, you can post new messages and respond to messages other users post. You can read messages at any time on the Web. If you would like to have new messages from a particular forum e-mailed to you, click the Subscribe to this Forum icon by the forum name in the forum listing.

For more information about how to use the Wrox P2P, be sure to read the P2P FAQs for answers to questions about how the forum software works as well as many common questions specific to P2P and Wrox books. To read the FAQs, click the FAQ link on any P2P page.

Shipping Software

WHAT'S IN THIS CHAPTER?

➤ Understanding what you need to ship software: vision, insight, resources, planning, and product features.

➤ Understanding three approaches to management methodologies: Scrum, MSF, and Waterfall.

➤ Comparing the three project management methodologies.

This chapter covers the high-level process of shipping software. You'll learn how to start with a compelling vision and the resources you need to build a product. You'll also learn about the relationship among competing constraints. You'll read about three popular software project management techniques: Scrum, Microsoft Solutions Framework (MSF), and Waterfall. By the end of this chapter, you'll be able to use what you know about the MSF and Waterfall methods to gain insight into Scrum.

This book is about using a specific tool, Visual Studio Team Foundation Server (TFS), to support the Scrum process for shipping great software. The fundamental concept is to put customer value at the center of everything you do. While maximizing customer value, you also maximize your team's productivity and predictability with each release, creating a sustainable team environment for shipping great software. In this book, you'll learn how to use the tools in TFS to manage a software development project using Scrum.

WHAT DO YOU NEED TO SHIP SOFTWARE?

Before you can ship great software, you need to build it. Before you can build it, you need to envision how it might work and look. Before you can envision it, you need to know why and how someone would use it. And before that, you need insight into the problem you're trying to solve. So, shipping great software really begins with vision and insight into how something works, how it can be improved, and why people care.

This section discusses the following requirements for shipping software:

➤ Vision

➤ Insight

➤ Resources

➤ Planning

➤ Product features

Vision

Great software starts with a great vision. It starts with a simple description of what you're setting out to build, for whom, and why. If you can't define this before starting the project, you should think about it some more. Creating software requires a surprising amount of resources, and you need to have a compelling vision in order to attract and allocate the resources you'll need.

The *vision* should be a meaningful description of the product goals and an inspiring outcome. It doesn't need to be melodramatic — helping the world's neediest people or creating the world's newest billionaire — but it must resonate with all stakeholders. The vision should describe the needs and benefits in terms that the user cares about. It should describe the problem being solved and the opportunity in solving it. The vision should pique the interest of customers, sponsors, and the project team.

The product vision should be relatively short; a few paragraphs generally suffice. It should include a description of the problem and opportunity as well as the solution and the benefit. Everyone on the project team will read it. They will talk to their colleagues, friends, and families about it. It should be clear yet comprehensive enough to resonate with these audiences.

The product vision is typically accompanied by a definition of scope. The *scope* clearly sets the path for the vision, from problem to solution. It should include high-level features, time lines, and constraints. You can define the scope of a prototype, a beta, and the first few releases. Earlier milestones should have greater granularity; later milestones can be more vague. The scope should clearly define what is being proposed and what is not being proposed.

Often, the vision and scope are combined into a single document, cleverly called a *vision/scope*. This document is the first opportunity to define a series of releases. Thinking and communicating in terms of successive releases is critical with Scrum. You can define the rough features that will be in each release, so everyone learns to expect incremental progress as the team iterates toward the solution.

For example, say you enjoy fantasy football, a game in which you create virtual football teams that compete based on the statistics of the individual players. The fantasy football sites have great features for building teams and leagues, but they don't combine that with great search capabilities. Using Google or Bing for searching just doesn't give you the data you want. In a moment of inspiration, you decide to fix the problem by building a search engine for this purpose. You could create the following vision for this product:

Create a search engine for fantasy sports enthusiasts.

Based on your vision, the reader will conjure up ideas about what the product may do. It's a good start, but this vision, as stated, is much broader than your intent. Your idea involved fantasy football, and the vision you've created could be interpreted much more broadly. Therefore, you might rewrite the vision as follows:

> *Many websites are available for fantasy football leagues. They have great features but lack powerful search capabilities. We will create a fantasy football search engine so that fans have access to more data and can create the best teams.*

This is better, as it constrains the problem to what you initially had in mind — fantasy football. It also adds a purpose: creating the best teams. Now you need to scope the problem. You want to solve the problem for fantasy football, but you also realize that the solution would work just as well with other sports. So you can broaden the vision and then constrain it with the scope:

> *Many websites are available for fantasy sports leagues. They have great features but lack powerful search capabilities. We will create a fantasy sports search engine so that fans have access to more data and can create the best teams.*

> *The immediate market for fantasy sports is 50 dedicated websites, reaching over 3 million users. The indirect market, including news and sports sites, is approximately 500 sites that reach over 20 million people.*

> *The first release will target American football and provide an interface for existing websites. It will contain data for all NFL teams and will support parametric searches on player characteristics. Subsequent releases will add more sports leagues; will support features for managing teams, players, standings, and trading; and will have an interface for mobile apps.*

From this vision/scope, the reader will have an idea of the problem being solved, the benefit of the solution, and the iterative path for expanding the product over time. After this, you can define a business case, technical solution concept, and critical assumptions.

 There are many examples of vision/scope documents online. They commonly have sections for vision, requirements, solution, assumptions, limitations, and risks. While Scrum doesn't prescribe a vision/scope document prior to initiating a project, it's a best practice to create one in software project management as it forces you to articulate the big picture.

Insight

It's one thing to have a great vision; it's quite another to turn that vision into a great product. This is true of engineering in general and software engineering in particular. Product management has a broad role in engineering and design. It involves translating the needs and desires of the user or market into instructions for engineering. (We use the term *instructions* very loosely here, as it may take the form of requirements, storyboards, user stories, mockups, visual comps, or other design artifacts.)

As you'll read in Chapter 2, product management is an essential element of Scrum. Say that you're working with a highly skilled, cohesive, experienced engineering team. And say that the working environment allows the team to flourish. This is a great start, but it's insufficient to build a successful product. In this case, the success of the product depends on product management. Specifically, it depends on product management to determine what's needed, by whom, why, and at what cost.

The product owner, who fills the product management role in Scrum, is embedded in the Scrum team and is counted on to know the user intimately. This person must know the user's likes and dislikes, tolerances, and aspirations. The product owner must know what the users love, what they don't like, and what they don't care about. Essentially, the product owner must have insight into how the user will value the product.

As you'll read further in this chapter and Chapters 2 and 3, Scrum is an Agile process for developing software. It prescribes planning and design up front, and it involves more planning and design as you iteratively build the solution. It's far from random and far from chaotic, but it does move fast and allows for unexpected results. Because of this, the product owner's insight into user needs is essential.

Several factors drive the need for insight in the product owner role in Scrum:

- ➤ **Decision making** — One person, rather than a group, makes product management decisions. Decisions are made faster than in traditional software creation, but if the product owner lacks sufficient insight into the problem, he or she will make wrong decisions or lack confidence to make any decisions at all.

- ➤ **Minimal prototyping** — There is minimal prototyping before the project starts because it's done in early sprints of the project. This means the product owner's insight will quickly be reflected in the product.

- ➤ **Iterative nature** — The product features are defined iteratively and frequently. They come in and out of scope based on product owner decisions, which directly impact the value of the product.

- ➤ **Customer feedback** — Customer feedback comes early and often. Good insight is necessary to sift out valuable data from extraneous data.

Resources

Building a software product is a very resource-intensive activity. It requires people from many different disciplines working together toward a common goal. These people include visual designers, domain experts, software developers, and product managers. Depending on the domain, building software may also require business analysts, security experts, information architects, and marketing specialists.

It's easy to underestimate the true cost of building production-quality software. When you wrote your first computer program, it was pretty easy: You were the designer, developer, tester, and possibly customer. Indeed, it was a lot of fun, and that's how many of us got hooked on creating software.

Building a commercial product is much more difficult than creating software for yourself. You need to clearly understand what the customer wants before you can start building. You need to know how much the customer is willing to spend before you begin to buy technology or hire the team for the job. Whether you're building something for just one customer or thousands, the work requires significantly more resources than building something for your own use.

> *As you'll see later in this chapter when we compare different strategies for software project management, Scrum optimizes resources by iterating toward a solution. This enables you to adjust your plans along the way, based on the realities you encounter with technology, the team, and customers.*

Time and Money

You need many resources to build and ship a great software product. At the highest level, you need time and money. To be sure, these are not interchangeable, no matter how much you have of either.

The saying "Timing is everything" holds quite true in software development. A perfect product released at the wrong time is generally not very useful. It may be interesting or thought provoking, and it may even be amusing, but if the timing is wrong, the product won't be useful. Similarly, the wrong product at the right time isn't very useful either. It may garner a lot of attention because of its potential, but if the product is lacking some critical element, it won't be very successful. On the other hand, the right product at the right time is very valuable: Even if it has flaws, if you release the right product at the right time, you'll have a success on your hands.

AN EXAMPLE OF A GOOD PRODUCT WITH PERFECT TIMING

One example of the right product at the right time was Microsoft Windows 95. It was a good product with perfect timing. It was the early 1990s, and Microsoft was developing Windows 95 as the next operating system for personal computing, gaming, and business productivity. But a confluence of events occurred during its development cycle that made Microsoft rethink its plan. The Mosaic browser was written and distributed as Netscape Navigator; Senator Al Gore sponsored legislation to increase investments in the publicly funded Internet; and consumer websites such as Amazon, eBay, and Yahoo! began to create real value. Microsoft faced a dilemma: Should it delay Windows 95 until it could include a web browser, or should it ship Windows 95 without one and continue to develop an integrated browser in parallel?

Microsoft knew that people would be upgrading their PCs to get to the Internet, and the company didn't want to miss the opportunity to sell those people an operating system. Microsoft chose the latter route and released Window 95 without a browser but in time to catch the Internet wave. While Windows 95 was far from perfect, its timing was ideal. Windows 95 was included on hundreds of millions of computers, and this cemented Microsoft's place as the desktop of choice for the next decade.

People and Technology

Unlike time, money can easily be converted to other resources you might need. Two obvious resources you need for software development are people and equipment.

For people, you'll likely want a mix of generalists and specialists. You'll need product managers to define the feature set that exactly meets your client's needs. You'll need software architects to stay with the project from beginning to end and to define the technical architecture and design patterns for the product. You may need user interface specialists, database specialists, security experts, and performance-tuning engineers. The bulk of the technical work will likely be done by generalists: engineers skilled in coding and testing.

If your project needs a high percentage of specialists rather than generalists, you might want to increase your time and cost estimates. Finding and replacing specialists can be a more time-consuming and costly activity than swapping generalists.

You can convert money into people by hiring a team. Some team members will be employees — people you want to retain for the duration of the project and beyond. Others will be contractors — people with specialized skills that you need during certain phases of the project.

You'll also need to convert money into technology. You can buy it, lease it, or rent it for remote access. This is true for both hardware and software. You can allocate technology to problems as they arise and then shift resources (such as money) as circumstances change. For instance, you may need significant hardware capacity during a performance-testing phase of a project. In this case, you can acquire the technology on a temporary basis and then shift it elsewhere when you're done.

Planning

Planning is an essential ingredient in shipping great software. Planning takes a great deal of time before a project begins and even more time once a project is under way. This is true whether you're using Scrum or another project management methodology. Depending on which methodology you use, the specific planning activities will vary dramatically.

For instance, planning a project using a traditional software development methodology involves allocating time for requirements definition, design, development, testing, user acceptance, release management, and support. Software development occurs solely during the development phase. Planning a project using Scrum involves allocating time to build features in fixed-duration "sprints." During each sprint, the team conducts the same activities as in the Waterfall method, but it does so in a small set of features. Figure 1-1 shows a high-level view of Waterfall and Scrum planning.

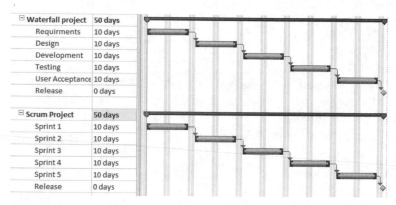

FIGURE 1-1: Waterfall and Scrum planning.

 The Waterfall method of project management is the method most commonly used to run software projects. When using the Waterfall method, you schedule tasks sequentially, completing one phase of activity before beginning the next. Later in the chapter, in the "Approaches to Project Management" section, we'll look more closely at the Waterfall method and compare it with Scrum.

One place where Scrum is different from traditional software project management methodologies (such as the Waterfall method) is with respect to predictability. Waterfall assumes that you can predict how long tasks will take. You allocate people and time to tasks and then schedule them accordingly. Scrum assumes the opposite. You cannot accurately predict how long something will take unless you've done it with the same resources (technology and people) before.

If you cannot predict how long a single task will take, how can you predict how long a whole series of tasks will take? Using Scrum, you accept the fact that you can't. Rather than predict the product schedule, you predict smaller units of work that can be completed within a sprint. At the end of each sprint, features are complete and can be included in a potentially shippable product. This way, you predict features by time rather than predicting time by features, which is essentially a time-box approach.

A sprint is the smallest cycle time within Scrum. Chapter 9 focuses on running sprints. Sprints can be as long as a month or two and as short as a day or two. The ScrumMaster decides the duration before the sprint begins. Each sprint starts with a sprint planning meeting, during which the team looks at the product backlog and decides which features to build during the sprint. The team members use their experience in the previous sprint(s) to predict how much they can accomplish in the next sprint. This is significantly different from the Waterfall method, which involves predicting the release and features up front and allocating time and people to the tasks.

Figure 1-2 shows a Gantt chart from a project planned using the Waterfall method. Note that each task is scheduled with a known duration. If a task completes early or late, this will impact all other tasks in the release. This works well if you have a high degree of confidence in your task estimates, but it falls apart quickly if the estimates are incorrect.

In a Scrum project, you must plan tasks. Software project management requires a lot of planning, and Scrum doesn't change that need. However, rather than plan tasks to manage dependencies, you plan tasks to manage feature delivery. The team focuses on building the product rather than keeping to the schedule. The schedule in Scrum is simple: It's the sprint cycle. Planning within a sprint focuses on the product

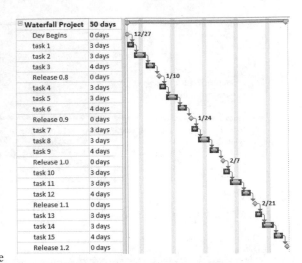

FIGURE 1-2: Waterfall method Gantt chart.

rather than the schedule because the schedule is so simple. Figure 1-3 shows a project artifact that you'll use for intra-sprint planning. This report, and many others like it, is covered in Chapter 6.

	A	B	C	D	E	F
			Project: TFSBook **Server:** tfs01.tfsmadeeasy.com\BluemetalCollection **Query:** PBIs Committed and their Tasks **List type:** Flat			
2	ID	Work Item Type	Title	Assigned To	State	Remaining Work
3	316	Product Backlog I	Find orders	Aaron Bjork	Committed	
4	317	Task	Build the find control	Michael de la Maza	In Progress	2
5	318	Task	Exploratory testing on the find control	Steve Resnick	In Progress	1
6	319	Task	Design the order find results	Michael de la Maza	In Progress	2
7	320	Task	UX review on all find features	Steve Resnick	To Do	2
8	321	Task	Build the controller for the find results page	Steve Resnick	To Do	3
9	322	Task	Exploratory testing on the find resutls	Michael de la Maza	To Do	3
10	334	Task	Build the search algorthim	Michael de la Maza	To Do	5
11	323	Product Backlog I	RSS feeds	Aaron Bjork	Committed	
12	324	Task	Build SOAP handler	Michael de la Maza	To Do	5
13	325	Task	Build the RSS service provider	Steve Resnick	To Do	3
14	326	Task	Optimize database calss for RSS results	Aaron Bjork	To Do	3
15	327	Task	Test the feed with different clients	Michael de la Maza	To Do	2
16	328	Task	Run the feed through perf scenarios and measure res	Aaron Bjork	To Do	1
17	329	Task	Enable for all types of data	Steve Resnick	To Do	1
18	330	Task	Exploratory testing for all	Aaron Bjork	To Do	2
19	331	Product Backlog I	Customer search	Aaron Bjork	Committed	
20	332	Task	Build and review the data interaction layer	Michael de la Maza	To Do	2
21	333	Task	Implement search from the landing page	Steve Resnick	To Do	4
22	335	Task	Design the search results screen	Steve Resnick	To Do	2
23	336	Task	Design the UI interactions	Steve Resnick	To Do	1
24	339	Task	Run example queries	Michael de la Maza	To Do	10
25	340	Task	Verify page load speed	Michael de la Maza	To Do	20
26	361	Task	Implement Autofill for as many fields as possible in c	Aaron Bjork	To Do	

FIGURE 1-3: A Scrum project artifact.

An artifact *is something that is useful to a project but isn't part of the product itself. Common examples of artifacts are task lists, schedules, and test cases. Figure 1-3 shows a list that combines backlog items and tasks, to easily organize and use them together.*

Budget Planning

It is extremely difficult to accurately forecast the cost of software development before you start. We all wish this weren't the case, but indeed it is. There are many unknowns in the factors that impact cost, such as requirements, technology choices, and team composition. For instance, while you may have a list of high-level or even detailed requirements, you may be two or three steps removed from the source of the requirements when you're preparing the estimate. Or, while you may assume that technology used on a previous project is good for this one, you may get into unfamiliar territory when working on specific features for this new project. And, in the realm of people, you may not be able to assume that a specific person will be on the project team. Rather, you tend to work with roles such as senior architect or database developer when estimating projects.

The project management triangle in Figure 1-4 depicts the three constraints that define a project: cost, time, and features. If you have a full understanding of the features, you'll be able to provide an accurate estimate of the cost and time. This is the case in auto repair and home renovation, so why not with software? The answer has to do with unknowns; in the world of software, you can't know everything before you start. And what you don't know will have to be factored into the triangle, resulting in varying costs, times, and features.

 Some people and texts refer to the project management triangle as an "iron triangle" to highlight the fact that you cannot bend it to suit your needs.

Because of these unknowns and the fixed constraints in the triangle, you simply cannot offer a fixed-cost commitment for a fixed-feature product. You therefore have two alternatives: Vary the cost or vary the features. If you must deliver a fixed budget, then the answer is simple: Vary the features.

Scrum offers this alternative. The cost of a Scrum team can be fixed. If you have two product owners, six team members, and one ScrumMaster, then you can add up their weekly wages to determine the weekly cost. If sprints are fixed at four weeks, then you know that a sprint will cost four times the weekly cost of the team. Now you can accurately predict the cost and duration of a sprint. However, customers rarely pay for sprints; they pay for products. This leaves the third element of the triangle: features.

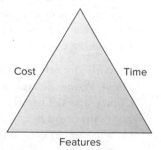

FIGURE 1-4: The project management triangle.

You need a well-developed product backlog. The backlog items must be ranked into a list, based on the value they deliver to the customer. By looking at the prioritized backlog, you can identify the first set of backlog items to implement. You might even be able to identify the second or third set of related backlog items. In other words, by working with the backlog, you can make a reasonable estimate of how much you can get done within a fixed time period. Your estimate is for a fixed time period with a fixed team, but the feature set that you deliver will vary. The Scrum approach therefore meets the goals of budgetary control and also addresses the realities of software development with respect to unknowns.

People Planning

Scrum projects are inherently team-driven activities, with all members involved with all aspects of the project. The team composition is simple, with just 3 roles defined. Team size tends to be small — up to 10 people or so. Because there are so few roles and so few people, team members are highly interdependent. The individuals on the team will succeed or fail together.

Scrum requires a cohesive team, one that is assembled early in the project and remains consistent from sprint to sprint. Of course, people will come and go, as families, careers, and projects take us in unexpected directions, but team consistency is more important in a Scrum project than in other project management methodologies.

In later chapters, we describe how sprint planning begins with a measure of *velocity*, the speed at which a team can implement items on the product backlog. With each sprint, the team estimates the effort needed to complete a set of backlog items. The team commits to completing the items, and then it actually does the work. The team's estimates improve with each sprint, as long as nothing dramatic changes. The measure of velocity becomes more accurate as the team executes sprints.

Changing the team between sprints negatively affects the predictability of the sprints. For instance, if Manny, Moe, and Jack are replaced with Tom, Dick, and Harry, is it fair to assume that they'll complete the same amount of work as the original team? Without knowing how much work these new team members can do, the team will have a difficult time committing to backlog items.

While changing team members between sprints is disruptive and negatively affects productivity and predictability, it's far worse to change team members within a sprint. You should avoid this if at all possible. Changing people will have a ripple effect not only within the team but also potentially within the customer base. For instance, if the product owner told some customers that they can see a feature at the end of a four-week sprint, and team changes within the sprint prevent that feature from being complete, the customer will be dissatisfied.

As with any other process, it's important that participants know who's supposed to do what and when. People do well when they know what's expected of them. The alternative — uncertainty — causes stress. Therefore, you should plan to educate the team on Scrum prior to the project. There are many good books and resources on Scrum methodologies that you can use to help train the team on what to expect. Appendix B provides suggestions on where to begin.

Product Features

Time and money — the latter being converted to people and equipment — are the limited resources for building a product. These resources have a direct relationship to the feature set that ultimately defines a product. Assuming that there is variability in terms of product features, your job is to optimize the use of time and resources to build a feature set that maximizes the value of the product.

In some business discussions, people are referred to as resources. *This is offensive to some and misleading to others. Here, we refer to resources as just what it sounds like — sources of supply. A resource can be a supply of labor, money, or equipment. Resources can be exchanged, either directly (for example, paying a wage changes money to labor) or indirectly (for example, paying a wage to build equipment changes money to labor to equipment).*

Quality is a feature you can control. You can create a product with more quality or less, depending on how you allocate the resources of time and money. If you run out of time before completing adequate testing on a project, you may implicitly decide to cut quality. The project team has complete control over how much quality to build into a product, as long as quality is considered a feature that requires resources to complete.

Shipping is another feature that you control. You can build a product and not ship it. You may not get paid very much in this case, but it is important to realize that it's a feature. Like quality or other features in the product, shipping takes time and money, so it's important to allocate both. For instance, if you're working on a minor release of a product and you choose to not ship that release, you can re-allocate the time planned for shipping activities ("release" build, final regression test, escrow code, and so on) to other features.

If you have more time or money, you can build more features and quality into a product. Conversely, if you have less time or money, you can either cut features or reduce quality.

The geometry of the project management triangle, with constant angles, dictates the fact that you cannot change just one side of the triangle without adjusting the others. If you increase the features, then you'll have to increase the time and cost lines. If you increase time, then you'll get more features, but it will cost more. If you want to decrease cost, you'll spend less time and get fewer features.

FEATURES VERSUS SCOPE

In general, products have features, and projects have scope. *Features* refer to attributes of the product — such as functions, style, security, or performance. *Scope* refers to the work or effort associated with a project. As constraints on the project management triangle, they're synonymous. But because Scrum is product focused rather than project focused, it's common to think in terms of features rather than scope.

Using Scrum doesn't change the reality of the constraints that define a project. However, Scrum is designed to react to changes gracefully. With respect to scope, Scrum assumes that the feature set is not fully defined up front. Rather, as the product emerges with successive sprints, features are added to and cut from scope. Scrum also assumes that building a product will take a variable amount of time and that you cannot predict the amount of time too early in the project. Once you have achieved a predictable burndown velocity, you can begin to predict scope completion dates. Scrum can work quite well on fixed-budget projects because it enables you to move features in and out of sprints and move sprints in and out of releases.

 Burndown velocity *refers to the rate at which you complete product features during each sprint. This is covered in Chapters 8 and 9.*

APPROACHES TO PROJECT MANAGEMENT

This section looks at the three most common approaches to project management:

➤ **Scrum** — Scrum is the newest approach. Scrum came on the scene around 2000 and is rooted in Agile programming.

➤ **MSF** — Microsoft Solutions Framework (MSF) was created in the early 1990s. Like Scrum, it is an iterative development method.

➤ **Waterfall** — The Waterfall method is the most mature process and is firmly established in software and other engineering disciplines.

Scrum

This book is all about using Visual Studio TFS to run a Scrum project. It assumes that you're somewhat familiar with Scrum and are looking for advice and guidance on using the tool to facilitate the process. If you're not familiar with Scrum but know how to use Visual Studio TFS, don't worry. By the time you finish this book, you will know more than enough to begin.

This section presents a very brief summary of Scrum in order to help you compare it with the other software project management methodologies. The subsequent chapters cover specific techniques for using Visual Studio TFS to implement the concepts introduced here. If you're new to Scrum, you might want to check out the many great books, websites, and other resources that we list in Appendix B.

The Theory of Scrum: The Agile Manifesto

The Agile Manifesto is a great starting point for understanding the principles on which Scrum is based. You can find it online at `http://agilemanifesto.org`.

Four high-level values frame the methodology:

➤ Individuals and interactions over processes and tools

➤ Working software over comprehensive documentation

➤ Customer collaboration over contract negotiation

➤ Responding to change over following a plan

These are not values in any moralistic way but preferences for working with products, individuals, teams, and customers on Agile projects. In addition, 12 principles guide Agile software development:

➤ Our highest priority is to satisfy the customer through early and continuous delivery of valuable software.

➤ It's important to welcome changing requirements, even late in development. Agile processes harness change for the customer's competitive advantage.

➤ It's important to deliver working software frequently, from a couple weeks to a couple months, with a preference to the shorter time scale.

➤ Businesspeople and developers must work together daily throughout the project.

➤ An organization should build projects around motivated individuals. Give them the environment and support they need and trust them to get the job done.

➤ The most efficient and effective method of conveying information to and within a development team is face-to-face conversation.

➤ Working software is the primary measure of progress.

➤ Agile processes promote sustainable development. The sponsors, developers, and users should be able to maintain a constant pace indefinitely.

➤ Continuous attention to technical excellence and good design enhances agility.

➤ Simplicity — the art of maximizing the amount of work not done — is essential.

➤ The best architectures, requirements, and designs emerge from self-organizing teams.

➤ At regular intervals, a team should reflect on how to become more effective and then tune and adjust its behavior accordingly.

The following section describes the high-level process that Scrum follows, from planning through execution.

The Practice of Scrum

Scrum is an *iterative* software development process. In an iterative process, a product undergoes many releases, some major and some minor, with each release adding more value to the product. This type of process enables a team to deliver value to the customer early and to get feedback that can be quickly incorporated into future product development.

In the Scrum method, the product feature set is defined by *user stories*, which are brief narrative descriptions of how the product will be used, by whom, and why. As features are scheduled for development, user stories are decomposed and augmented with increasing levels of detail.

The product release cycle in Scrum is divided into sprints. These are fixed durations, typically two to eight weeks, in which all development activities take place. Each sprint produces a potentially shippable product that contains features which meet customer expectations. After a number of sprints, typically 3 to 10, the product contains enough value to warrant deployment. Figure 1-5 shows the release and sprint cycle. (Chapters 8 and 9 cover using Visual Studio TFS for release and sprint management.)

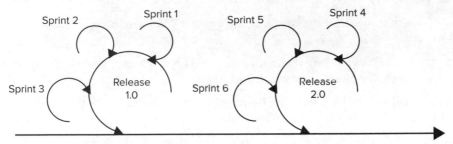

FIGURE 1-5: The Scrum release and sprint cycle.

You can observe the high-level activity of a Scrum project by reviewing three characteristics:

➤ **Project artifacts** — The artifacts are the lists, charts, and documents that the team uses to run the project.

➤ **Roles** — The product roles are simply the job descriptions that show who is responsible for what on the team.

➤ **Ceremonies** — The ceremonies are the rituals that mark the beginning and end of a particular activity.

The following sections look at each of these characteristics in more detail.

Project Artifacts

The product backlog is the list of all features waiting to be built. A team prioritizes the product backlog by business value and ranks it according to which features should be delivered to the customer. Scrum assumes that the list will grow and shrink throughout a release, as the team learns more about the features and the customer learns more about the product. Initially, there is just enough detail associated with each backlog item to begin the discussion between the product owner and the development team. The primary communication mechanism between groups is face-to-face interaction rather than documentation.

The product backlog is the sole input directing work streams of the Scrum team. If a feature isn't on the backlog, it won't be scheduled or built. At the beginning of each sprint, the team moves items from the product backlog to the sprint backlog to indicate the features that will be built in the current sprint. At the end of each sprint, the team produces a potentially shippable product. Bugs that exist at the end of each sprint are added to the product backlog, so work can be scheduled to complete those items in future sprints. (Chapter 6 covers using TFS to manage and track the product backlog.)

Roles

Scrum has a very simple team structure that involves just three roles. This structure generally doesn't translate to an organization or a reporting structure within a company, but it clearly defines who does what on the Scrum team. These are the three roles:

➤ **Product owner** — The product owner is responsible for all aspects of product definition. This person is the voice of the customer and is always available to meet directly with the development team to discuss and review features. There must be at least one product owner on a project at all times.

➤ **Team members** — Team members are responsible for building the product. They may follow Agile engineering methods (such as test-driven development or paired programming), although this isn't a requirement. Team members are the architects, developers, and testers. There is no outside group performing these tasks.

➤ **ScrumMaster** — The ScrumMaster is responsible for the cadence and productivity of the project team. The ScrumMaster defines the sprint duration (generally two to four weeks), runs the daily standup meeting, and helps to keep all team members working productively.

Chapter 2 covers team organization in detail.

Ceremonies

At the beginning of each sprint, the team holds a sprint planning meeting to review the backlog and estimate how much it can accomplish. The team identifies the items it will build in the sprint, and it commits to completing those items. Because each sprint has a fixed set of resources, the number of features must vary (refer to Figure 1-4).

Each day of the sprint, the ScrumMaster leads the daily Scrum, or standup meeting. This is a short (15- to 30-minute) meeting to ensure that everyone on the team is productive and to identify dependences that are impeding progress.

At the beginning of each sprint, the team holds a retrospective in which it looks back and discusses what went well and what didn't, in an attempt to improve productivity. Chapter 10 covers using TFS to conduct effective retrospective meetings.

Microsoft Solutions Framework

MSF is a framework for building and shipping software in an iterative series of releases. Microsoft Consulting Services developed MSF, based on best practices from Microsoft product teams. Its goal is to help a team build and ship software for enterprise customers in a rapidly changing world while reducing risk at each stage. It assumes that there will be changes in scope, technology, and people throughout the project.

Iterative software development focuses on delivering small pieces of functionality frequently in order to solicit and react to feedback, thereby reducing risk. Rather than shipping one release over a two-year project, MSF breaks a release into four smaller projects, each of which delivers a subset of the features. With this method, the end user can see the product in an earlier stage of development and provide feedback before additional features are built.

The MSF Process Model

MSF uses a well-published process model, shown in Figure 1-6. MSF contains five distinct milestones in each iteration, represented in the figure by black diamonds and labeled outside the circle. There are five corresponding project phases in each iteration. These are labeled on the inside of the circle. The project moves from one phase to the next as each milestone is achieved:

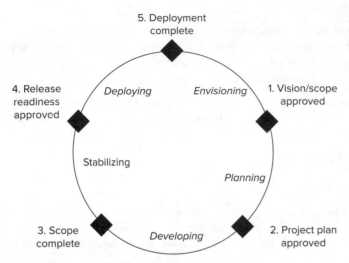

FIGURE 1-6: The MSF process model.

1. **Vision/scope approved** — This milestone is reached at the end of the envisioning phase, after the vision/scope document is reviewed and approved by the project sponsor and user community. In contrast to the Waterfall method, the vision/scope document is typically not an exhaustive list of requirements. Instead, it captures the high-level vision for the release and the specific scope that will be implemented. It may have screen shots of competing systems or of prototypes. It may define high-level use cases, business workflows, or personas to indicate how the system will be used and by whom.

2. **Project plan approved** — This milestone is reached at the end of the planning phase, after the functional spec is written and a concrete project plan is approved by the project sponsor. This is typically a relatively long phase. It involves prototypes and detailed design activities. The more technical work that is completed in this phase, the more accurate project plans will be.

3. **Scope complete** — This milestone is reached after the components are built and unit tested during the developing phase. All major software development is complete at this point.

4. **Release readiness approved** — This milestone occurs after the stabilizing phase, when the system is tested for end-to-end correctness and workflows. This phase also typically includes stress and performance testing. In addition, production-readiness activities, such as run books for operations and configuration tools, are built.

5. **Deployment complete** — This milestone is reached after the deploying phase, when the software is deployed to the target operating environment.

The MSF Team Model

MSF uses a well-published team model, shown in Figure 1-7. MSF defines six roles, all of whom are peers on the project team. Each of these roles should be filled at the beginning of the project, although full-time involvement will vary during each cycle:

FIGURE 1-7: The MSF team model.

➤ **Program management** — Program management is responsible for the project plan. Their central job is to balance the project constraints of time and money against the feature set to deliver the product on time and on budget. What makes this difficult is that the program manager does not control the resources or the feature set; the other roles control the resources and feature set. Effective communication and negotiation are hallmarks of this role.

➤ **Product management** — Product management is responsible for specifying a product that meets customer expectations. Product managers deeply understand customer needs and usage patterns. They instinctively know what is good, what is great, and what is awful. They contribute heavily early in the project, a bit less in the middle, and then significantly again toward the end.

➤ **Development** — The development team is responsible for the architecture, design, and software construction activities. This team works closely with all the other teams to build a top-quality product. It is organized along functional or technical lines so it can scale well.

➤ **QA** — The quality assurance team works very closely with the development team and is responsible for tracking and reporting quality to program management. This team develops and executes test plans to ensure that the product meets functional specifications and user expectations. It works closely with the development team to test the product throughout the developing and stabilizing phases.

➤ **Release management** — Release management is responsible for the logistics of deploying the product in a target environment. This often includes writing and testing the installation instructions to ensure smooth rollout. It also includes working with operations teams to ensure compliance with local procedures and policies in the target environment. Release management contributes heavily near the end of a release, but earlier involvement greatly increases the likelihood of successful deployment.

➤ **User experience** — The user experience team is responsible for the overall experience users have with the product. At the software level, it includes visual design, information architecture, feature usability and discoverability, and the overall look and feel of the system. In addition to software, the user experience team delivers documentation, help text, and training. Making this function a peer with other team roles enables these critical functions to be planned for and budgeted throughout the project.

The Waterfall Method

The Waterfall method is a proven technique for engineering and construction management. It breaks a project into a series of phases, each one conducted by a specialized team with specific outcomes and deliverables. The term *Waterfall* refers to the visual structure of a Gantt chart, which is commonly used for planning. Figure 1-2, earlier in this chapter, depicts the waterfall shape of the Gantt chart.

The Waterfall method is very effective under certain circumstances, although it has had limited success in producing modern software. It's used in situations in which there are well-understood requirements and the solution uses proven, mature technology. The Waterfall method favors stability over agility, planning over experimentation, and documentation over discussion. The following sections discuss these three concepts.

Stability

If system requirements are stable, you can predictably engineer a solution that meets those requirements. For example, if you're hired to build a bridge across a river, you will be given some very concrete requirements. You will be told where the bridge should begin and end. You'll be told the volume and makeup of traffic it must carry. There are dozens of other requirements, but for the sake of this example, let's ignore them and assume that they are relatively predictable. With stable requirements and stable technology, an experienced engineering firm should be able to prepare a reliable estimate for completing the work.

If the requirements are more dynamic, then it becomes increasingly difficult to estimate the time and cost of the project, and the Waterfall method fails. For instance, if you are hired to "move people between Boston and Cambridge as efficiently as possible," you cannot predict when you will be finished because you don't yet know if you'll be carrying foot traffic, cars, or trains and whether one bridge is more desirable than two. In this case, an experienced engineering firm would propose a discovery phase, possibly for a fixed price, but could not accurately plan the project further.

With software, customers typically describe the solution they want ("move people") rather than the product they want ("a bridge"). This makes using the Waterfall method difficult because there are simply too many unknowns at the start of a project.

Don't underestimate the language barrier between customers and engineers. Customers may have difficulty articulating what they want, and engineers may not fully understand what they need to build. If these people are speaking different languages, each will be misunderstood.

Planning

Each phase in the Waterfall method is predicated on successfully completing the prior phase. Each phase builds on the work and decisions made in the prior phase, and the team can adjust its plans accordingly. This implies that decisions made in early phases have an increasingly large impact in later phases. That being the case, earlier phases focus on solidifying the requirements and design of the system, with little code or engineering work taking place until later.

A central concept in this method is that problems uncovered earlier in the process are much easier to correct than those found later. For instance, in the bridge example, it would be very expensive to move the bridge once constructed, so the engineering team has to be 100% sure of the location before the first stone is moved. The same concept can also be applied in some software projects. If the requirements are very stable and clearly understood, then a lengthy design phase, including prototyping and feedback, followed by a shorter development phase, can deliver a product for a predictable cost.

Documentation

Documentation is the primary communication vehicle between phases of the Waterfall method. Heavy reliance on documentation allows project phases to start, be staffed by experts, produce a result (a document), and then wind down in a predictable manner. It also enables a large team to switch players throughout a project in order to maximize people's time. Finally, it provides a written record of progress so there is transparency into why, when, and by whom decisions are made.

Requirements gathered from stakeholders are cataloged and assembled into a document that becomes the definition of success. This primary document is called the requirements definition, business requirements document, or something similar. The document essentially becomes the contract between the business users and the technical implementation team. If, when the system is deployed, it meets the requirements listed in this document, the system is deemed successful. Therefore, both teams must fully understand this document.

After the requirements definition is reviewed and approved by the business users, a more technical team translates it into a functional specification (or spec). The functional spec describes what the system will do. It depicts screens, database tables, field-level validation, and workflow. It translates the business requirements into something that the team can build. The business user must also review and approve this document, since it precisely describes the system that will be built. The functional spec also typically includes a traceability matrix that references the requirements document. This matrix ensures that the functional specification addresses all business requirements.

Following the functional spec is a detailed design document, the first document that addresses the technology. Its purpose is to map the functional spec into a blueprint of a system. After system architects approve the detailed design, construction begins.

While heavy documentation has advantages in terms of oversight and traceability, there are major problems with it. First, it assumes that people will read the documents. This is rarely the case, as documents frequently exceed hundreds of pages. Second, it assumes that the reader can understand the documents. This is also rarely the case. Business users don't speak or write in terms of "requirements," yet they are expected to approve a document written in that language. They generally approve a document based on their trust of the people writing it, but this allows errors and omission to easily slip past review. Finally, the more the team focuses on documentation, the less it focuses on the actual task at hand — building great software.

COMPARING METHODOLOGIES

The following sections compare the three project management techniques according to primary characteristics. The intent is to help you understand the similarities and differences, so you can use your experience with Waterfall or MSF to gain insight into Scrum.

Product Definition

How, when, and by whom is a product defined? How are the user needs and expectations captured? How are requirements communicated to the technical team? How does the technical team communicate with users? The three project management methodologies address product definition as follows:

➤ **Waterfall** — Product requirements are extensively documented during the first phase of a project. They are generally expressed in a technical grammar rather than natural language, although they are describing business goals rather than technology. At the end of the requirements definition phase, the capabilities of the system are fully specified. The requirements document can be used for tendering proposals from competing vendors to do the implementation.

➤ **MSF** — The product definition begins with a vision/scope document, which is a narrative description of the high-level goals and motivations of the project. This document is used to build a functional specification that fully describes the product. The functional specification can be used for tendering proposals from competing vendors to do the implementation.

➤ **Scrum** — The product definition is captured as user stories and expressed in natural language, in the form `<someone> wants to do <something> because <reason>`. User stories are decomposed and expanded closer to implementation. The feature set for the system is dynamic and changes throughout the project life cycle.

Adaptability

How does each methodology work with changing requirements? Does the methodology favor a stable or changing landscape? The three project management methodologies address adaptability as follows:

➤ **Waterfall** — Requirements are locked down early in the project life cycle. Changes introduced later in the project can have a large ripple effect on time and cost. Change orders are used to track and schedule cost and features. A big design phase up front can produce a predictable cost and schedule.

➤ **MSF** — MSF features iterative development that reacts well to change. Requirements are locked at the beginning of a release but can be added in subsequent releases. Major and minor releases can be scheduled based on new requirements.

➤ **Scrum** — Scrum assumes that features will be added to the product backlog after work begins. Because change is expected, it has less of a ripple effect throughout the system. Instead of change orders, additional sprints or releases are added to the schedule to implement new features.

Scheduling

What is the basis for scheduling features or people? When will you know if the project is slipping? The three project management methodologies address scheduling as follows:

➤ **Waterfall** — Scheduling is predictive. Using a known team and known technology, an experienced team can predict the duration of each phase and task. This method doesn't respond well to slippage, as dependencies among tasks and phases are often very complex.

➤ **MSF** — Scheduling is predictive, as in the Waterfall method. However, because MSF is iterative, with more frequent releases, schedule slippage is more manageable. Subsequent releases can add or remove features to react to prior impact.

➤ **Scrum** — Scheduling is empirical. Work is scheduled based on the Scrum team's velocity. Estimation becomes more accurate with each successive sprint, based on actual work completed. Scheduling is very reliable because of the fixed-duration sprints. The scope is less reliable because features will move in and out of sprints and releases to accommodate the fixed schedule.

People

How are teams organized? When are people added to and removed from projects? The three project management methodologies address people as follows:

➤ **Waterfall** — Specialized teams work on different phases of the project. Business analysts perform the requirements definition work early, often before technical experts have been assigned to the project. Once development begins, business analysts have a reduced role. Testing begins after development completes. Project management is a specialized role, often staffed by a project management office.

➤ **MSF** — Specialized teams work on different aspects of the project but all at the same time. Roles are clearly defined and cover the full spectrum of what's necessary to build and ship products in a predicable manner. The project is run by a team of peers, with each discipline contributing to each phase.

➤ **Scrum** — A single team is involved throughout the project life cycle. Within the team, just three roles are defined. The work is very collaborative within and across roles. The team is self-organizing, and team members have full visibility into the product backlog and commit to completing scope. The team is involved in planning, estimating, developing, and testing. The team remains customer focused throughout the project.

Documentation

What form of documentation is needed and produced? The three project management methodologies address documentation as follows:

➤ **Waterfall** — Documentation is the rule of law. Documents describe what's needed and how the system will work. Documents enable team members to come and go because they provide a permanent record of decisions. Microsoft Project and Gantt charts are tools commonly used for documenting the project schedule.

➤ **MSF** — A prescribed set of documents guide an MSF project. Beginning with a vision/scope and concluding with release documentation and the Microsoft Operations Framework, these documents provide a common language for teams familiar with MSF. Because MSF is primarily used on Microsoft-focused projects, documents are frequently stored in SharePoint or Visual Studio. Microsoft Project and Gantt charts are tools commonly used for documenting the project schedule.

➤ **Scrum** — Discussion and informal communication are favored over formal documentation. User stories are decomposed into a scope that is scheduled for development. Before work can begin, the product owner and team members discuss the features in detail. Visual Studio TFS is a very effective tool for communicating user stories, features, and tasks. When using Visual Studio TFS for Scrum artifacts and activities, documents are frequently stored in SharePoint.

Project Duration

What is the typical duration of a project? The three project management methodologies address project duration as follows:

➤ **Waterfall** — Waterfall typically involves longer development projects, often measured in years. It's not uncommon to spend 3–4 months defining business requirements, followed by 3–4 months defining the functional requirements and then 3–4 months defining the technical design, all before the software development phase.

➤ **MSF** — MSF uses an iterative framework, with releases shorter than those in Waterfall projects. Typical durations are 6–12 months for a major release and 3–6 months for a minor release. This pace balances design with delivery and user feedback with product improvement.

➤ **Scrum** — Scrum excels with projects of variable lengths and scopes, especially those that deliver value to the customer early, with rapid iteration and product improvement. Releases typically last 6–12 months, and sprints last 2–4 weeks.

SUMMARY

Shipping great software requires a lot more than writing great code. It requires all of the following:

➤ **Vision** — A great product starts with a compelling, concise description about what you're building, for whom, and why. This is written or heavily shaped by the project sponsor.

➤ **Insight** — Shipping great software requires a deep understanding of the desires, needs, and tastes of the customers. It is the product owner's job to have this understanding.

➤ **Resources** — It takes a surprising amount of resources — including time, money, people, and technology — to build and ship software. You need to allocate and spend resources carefully.

➤ **Planning** — For planning, you need a process, and you need tools. Scrum is a planning process, and TFS is a planning tool.

➤ **Features** — Ultimately, the success of your software is measured by the usefulness and quality of what you produce. It can be considered useful in terms of productivity, education, entertainment, or any other attribute your customers value. Scrum is a product-focused method for producing products with the right features for your customers.

With all this in place, you have the raw ingredients to ship great software.

Several project management methodologies are commonly used in shipping software. This chapter discusses three of them: Scrum, MSF, and Waterfall. It presents highlights of the three methodologies and compares their significant project attributes.

You're now ready to begin learning more about running Scrum projects. In Chapter 2, you'll learn about the organization of a Scrum team.

2

Organizing a Scrum Team

WHAT'S IN THIS CHAPTER?

➤ Organizing a Scrum team and understanding the roles of the team members.

➤ How to scale a Scrum team.

➤ Comparing Scrum team organization with the Microsoft Solutions Framework organization.

➤ How other IT roles work with a Scrum team.

➤ Transitioning to Scrum.

Team organization in Scrum is quite different from team organization in traditional software development projects. Rather than analysts, developers, testers, release engineers, and project managers, Scrum involves a core team of peers who are responsible for building, testing, and shipping a great product. The roles are clearly defined, but each person is responsible for a wide variety of tasks. When moving from traditional software development to Scrum, a team's composition shifts from having many roles, each with narrow responsibilities, to having fewer roles, each with broader responsibilities. This shift leads to a more collaborative, empowered team.

This chapter defines the project roles in Scrum, both in terms of their responsibilities on a project and in the context of traditional software project management strategies.

SCRUM ROLES

There are just three roles defined in Scrum:

➤ **Product owner** — The product owner determines what features go into the product.

➤ **ScrumMaster** — The ScrumMaster is responsible for project status and coordination, team productivity, and removal of impediments to progress.

➤ **Team members** — The team members are responsible for building and testing high-quality software.

Of course, many more people have a significant impact on a project. People outside a Scrum team are responsible for funding, acceptance, delivery, and support. But although these people are important to the success of a project, they're not part of the Scrum team. This is one reason Scrum can be so effective: It limits the crossfire that a larger constituency generates.

Figure 2-1 depicts a typical Scrum team. This example shows one product owner, one ScrumMaster, and six team members doing development and testing.

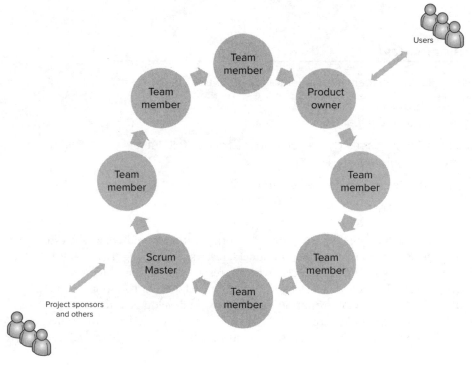

FIGURE 2-1: Scrum team organization.

The ScrumMaster

The ScrumMaster has two primary responsibilities: ensuring team productivity and tracking project status through release. These are not easy tasks, but when treated as top-line job responsibilities, they are quite achievable.

ScrumMasters can facilitate team productivity in a number of ways, as shown in Table 2-1.

TABLE 2-1: Ways a ScrumMaster Increases Team Productivity

GOAL	SCRUM ACTIVITY
Maximize productivity in meetings	The daily Scrum is a 15-minute meeting to discuss coordination, dependencies, and roadblocks. Keeping it short keeps the team moving and prevents the team from wasting time.
Promote effective inter-team communication	The simple organization structure of a Scrum team keeps communication lines open. The ScrumMaster ensures that people are talking.
Eliminate impediments to progress	The ScrumMaster tracks and attacks any impediments. This includes simple tasks such as keeping the team caffeinated and working with good equipment, as well as complex coordination and reporting.

Before looking at techniques and attributes of productive teams, it helps to think about the negative. Unproductive software teams have a number of common attributes, as described in Table 2-2.

TABLE 2-2: Ways a ScrumMaster Decreases Unproductive Behavior

COMMON UNPRODUCTIVE BEHAVIOR	HOW A SCRUMMASTER AVOIDS IT
Ineffective meetings — that is, meetings that occur too often, are too long, and are inconclusive	The ScrumMaster sets the pace for the team and runs the daily Scrum. The ScrumMaster and the product owner empower the team to build the product. The Scrum team is empowered to make virtually all decisions about the product, which streamlines decision making.
Individuals making decisions without all available information	Because the team structure is relatively simple, information flows freely. The daily Scrum enables a very rapid exchange of ideas, concerns, and dependencies.
Large teams that prohibit progress	A Scrum team is small — typically fewer than 10 people. You can build more complex products by scaling with Scrums of Scrums, but the basic unit remains small and agile.

The ScrumMaster's job is to provide the structure and communication channels to avoid these unproductive activities. The ScrumMaster can do this by using formal and informal techniques, but whatever techniques are involved, the ScrumMaster is responsible for creating a productive environment.

The following sections describe the activities of the ScrumMaster:

➤ Running the daily Scrum

➤ Involving others

➤ Fostering effective communication

➤ Determining team size

Running the Daily Scrum

The daily Scrum, sometimes referred to as the daily standup, creates a hyper-productive environment for communication within the Scrum team. The entire team attends this 15- to 30-minute daily meeting, which is typically held in the morning. The purpose of the daily Scrum is to discover issues that are blocking progress and to request assistance or adjustment to overcome these issues. Easy solutions are resolved at this meeting, and more difficult topics are scheduled for later follow-up.

 At the daily Scrum, a quick inexpensive snack helps the mood of the meeting.

With everyone in the room, it's easy to identify dependencies that could impede progress throughout the day. For instance, if Bill is waiting on Hannah to check in some code, but Hannah isn't planning to finish testing until the end of the day, Bill can work on something else for the day rather than wait and pressure Hannah. Simple planning and discussion make the daily Scrum a very effective use of everyone's time.

For topics that require follow-up, the ScrumMaster may or may not stay involved. For topics that the team can resolve — such as technical discussions, refactoring, common components, or performance — the ScrumMaster is not needed. Team members can hold these discussions following the daily Scrum or schedule meetings for later in the day.

The ScrumMaster sets the pace of the sprint during the daily Scrum. If necessary, the ScrumMaster should get commitments from people to ensure that everyone is focused on the most important backlog items. The point of the meeting is to remove roadblocks and impediments and to ensure that the team is working toward the common goal of the sprint. It is a great opportunity to keep a sprint productive and collaborative.

 Demonstrating progress is an easy way to motivate people. If someone just finished a backlog item that makes a good demo, have that person spend a few minutes showing it off during the daily Scrum.

Involving Others

The daily Scrum occasionally raises issues that people outside the team must help resolve. These issues might involve clarification of product features, the budget, or the deployment environment. For issues that require resolution by people outside the team, it's the ScrumMaster's job to understand the impediment facing the team and to bring in outside expertise to resolve the issue. The team members can quickly return to the features they're currently working on from the product backlog while the ScrumMaster researches the issue and tracks down the necessary constituents. The research may take days, but the team productivity is not impacted.

 When a team faces technical unknowns or issues that require outside help, it's important to address them head-on, by bringing in additional expertise and resolving any questions. Often, this is done in a spike, *a short sprint focused on a single issue. See Chapter 11 for information on running spikes.*

This division of labor keeps the team productive. Team members focus on building software, while the ScrumMaster tracks down the right people for a decision. The ScrumMaster identifies and briefs the appropriate people on the issues and the decision that must be made. Then the ScrumMaster brings those people together with the team to reach or review the decision.

Fostering Effective Communication

The ScrumMaster must ensure team productivity, and this requires effective communication. There are numerous impediments to effective communication, including cultural differences, interpersonal skills, time/distance differences among the team members, and job expectations.

The ScrumMaster must keep a constant watch for communication enablers and inhibitors. Who are the connectors on the team, the individuals who work well with everyone and are quick to convey information or provide insight? Are the technical leaders adequately coaching the junior team members? Is everyone contributing to his or her best ability? Is everyone actively participating at the daily Scrum? Is anyone spending days or weeks on a problem without communicating or demonstrating progress?

The ScrumMaster must ensure that communication lines are open among team members and between product owners and the team. Failure in this area may not be recoverable. If the team doesn't understand the way in which the product will be used, it is extraordinarily difficult to build the product optimized for that usage.

Determining Team Size

Large projects that have increased scope and complexity generally require larger teams. Larger teams involve more people, more diverse skills, and often more locations.

Scrum projects tend to be smaller. They tend to focus on product features and on shipping quality software. If Scrum is done right, it involves less process and more result. The ScrumMaster is responsible for scaling a Scrum project, and he or she must do this carefully.

The Product Owner

The product owner is responsible for ensuring that product features meet customer expectations. The product owner can be a leader in the user community, someone from marketing, a business analyst within the IT arena, or any other individual who can effectively communicate business needs. Regardless of this person's training or the organizational hierarchy, the product owner must have the ability to provide deep insight and understanding of product usage and benefits to the Scrum team.

Table 2-3 describes the characteristics of a good product owner.

TABLE 2-3: Characteristics of a Good Product Owner

CHARACTERISTIC	DESCRIPTION
Deep domain knowledge	The product owner's primary role is to translate business needs into technical requirements. Having a deep understanding of the business is crucial to success.
Strong verbal and written communication skills	The product owner will spend time with users, business decision makers, clients, and the Scrum team. The various constituents speak different languages, and the product owner must be able to communicate with them (talk, present, write, e-mail, IM) at all levels.
Presence	The product owner must be physically or virtually present on the team. He or she must be available to answer questions quickly and decisively. The product owner may not have all the answers but should be able to get them on short notice in order to prevent impediments.
Empowerment	The product owner defines the feature set, so not only must this person understand the need, he or she must be empowered to determine how that need is met in the product.

At a high level, the product owner has the vision for the product. He or she describes the end state for the system and how it will benefit the users. More tactically, the product owner has details about what specific features must do. The product owner will not be the expert on all features, but when this person does not know something, he or she needs to be able to find answers from someone who does.

A product owner is involved in three primary activities:

➤ Specifying and prioritizing features

➤ Planning sprints and releases

➤ Testing features

The following sections discuss these activities.

Specifying and Prioritizing Features

The product owner, or project sponsor, writes the product vision to describe the overall goals of the product. The *product vision* should convey who uses the product, what benefits the users derive, and what competing options exist. (The competition may be another software product, or it may be another way of doing something that doesn't require software at all.) In total, the product vision describes the context in which the product exists.

The product vision is then bound by a project scope. The *scope* defines the level of effort, emphasis, and constraints that guide the early sprints and releases.

With the vision and scope in hand, the product owner creates the product backlog. The *product backlog* is the master list of all potential features for the product. The items in the product backlog, also known as *product backlog items (PBIs)*, must be specified with enough detail so that the team can understand and discuss them.

It is common for PBIs to be expressed in user stories. PBIs can be very high level or can provide more detail. In either case, they should contain just enough information for everyone to understand the feature. As Albert Einstein might have said, PBIs should be made as simple as possible, but not simpler.

USER STORIES

A *user story* is a short description of a product feature. It starts as a simple sentence or two, often on a note card, and is used as a reminder that more detail is needed. It culminates in a rich understanding between the product owner and the team, with just enough documentation of what is needed and how it will be tested.

Prior to the first sprint of a release, the product owner populates and prioritizes the product backlog so the team can gain insight into the overall scope of the release. Prioritizing the backlog is crucial because it enables the team to commit to the items of the sprint.

The backlog priority indicates the order in which PBIs should be scheduled into a sprint. The priority is a relative value, where lower numbers have great priority. For example, an item with a priority setting of 50 will be scheduled before an item with a priority of 1,000.

BACKLOG PRIORITY VERSUS BUSINESS VALUE VERSUS EFFORT

Backlog priority is different from business value. *Business value* is a measure of importance for a feature. A feature may be very important to the business, but it may not be needed or even feasible until a later sprint. The priority directs the order in which features will be built — not their intrinsic importance to the product.

Similarly, the backlog priority is also different from effort. *Effort* is a rough estimate of how difficult it is to build a feature. The team may not have enough information to make a good guess, but it can at least make a guess. The estimate is typically not in terms of time or money; it's just a relative estimate used to scope sprints and releases. We cover estimation in Chapters 3–6.

Planning Sprints and Releases

At a high level, a release is composed of a series of sprints. A *sprint* is a unit of work, typically lasting two to four weeks, that delivers a set of features in a potentially shippable product. The product owner delineates what features will be in each release and works with the team members to schedule those features into sprints. Chapters 8 and 9 describe this process in more detail.

Whereas a sprint is a potentially shippable product, a *release* is a product actually ready to be shipped. There are big differences between the two. "Potentially shippable" refers to the fact that the features have been tested. Most products cannot ship until a set of related features are complete, hardened for production, reviewed for security, and packaged for deployment. The product owner defines the release by determining the set of features that he or she would like to ship as a unit. The team then iteratively builds those features in sprints.

At the sprint planning meeting, the team selects PBIs and commits to completing them within the sprint. One by one, the team removes items from the product backlog and places them on the sprint backlog. The sprint backlog is an outcome of the sprint planning meeting.

The sprint planning meeting is a group exercise, with the product owner, ScrumMaster, and team all participating. The product owner prioritizes the product backlog. The team commits to specific items it will complete within the sprint.

Testing Features

In the customer's eyes, the product owner is responsible for delivering a high-quality product. The product owner will have enormous pride in what the team produces, and just as he or she is the customer's advocate inside the team, the product owner is the team's external face to the customer.

The product owner starts thinking about testing while initially writing the user stories. Going from note cards on a board to redundant PBIs in TFS, user stories incrementally define the quality level that meets the customer's expectations.

First, the product owner defines a test plan, indicating the success criteria for each PBI. Then the product owner defines test cases. There may be just a few test cases, or there may be dozens. The goal of the testing is to ensure that the product performs as expected.

As described in Chapter 1, Scrum minimizes documentation. Therefore, the test cases are often the most concrete definition of a product feature's function. The product owner has huge incentive to be explicit and thorough in defining test cases because the team will build features that pass the tests.

The team will create many automated tests, and the product owner may create hundreds of manual tests. It is the product owner's responsibility to see that the tests are run as the product emerges. Chapter 7 covers quality assurance in detail.

Scaling Product Owners

A traditional software project may involve months writing specifications (or specs) before anyone begins to write any code. With Scrum, you try to minimize specs in order to write code earlier. The high-level information that used to be in the spec is now headlined in the product backlog. The additional details that used to be in the spec are available on demand from the product owner. Therefore, the product owner can quickly become a bottleneck in a project.

Larger Scrum projects often need more than one product owner. In fact, the product owner is often the first person to be overwhelmed, since all team members tend to require this person's input. If you need one additional product owner, you can simply add one to the Scrum team. You may need an extra product owner for just one or two sprints, or maybe for an entire release. In either case, as long as the overall Scrum team isn't too big, you can add product owners to the team.

Figure 2-2 shows a Scrum team with two product owners. In this scenario, each product owner would be responsible for a set of sprint backlog items.

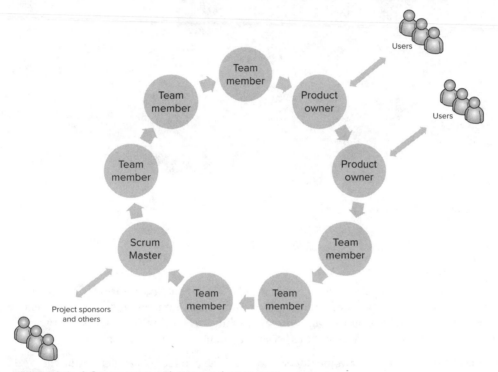

FIGURE 2-2: A Scrum team with two product owners.

For a large project that requires more than two product owners, the team may want to add a hierarchy of product owners. For instance, if the project is to build a retail website, one product owner may be in charge of inventory, one may handle marketing, and one may be responsible for customer management. You may also have a product owner for performance. In the case of multiple product owners, one of them should represent the others at the daily Scrum meeting.

Figure 2-3 shows a Scrum team with four product owners. In this case, each product owner would be responsible for a set of sprint backlog items, but only one would need to attend the daily Scrum. Issues raised during the daily Scrum would be resolved directly between the team members and the attending product owner.

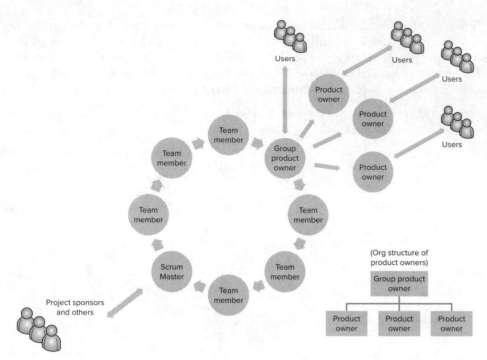

FIGURE 2-3: A Scrum team with four product owners.

Team Members

As stated at the beginning of this chapter, Scrum teams have a simple organization. Each team is composed of a ScrumMaster, a product owner, and a number of team members. The team members typically have skills in software engineering, software architecture, business analysis, software testing, database tuning, IT operations, user experience, and user interface design.

The primary responsibility of the team members is to build the product. They determine the architecture, component design, and user experience. They work within boundaries of time and cost and are empowered to make trade-offs to build the best possible product within those limits. Both development and testing occur within the team. Because there is no separate QA group, the team members are both empowered and responsible for their own testing.

The team members participate in sprint planning activities. Since they are the ones building the product, one sprint at a time, the team members are the only ones who can truly commit to completing PBIs within the sprint. This is a radical departure from traditional software development, where managers commit to time schedules and allocate tasks to developers and testers.

A Scrum team typically contains a mix of senior, more-experienced members and junior members who are earlier in their careers. In a more traditional management structure, senior members may be on an architecture board that defines the architecture, with product development team members following that architecture. In contrast, a Scrum team brings together different skill sets and levels.

As described in the following sections, the team focuses on the following activities within a sprint:

- ➤ Committing to delivery
- ➤ Focusing on the features
- ➤ Improving as a team

Committing to Delivery

At the beginning of a sprint, the team collectively determines which PBIs it will complete. This list becomes the sprint backlog that the team commits to completing. From this point until the end of the sprint, the team is responsible for delivering the items on the spring backlog.

The team members must drive toward sprint completion as a group, and they will succeed or fail as a team. There will be top performers within any team, but it's the team result that makes Scrum work. If the team commits to completing 10 items but completes only 5, the failure to meet the commitment has cost the project something — in terms of time, money, or trust. Because of the group focus and collaboration of the sprint, it is in everyone's interest to complete items and to help teammates do the same

Focusing on the Features

A Scrum team should be focused on a cohesive set of PBIs within a sprint. All team members must actively engage in discussion. Their discussions, both across the desk and at the lunch table, will wander from technical details to user expectations. Someone will be working on a user interface element, someone else on a business rule, and maybe a third person on a caching technique. Along the way, collaboration is natural. The alternative, which is to make progress in many disparate areas of the backlog, tends to be isolating and may lead to fragmented results.

TEAMWORK AND RELATED FEATURES

When team members focus on related items, they can easily find opportunities to improve each other's work and deliver a more cohesive and comprehensive product. Consider a team building a retail website. If one person is working on the product catalog, another on user registration, and a third on coupons, there's very little need for these three people to discuss their work. A fourth person working on performance optimizations may just have his or her head down in profiling and monitoring tools.

Now imagine that the four team members are working on just the inventory system. One may focus on bulk updates, another on cross-sell catalog links, a third on image attributes in the catalog, and a fourth on query optimization in popular categories. At the end of this sprint, the four team members will know a lot about tracking inventory. They'll also know more about each other.

Improving as a Team

A product is only as good as the people who build it. A top-performing technical team has the capability to build a great product. A team lacking important skills can rarely build anything great. Therefore, the final product is directly related to the technical wherewithal of the team.

Team members have an opportunity to improve their skills with each sprint. Close collaboration encourages cross-learning, so the team should take every opportunity to foster this. The following are some simple techniques:

➤ Include both senior and junior engineers on the Scrum team

➤ Encourage team members to be responsible for small PBIs outside their core competency

➤ Encourage one-on-one follow-up meetings to discuss topics raised at the daily Scrum

➤ Hold informal design reviews and code walkthroughs

SCALING A SCRUM TEAM

In projects that require teams larger than 8 or 10 team members, it is necessary to scale the team. Earlier, this chapter discussed ways to scale the product owner role. Scaling an entire Scrum team requires a different approach: You need to define multiple Scrum teams.

Having multiple Scrum teams can greatly accelerate progress. If done right, you can scale from 8 to 80 team members and burn down the product backlog at a corresponding pace. If done wrong, it will grind progress to halt.

When defining multiple Scrum teams, the goal is to have teams that can work independently. At the same time, the teams must coordinate on technology and integrate as early as possible. If the teams do not coordinate on technology, the resulting product may have architectural differences that are difficult to resolve. The longer the teams go without integration, the greater the risk that integration will be difficult.

As discussed in the following sections, to ship a great product that is produced by multiple Scrum teams, you need to address the following topics:

➤ Team specialization

➤ The Scrum of Scrums meeting

➤ The product backlog

➤ Sprint synchronization

➤ A common architecture

Team Specialization

To scale a Scrum team, you need to establish multiple Scrum teams that will work independently yet come together to produce a single product. How should the team be split? Should it be split by feature, by cross-cutting concern, or by technology? The preference should be by feature, and then by cross-cutting concern, and then by technology. Table 2-4 summarizes the decision process.

TABLE 2-4: Specialization Across Scrum Teams

SPECIALIZATION	EXAMPLE	ADVANTAGES	DISADVANTAGES
By feature (best choice)	In a retail website, one team may deliver cart and checkout features, while another team may deliver inventory and merchandising features.	Reduces dependencies on other teams. Focuses on product features. Improves acceptance testing.	Architecture and technical design could bifurcate across features, increasing support costs. Each team may need to reinvent the wheel.
By cross-cutting concern (second-best choice)	In a retail website, one team may deliver the caching objects, and another might deliver the security infrastructure. Artifacts from these teams are delivered to other teams, not to the customer.	Reduces cost and maximizes quality for complex technical capabilities. Ensures architecture consistency across features.	This division is not customer driven. Scrum teams are less empowered because they don't see the full scope of the product. Need to define and lock down the interface early; changes are expensive.
By technology (last choice)	In a retail website, one team may focus on the web tier, another on the mid-tier, and a third on the database.	Maximizes skills of specialists. Improves unit testing because team members are experts in their technology focus.	This organization maximizes inter-team dependencies. Nobody is responsible for feature delivery. Each team will produce solutions that maximize reliance on their technology, while nobody is paying attention to the complexity of technical cohesion of the product.

The specialized Scrum teams will work largely independently of each other. Coordination between them is important, but the daily work and communication will primarily be focused within the team. The way you choose to specialize will impact the degree of coordination, as outlined in Table 2-4. Consider the following:

➤ If you specialize by feature, then you will coordinate on cross-cutting concerns and technology, discussing how to use common components and how to use technology.

➤ If you specialize by cross-cutting concern, then you will coordinate on features and on technology.

➤ If you specialize by technology, then you will coordinate on features and on cross-cutting concerns.

Regardless of how you specialize the teams, each Scrum team operates as its own unit, with a product owner, a ScrumMaster, and team members. Each Scrum team has a daily Scrum, PBIs, bugs, tasks, burndown charts, and sprints.

The Scrum of Scrums Meeting

With multiple teams specialized to implement different aspects of the product, the teams must coordinate and integrate in order to produce a cohesive result. The Scrum of Scrum meeting is where this coordination takes place.

Representatives from each Scrum team attend the Scrum of Scrum meeting. Each team sends an emissary to the meeting. Each team can send more than one person, but one is usually sufficient. The representative could be the lead developer or architect, the product owner, or the ScrumMaster. You should choose carefully because this person will spend significant time coordinating.

The Scrum of Scrums is a meeting — not a team. It does not have a ScrumMaster, a product owner, or team members. It's a meeting that occurs regularly, either daily or a few times per week. It is longer than the 15-minute daily Scrum, but not much longer. The purpose of the meeting is to identify and mange dependencies, coordinate work where necessary, and resolve impediments.

Figure 2-4 depicts a Scrum of Scrums meeting, with an individual from each Scrum team participating. This example shows three team members attending the Scrum of Scrums, but the ScrumMaster or product owner could just as easily be the participants.

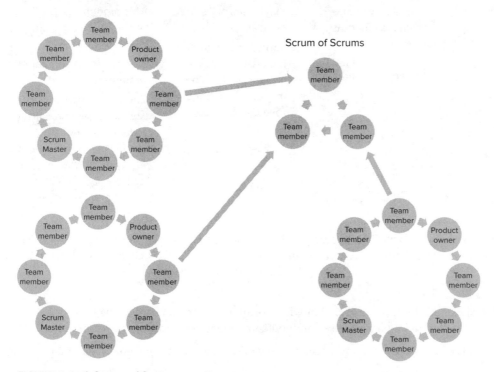

FIGURE 2-4: A Scrum of Scrums meeting.

The Product Backlog

Each product has one product backlog. This is an essential concept in Scrum: The product backlog is the single input queue to the team. This remains true when the product is being built by multiple Scrum teams and is even more important as the aggregate team grows.

The product backlog scales quite well with multiple Scrum teams, especially if they're each focused on a different set of features. It may grow large, but with each team owning certain PBIs, it is very manageable. Each team manages its own PBIs. As if other teams didn't exist, each team assigns business value, estimates effort, and prioritizes the list to determine the order in which features should be implemented.

Using the Area Path field in TFS becomes very important with multiple Scrum teams, as it's often used to group PBIs. If there are dozens of PBIs within each functional area of the product, in a product backlog that contains hundreds of items, using the Area Path field becomes the simplest and most consistent way to delineate work across teams.

 In TFS, the Area Path field in a PBI identifies a component or functional area of a product. The PBI fields are discussed in more detail Chapters 3 and 6.

Sprint Synchronization

Each Scrum team executes sprints independently. Each team has a sprint planning meeting at which it commits to PBIs. Each team also has tasks that implement the PBIs, test cases that verify their correctness, and bugs that need to be tracked and resolved. Each team also has a retrospective meetings to identify ways to improve productivity, quality, and velocity.

It is not necessary to synchronize sprints across teams all the time, but it is crucial to do it some of the time. One team may prefer two-week sprints, with a one-week integration sprint after each two-week sprint. Another team may prefer two-week sprints, with a two-week stabilization sprint after three successive two-week sprits. Variation is okay, as long as it's tuned to the needs of the team and product features.

However, there must be times when all teams are stable and can integrate each other's work. Sprints should be synchronized to facilitate this integration. Every few months, there should be sync points at which each Scrum team is finished with its sprint and can integrate its work with the work of the other Scrum teams.

Common Architecture

As Table 2-4 shows, one risk of having specialized Scrum teams that are organized by product feature is that each could develop its own technical architecture and solution to common problems. This risk can be addressed through organizational alignment and a common process.

Organizationally, in addition to defining Scrum teams by feature, you can also define core teams by component. For instance, you may have three features teams building a commercial website: one working on the catalog, one on the commerce functions, and one on personalization and merchandising. You may add a fourth team to focus on cross-cutting concerns such as database tuning and caching. You may add a fifth team for user experience. This way, each feature team still estimates and commits to its PBIs, but each team also works with a common team for core technology infrastructure.

For process, the product owner on a core team gets input from the feature teams' ScrumMasters, product owners, and team members. He or she creates PBIs for the core team, and then that team estimates, prioritizes, and commits to those items.

 Having core teams with a larger Scrum project is critical for ensuring architectural integrity of the product.

So far this chapter has covered how to organize a Scrum team in isolation of other project management techniques and enterprise IT. The remainder to the chapter highlights how Scrum compares with MSF and how it fits in with IT.

COMPARING MSF AND SCRUM

If you're reading this section, you have probably built software following the Microsoft Solutions Framework (MSF) methodology. Maybe you have been rewarded for using MSF in the past and now you are considering doing things differently. Or maybe it didn't work out too well for you, and you are looking for a better way.

This section serves as a map from using MSF to using Scrum. When transitioning to Scrum, lines of responsibility change. Your interaction with colleagues changes. Your title changes. The way you plan the project changes. The way you measure progress changes.

Figure 2-5 shows the six roles in a typical MSF team organization.

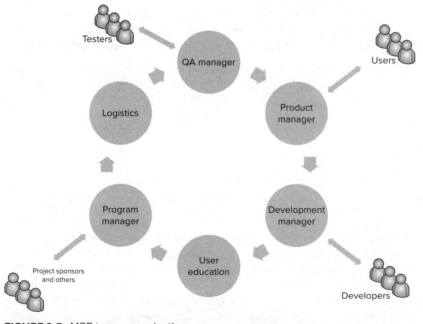

FIGURE 2-5: MSF team organization.

Like Scrum, MSF also favors peer relationships. However, unlike Scrum, with MSF the peers can be managers. Using a more traditional organizational structure, managers direct individuals to work on different parts of the system. The individuals interact closely with people on their team but not necessarily with people outside their team.

MSF has a natural ability to scale, leveraging organizational hierarchies for major responsibilities. It relies more on specifications than on face-to-face communication. Specs facilitate communication across time and distance.

There are six roles in MSF:

➤ Product manager

➤ Program manager

➤ Development manager

➤ QA manager

➤ Training manager

➤ Release manager

Each is a peer on the team and has distinct responsibilities. The following sections describe each of the roles and compare them to their counterparts in Scrum.

The Product Manager

The product manager role in MSF maps to the product owner role in Scrum. Individuals in each role draw from their experience and insights in the domain. They often come from the user community or have very deep roots there. The practices and tasks differ significantly between the MSF and Scrum roles, but the individuals filling these roles are generally the same.

The MSF product manager writes the vision/scope, writes the requirements, and manages all aspects of customer relationships (including marketing, communication, and advocacy). This person is responsible for marketing and product planning.

One difference between the product manager role in MSF and the product owner role in Scrum is that the MSF product manager does not generally have much exposure to the development team. Rather, this person provides input to the program manager, who writes specs for the developers. In other words, there's someone between the product manager and the development team.

Scrum optimizes communication by facilitating face-to-face collaboration between product owners and team members. It eliminates the need for an in-depth specification and the possible misinterpretations of such a spec. This is not to say that specs are bad. They are critical in certain situations. However, they do not need to be the primary communication vehicle between the product owner or manager and developers in creating a product.

Table 2-5 compares the activities of an MSF product manager with those of a Scrum product owner.

TABLE 2-5: Comparing the MSF Product Manager with the Scrum Product Owner

RESPONSIBILITY	MSF PRODUCT MANAGER	SCRUM PRODUCT OWNER
Customer advocacy	Yes	Yes
Writing the vision/scope	Yes	Yes
Capturing product needs	Writes requirements	Writes user stories
Working with developers	No	Yes

The Program Manager

The program manager role in MSF is responsible for driving the development process. This person is the heartbeat of the team, whether with daily Scrums or with weekly meetings. The program manager maintains the high-level schedule for the overall release.

The program manager role maps most closely to the ScrumMaster role in Scrum. If you're a program manager today, you should look at the attributes and responsibilities of being a ScrumMaster. In both MSF and Scrum, this role is responsible for communication outside the team. This is the "go to" person that project sponsors rely on for status and significant changes to project scope, budget, or delivery.

However, there are significant differences between the program manager role and the ScrumMaster role. Because of the extreme collaboration and distributed responsibility in Scrum, there may even be more differences than commonalities between these roles. For instance, in MSF, the program manager owns the schedule, with input from the development team and product manager. In Scrum, the team is committed to the schedule, and the ScrumMaster just facilitates the process. As another example, in MSF, the program manager writes the functional spec, taking input from requirements and writing in terms that developers can follow. In Scrum, the ScrumMaster does no such task because communication is direct — between the product owner and the team.

Another difference between the roles is their position within the team. In MSF, the program manager is responsible for negotiating differences among competing interests. These often occur between product management and the development team and focus on features (for example, functional, operational, quality) and cost (for example, time, people, money). In Scrum, the ScrumMaster does not have this position of power. He or she may facilitate the communication but does not have any overriding power to decide what goes into each sprint or release.

Table 2-6 compares the activities of an MSF program manager with those of a ScrumMaster.

TABLE 2-6: Comparing the MSF Program Manager with the ScrumMaster

RESPONSIBILITY	MSF PROGRAM MANAGER	SCRUMMASTER
Driving product development	Yes, using status meetings, war rooms, and other techniques.	Yes, using the daily Scrum.
Functional specifications	Yes. The program manager writes or manages the spec.	No. In Scrum, the product owner is responsible for writing user stories and communicating them to the team.
Communication	Yes	Yes
Negotiating features/cost	Yes. The program manger is responsible for shipping the product on time.	No. This occurs within the team, often between the product owner and team members.
Maintaining the schedule	Yes. The program manager defines the iterations and work breakdown structure within iterations and release.	Yes, but in a limited capacity. The ScrumMaster defines the duration of sprints and release cycles, but the team owns the feature set of the work breakdown structure within each sprint. There is no master work breakdown structure.
Acting as solution architect	Yes	No. The solution architect is often a team member, with skills and interests divergent from those of the ScrumMaster.
Risk management	Yes	No. The team handles this, although the ScrumMaster communicates issues with project sponsors. In practice, however, the messenger is held accountable for the message, so the ScrumMaster is more involved with risk management than are other team members.
Delivery	No	Yes. The ScrumMaster is often responsible for PBIs during sprints.

The Development Manager

There is no development manager role in Scrum as there is in MSF. The responsibilities of the MSF development manger role are largely distributed among the team members in Scrum.

The technical work done by developers in MSF is similar to the technical work done by team members in Scrum. In both methodologies, developers are empowered and expected to build a product that meets customer expectations. They specify the product architecture and design, they estimate the time and cost required to complete each feature, and they prepare the product for deployment.

However, there are some significant differences between MSF and Scrum when it comes to development. In MSF, a development team works from technical specs written by the program manager. In Scrum, the team members work from the product backlog and must closely communicate with the product owner. In MSF, the development manager may supervise or outsource development of a feature, but he or she is still responsible for delivering that feature to the team. In Scrum, there is no such delegation: Instead, team members build the product. Outsourced feature teams are managed as self-contained Scrum teams, with integration happening in a Scrum of Scrums or through a designated integration team.

WHO'S YOUR BOSS?

Everyone has a boss. Developers work for managers, who work for directors, who work for vice presidents, and so on. Your boss is the only one who can promote you or fire you, so even when you're working on a Scrum team, you still must meet your boss's objectives. But within the context of Scrum activities, no one person manages the work for the developers.

Table 2-7 compares the development manager role with the role of the Scrum team member.

TABLE 2-7: Comparing the MSF Development Manager Role with the Scrum Team Member Role

RESPONSIBILITY	MSF DEVELOPMENT MANAGER	SCRUM TEAM MEMBER
Building the product	Yes	Yes
Following product specifications	Yes. The primary source of information is the functional spec written by the program manager.	Yes. The primary sources of information are the PBIs written by the product owner and direct communication between the team members and the product owner during the daily Scrum.
Primary communication	Works primarily with the program manager and testers.	Works primarily with the product owner and other team members.

Quality Assurance Manager

As President Ronald Reagan famously said regarding nuclear disarmament, it's best to "trust but verify" an adversary turned partner. The same can be said about system testing within Scrum. Scrum does not have an explicit QA role; instead, the product owner trusts that the team will deliver tested code and will then verify the product, using documented test cases.

As with the MSF development manager role, the responsibilities of the MSF QA manager role are largely distributed among the team members in Scrum. There is no explicit QA manager role in Scrum. Some team members do software development and some do software testing, but everyone is responsible for quality.

Testers on a Scrum team are essential for delivering quality. A general rule of thumb in software project management is to have one tester for every one to three developers. On a Scrum team, testers and developers are peers, working together early and often. Organizationally, they may be in different groups within a company, with developers reporting to a development group and testers reporting to a QA group. This poses no problem for a Scrum team, which can be assembled within a matrix-managed organization. Outside the Scrum team, individuals may have different career goals and job responsibilities, but inside the team, everyone has a common goal.

MATRIX MANAGEMENT

Matrix management refers to an organizational structure in which individuals with similar skills are grouped into functional departments but are assigned to projects outside their departments. For instance, developers may work in the "development group," and designers may work in the "creative group," and individuals from each group may work together each day on a Scrum team that reports to a business unit.

The product owner is ultimately responsible for delivering a great product to the user community. That community trusts that the product owner will advocate for their needs and help the Scrum team deliver a top-quality product. As much as anyone else, the product owner has a vested interest in testing. The product owner spends an increasing amount of time testing the product, filing bugs, and retesting after the bugs are fixed during each sprint.

While the product owner is responsible for delivering quality to the user community, the team members writing the code are delivering quality technology. The team members are the primary testers and first line of defense against bugs. They use automated and manual test methods, favoring automation wherever possible.

Table 2-8 compares how quality assurance is carried out in MSF and in Scrum.

TABLE 2-8: Comparing the MSF QA Manager Role with the Scrum Team Member Role

RESPONSIBILITY	MSF QA MANAGER	SCRUM TEAM MEMBER
Test planning	Yes. This is done separately from development activities. Test planning is usually competed before development begins.	Yes. This is done within each sprint. All team members working on a PBI conduct test planning, so they allocate time to build automated or manual tests. The product owner tests to ensure that each PBI meets the appropriate needs.
Test engineering	Yes. The test team does this.	Yes. Developers and testers on the team do this. Automated testing has far greater importance in Scrum than in MSF because of the short sprint times. Test-driven development is a hallmark of Scrum projects.
Primary communication	The test manger reports status to the program manager, who reports status to stakeholders.	The team reports automated test results to the product owner. The product owner verifies quality early and often with manual tests throughout a sprint.

The Training Manager

The training manager in MSF is responsible for all the activities necessary to train the user community to successfully use the product. This includes end-user training, such as online video and help text. It could also include installation if the product is installed and managed by an IT organization. The responsibilities of the MSF training manger are subsumed by the product owner. There is no training manager role in Scrum.

In Scrum, the product owner is responsible for inbound and outbound communication with the Scrum team. Inbound communication is all about the PBIs: capturing the essence of the need in a form that can be tracked, scheduled, and delivered by the team. Outbound communication takes many forms — from holding demo days, when team members demonstrate progress with each sprint, to more formal prerelease notes to get the user community excited about the product.

Training is another form of outbound communication that the product owner must manage. This person must produce sufficient material, but not too much, so that users can take full advantage of the features they rely on the team to build. If people don't know how to use the product, the product has failed in its mission. Therefore, training content is as important as any other aspect of a product.

Release Management

There is no specific release management role in Scrum. Instead of having a person focus on release responsibilities in Scrum, it's common to have a sprint focused on release activities. This is a consistent way to bring the Scrum philosophy and benefits to the release management discipline.

The Scrum team should add production deployment items to the product backlog and address them during sprints. This will ensure that the team is thinking of the issues and building the technology needed to make the product deployable. As with all PBIs, the product owner should write user stories and work with the team members to ensure that they know how to meet the need.

After a Scrum team has completed the PBIs that make up a release, the team may go through a final sprint to focus on release-specific activities. This typically includes preparing training materials, writing and testing installation documentation, and conducting final regression testing on the PBIs. This is a time of close coordination with the deployment team, whether that team is internal to the organization or at a hosting provider.

 Allocating a sprint to release management brings the best of Scrum to the release management process. Rather than having an operations team figuring out how to package and deploy a product, individuals from the operations team work closely with the Scrum team during the final sprint. They have ready access to developers, testers, and the product owner to get fast access to the information they need.

IT ROLES IN SCRUM

Scrum defines only three roles: ScrumMaster, product owner, and team member. However, there are many more critical roles in IT. These roles don't go away with Scrum, but they're outside the Scrum team. The following sections look at how the following IT roles interact with a Scrum team:

➤ Project manager

➤ Architect

➤ Release management

➤ QA manager

The Project Manager

The project manager role in IT is a tough job. It is the central control point for a number of competing interests — features, time, money, and people. Project managers rely on controls and metrics, written and oral communication skills, and technical depth and breadth to complete projects successfully. Seasoned project managers are extremely valuable in large organizations. Senior executives rely on them to deliver projects on time and on budget, which are two characteristics that are relatively easy to measure.

At a higher level, senior executives measure the return on investment (ROI) of a software project. The investment is primarily the cost of building and delivering the system, plus the cost of the intended users operating the system. A productive development team lowers the cost, thereby increasing the ROI, which is good. A product that reduces labor from another part of the organization also reduces the overall cost and increases ROI, which is also good.

But there's a problem: A project manager is typically rewarded for lowering the cost of software development but not for ensuring the effectiveness of the product. For instance, say that an organization sets out to build a new order management system to reduce the time it takes to place an order from five minutes down to three minutes. The benefit (return) of the system is to reduce the number of entry representatives and to increase the revenue per rep. The cost (investment) is the cost required to build and deploy the system. However, the project manager will probably not be measured by the benefit — just by the cost. So, if he or she produces a system on time, within budget, and with no bugs, yet the system doesn't do what is needed, the project manager is still considered successful. In this scenario, the team that provided the requirements or the one who footed the bill is the one who has failed.

Scrum addresses this problem by placing the product owner on the team, which eliminates two or three levels of indirection between the user and developer. This reduces the likelihood of the development team producing a system that doesn't meet the true needs of the sponsor and user.

Scrum does not have a project manager role on the team, but most organizations still maintain this role outside the team. The project manager role may be held by a stakeholder within IT to ensure proper governance in the team and results from the team.

The Architect

Four resources are required to ship great software: time, money, people, and technology. From a technical perspective, the architecture of a product has the greatest impact on a product's usability, flexibility, effectiveness, and cost of ownership. Therefore, every project that involves building software requires someone to fill the role of architect. The architect is typically one of the senior members on the team — someone who has "been there and done that" before. This person understands the full scope of technical implementation, from design through deployment. He or she is a mentor to more junior technical staff and acts as the go-to person for the product owner when determining what's feasible. This role is crucial whether you're using Scrum or not.

 The architect's role, regardless of project management methodology, is to manage the complexity of component parts of the system. Developers write the code, but the architect must be able to see the forest for the trees.

In Scrum, the architect is critical during release and sprint planning. This person often has the insight and depth needed to make the most reasonable effort estimates for PBIs. He or she also has input into PBI priority and understands the technical subtleties and dependencies among features.

The architect should not be the ScrumMaster. The architect must focus on technical solutions, while the ScrumMaster focuses on removing impediments and communicating with stakeholders. In general, a good software architect makes a good ScrumMaster, but in the ScrumMaster role, the person cannot be an effective architect.

 While an external architect may be involved in sprint planning, he or she should not participate in estimation. Only team members who are actually building the features should be estimating their complexity.

Release Management

Release management has an important role in Scrum. It changes somewhat from how it looks in other methodologies, but the core functions remain the same. A Scrum team needs to work with the production teams that will distribute, host, and support the product. The earlier this discussion begins, the easier it will go. However, there is no release manager on the Scrum team; this is an external role.

Early during a release cycle, a Scrum product owner should define the PBIs to meet the needs of the deployment team and the operations team. The more the product owner considers the needs of these constituents, the smoother the deployment will be. Failure to understand these needs will result in difficulties as the product moves to production, so this is an important step.

An important goal in Scrum is to have a potentially releasable product at the end of each sprint. There is a difference between "potentially releasable" and "production quality"; at the end of each sprint, the product is probably not ready for production deployment.

Table 2-9 summarizes the release management activities on a Scrum team.

TABLE 2-9: Release Management Activities in Scrum

ACTIVITY	WHO IS RESPONSIBLE	DESCRIPTION
Advocate for deployment teams	Product owner	Treats the deployment team as a user, creating user stories and adding items to the product backlog. This includes operational requirements such as "must use SSL" and "credit cards cannot be stored in the database."
Security review	ScrumMaster	Works with the operations team to schedule a security review after key sprints. Depending on the product, a team may choose to do it earlier.
Release documentation	ScrumMaster	Many IT organizations require checklists and supporting documentation before a product is released into a production data center. This responsibility generally falls to the ScrumMaster.
Verification and validation	Product owner	The Scrum team must build and unit test features. Ultimately, however, the product owner accepts each PBI, so this production requirement is generally met within the sprints.

The QA Manager

The discrete role of QA manager goes away with Scrum. Likewise, there is no "QA group." These functions are subsumed by the Scrum team members and product owner. These roles are no less important, but they become more efficient and empowered when they are part of the Scrum team. Efficiency comes from being just one "seat" away from the developer and one seat away from the product owner.

When testers have direct access to both sides of the testing (producer and consumer), they are more productive. Empowerment comes from running tests early in the development cycle. When software is late (which it often is), the testing window shrinks quickly. By being part of the Scrum team, testers can begin testing earlier and have a greater impact with the bugs they find.

The product owner also ensures that each PBI meets its exit criteria, as defined in the user story. This adds a layer of verification and validation on top of the testing that the team carries out. The product owner may involve users in testing after each sprint. The team tracks and adds bugs that surface during that testing as items to complete in the next sprint.

TRANSITIONING TO SCRUM

This section summarizes some of the changes that occur within an organization as it transitions to Scrum. It is not intended to be a road map as to how to transition but instead as a set of observations that help you know that you're heading in the right direction.

Increasing User Involvement

Scrum is very user-centric. The product owner tends to be in frequent contact with users throughout the sprints. After each sprint, when the product is in a potentially releasable state, the product owner should show off product features and get very fast feedback.

But with Scrum, the product owner is not the only one who works with the user community. The entire team is much more involved with users. Rather than discussing whether a feature meets the spec, a team discusses whether the feature meets the user's expectations. Nothing beats going to the source to get clarification on exactly what those expectations are.

> **INVOLVING USERS IN THE DAILY SCRUM**
>
> You may find that users want to attend the daily Scrum. This is okay, as long as they attend as observers and not active participants. From a scheduling perspective, you know that the team will be in the same place at the same time each morning, so it can be convenient for team members to meet with users right before or after the daily Scrum.

Decreasing Documentation

Scrum is very collaborative. It relies on clear communication among team members and between the Scrum team and the user community. Therefore, there's less use for formal documentation in Scrum than in other methodologies.

However, Scrum is not without documentation. Documentation is good. It's a record of what was needed, what was decided, and why. If a Scrum team fails to capture and record this basic information, the organization will have to retrace the team's steps the next time the question comes up. However, a 100-page business requirements document will not be helpful to a Scrum team. Scrum documentation is much shorter and to the point than this.

Scrum requires a minimum body of documentation to define the product vision and an increasing body of documentation to capture user stories for how the product will be used. Once user stories are captured and the technical features are defined, the Scrum team favors other forms of communication media, such as the following:

➤ Face-to-face meetings at the daily Scrum to remove impediments

➤ Whiteboards and sticky notes to refine user stories

➤ Whiteboards for architecture design sessions within the team

➤ Tracking tools (such as Team Foundation Server and Excel)

➤ E-mail and PowerPoint status given to project constituents

At the conclusion of each release, additional documentation may be required to deploy the product into production. This often occurs in the form of checklists and forms required by an external operations team.

Simplifying the Schedule

Sprints and releases are hallmarks of Scrum. There are specific ceremonies at the beginning of a release and after the release occurs, and there are specific ceremonies at the beginning and end of a sprint. These are described later in the book, in Chapters 8 and 9. A Scrum schedule is quite predictable and can be safely planned and budgeted with accuracy within a week or two.

A sprint is typically fixed at two to four weeks. In the case of a four-week sprint, there are generally three weeks of coding and testing, followed by one week of integration, the retrospective, and planning for the next sprint. Each day, the team meets for 15 minutes to discuss and remove impediments to progress. A Scrum team rarely extends the duration of a sprint because the cadence of the project depends on the sprint length remaining constant and predictable.

Uncertainty doesn't go away with Scrum; it just moves. Rather than being uncertain about when a release will ship, a project sponsor is uncertain about what will be in the release when the team says the release is ready. Uncertainty is generally reduced with each successive sprint, as more and more of the product emerges in a potentially shippable form. But from the standpoint of managing a schedule, things get easier with Scrum.

Finding Problems Earlier

With iterative development and a potentially shippable product with each sprint, the user community and project sponsors get to see the product much earlier than with traditional methodologies. This is good for everyone, as it enables the extended team to catch problems as they occur.

Consider a traditional Waterfall methodology. Analysts collect requirements from users and write a business requirements document that is often a lengthy document that becomes the contract between the user community and the project management team. If a requirement didn't make it into this document, then it becomes a change request. From there, the project team writes a functional specification, describing the design and data validation of a system that meets the requirements. The business requirements document is a deliverable from the project team to the user community, but rarely do any users read it, so the possibility for errors is quite high. The team builds a system to meet the functional requirements and then turns the system over to a QA group to ensure that the system meets the requirements in the functional specification. Again, nobody is checking whether the system is even close to what the users want.

Scrum improves on this process in a number of ways:

➤ Users get to see the system after just a few weeks (a sprint) and can identify problems or question assumptions.

➤ Integration among technical components happens during each sprint, so problems that would have been uncovered very late using a traditional methodology are visible early with Scrum.

➤ The team focuses on QA within each sprint, both with automated testing and with verification from the product owner, so problems surface early. This differs from traditional methods where QA happens after development is complete.

➤ There is no change order process, so the team can be more flexible in building a system that meets user needs. Scrum assumes that the product backlog is dynamic (within budget constraints), so the team is more aligned to the users for a positive outcome of the project.

SUMMARY

Scrum defines just three roles: product owner, ScrumMaster, and team members. Collectively, the team fulfilling these roles builds a potentially shippable product during each sprint. The users are at the center of everything the team does and are involved early and often in decisions and demonstrations.

It is possible to scale a Scrum team in two ways. The first way is to scale the product owner, since one product owner can quickly be overwhelmed when eight team members need clarification. Because the product owner is also responsible for signing off on PBIs, his or her time is quite limited, so it's common to add labor in later sprints. The next way to scale is by creating additional Scrum teams. It's typically best to create Scrum teams by feature, although sometimes it is more appropriate to partition teams by component or technology.

In understanding the three roles within Scrum, it's helpful to compare the responsibilities of these roles to roles in other software methodologies, such as MSF and IT in general. This chapter discusses how those MSF and IT roles relate to the functions of Scrum roles.

When transitioning from another methodology to Scrum, you see significant changes. Some (such as minimal documentation) can be unsettling at first, but the result of using Scrum is a product that better meets user expectations.

3

Tracking What's Important in Team Foundation Server

WHAT'S IN THIS CHAPTER?

➤ Understanding how project data is stored in Team Foundation Server.

➤ Looking at the artifacts that make up a Scrum project.

➤ Understanding the key activities of a Scrum project.

In Chapter 2, you read about different approaches to software development and how you can organize your team. This chapter focuses on the specifics of the Scrum framework, including the main activities and artifacts in Scrum. This chapter begins by looking at how your project data is stored in Team Foundation Server (TFS) and how team members can use this data. Then the chapter dives into the Scrum process and examines the key activities and artifacts that a Scrum team uses.

UNDERSTANDING YOUR DATA IN TFS

TFS is a Microsoft product that helps you manage and organize source code, project work items, project artifacts, and builds. This book focuses on project work items and how you enter them into TFS for tracking and reporting purposes. Work items are the main means for storing data in TFS. You can think of a work item as a single row in a database table, where the table name and table columns are defined by the process. A work item can by any type, but most work items fall into the common software project management categories requirements, bugs, tasks, and issues.

Within TFS, the team records its work in a team project. Each team project in TFS is created from a process template. A process template is a set of XML files that define the different components of the team project. For example, the fields displayed for a work item are defined in the process template.

TFS 2010 ships with two process templates:

➤ **MSF for Agile Software Development v5.0** — You can use this generic Agile best-practices template to implement different Agile methodologies (for example, Scrum, Extreme Programming [XP]).

➤ **MSF for CMMI Process Improvement v5.0** — This formal process template with deep traceability and auditability helps teams satisfy the requirements of the Capability Maturity Model Integration (CMMI) approach to process improvement.

Microsoft Solutions Framework (MSF) is a framework for building and shipping software in an iterative series of releases. For more information on MSF, see Chapter 1.

Microsoft released a third process template during the summer of 2010, shortly after the release of TFS 2010:

➤ **Microsoft Visual Studio Scrum 1.0** — This prescriptive template was built for teams practicing Scrum.

Off the shelf, TFS doesn't come with the Microsoft Visual Studio Scrum 1.0 process template. See Chapter 4 for details on how to download and install this template.

Microsoft Visual Studio Scrum 1.0 was the first template from Microsoft that departed from the MSF brand. The template shows Microsoft's commitment to the Scrum framework and Scrum teams, and it shows the continued trend toward Agile methodologies (specifically Scrum) in the software industry. This book examines Microsoft's Scrum process template and discusses details of how your team can set up, track, and execute a Scrum project in TFS 2010.

Reporting Capabilities in TFS

Every software project needs to be tracked. Without clear project metrics, it is impossible to measure a project's health or likelihood of success. TFS provides a SQL Server data warehouse that can be used for analytics and reporting. From this warehouse, a SQL Server Analysis cube is built that allows you to slice and dice your project data in a variety of ways. A *cube* is a data structure that allows for fast analysis of large amounts of data. This book takes an in-depth look at the reports provided with the Microsoft Visual Studio Scrum 1.0 process template. You'll discover how to use common tools such as Microsoft Excel to dig into the trends and metrics of your software project.

SQL Server Reporting Services

Each process template included with TFS comes with a set of SQL Server Reporting Services reports. These reports provide key metrics to support the process defined in the process template. Figure 3-1 shows the velocity report in the Microsoft Visual Studio Scrum 1.0 process template.

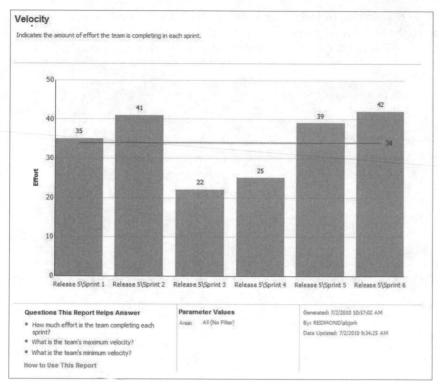

FIGURE 3-1: The velocity report.

The Microsoft Visual Studio Scrum 1.0 process template includes the following reports:

➤ Sprint burndown

➤ Release burndown

➤ Velocity

➤ Test case readiness

➤ Test plan progress

➤ Build success over time

➤ Build summary

In the chapters that follow, you will examine the sprint burndown, release burndown, and velocity reports and dig into how they provide valuable information to a Scrum team. You'll also examine the test case readiness, test plan progress, build success over time, and build summary reports and learn how they can help your team track progress and quality.

Excel Reporting

Excel is a powerful reporting tool that a team can leverage to track project progress and project health. Whereas SQL Server Reporting Services provides a platform for building professional and detailed reports, Excel is a great low-barrier-to-entry tool for browsing the data in the SQL Server

Analysis Services cube to examine project trends and metrics. Reports in Excel are built from PivotTables connected to the SQL Server Analysis Services cube. Figure 3-2 shows an example of a report built using Microsoft Excel. Chapter 5 discusses the details of creating reports in Excel.

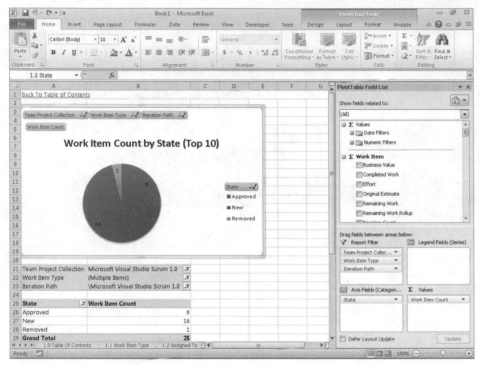

FIGURE 3-2: An example of a report built in Excel.

 To use Excel to build a report like the one shown in Figure 3-2, you right-click any work item query in Team Explorer and select Create Report in Excel.

CHOOSING SCRUM

Teams choose Scrum for many reasons. The most common reasons are controlling risk, improving predictability, and maximizing return on investment (ROI):

➤ **Controlling risk** — Scrum controls risk by time-boxing activities. Instead of making a few large commitments (high risk), a Scrum team makes a series of smaller commitments (low risk). The smaller the commitment, the smaller the risk. Scrum helps teams control and minimize risk by breaking large, complex problems into smaller, manageable pieces.

➤ **Improving predictability** — Scrum involves a repeatable process called a sprint. A *sprint* is an iteration of work that is time-boxed to one month or less. By continually working in sprints, teams improve their ability to plan, estimate, and make decisions.

➤ **Maximizing ROI** — A Scrum team trades value gained from traditional planning for the value gained by doing and learning.

FROM WATERFALL TO SCRUM

The most traditional software-creating process is the Waterfall method. The Waterfall method is a sequential process in which progress flows from top to bottom through a series of phases:

➤ Requirements

➤ Design

➤ Implementation

➤ Integration

➤ Verification

➤ Maintenance

In each phase of the process, the team completes a specific set of steps before moving on to the next phase. At the end of the entire process, the team delivers a piece of working software. Figure 3-3 shows these steps simplified: plan, review, execute, and manage change.

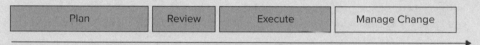

FIGURE 3-3: Traditional planning steps.

Scrum assumes that despite achieving the end goal (working software), the traditional steps create a significant amount of waste. Requirements are rarely perfect when handed off for design — and this equates to waste. In addition, implementations are often reworked after they start because initial designs were flawed — and this represents more waste. Scrum aims to eliminate waste by completing all these phases within the time box of a single iteration (that is, sprint). Figure 3-4 outlines how Scrum embraces change throughout the life cycle of a project.

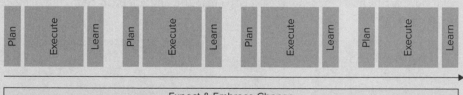

FIGURE 3-4: Scrum planning steps.

Scrum is a framework under the umbrella of Agile software development. *Agile software development* is a group of software development methodologies based on iterative and incremental development. As mentioned in Chapter 1, in 2001, a group of industry leaders gathered and published the Agile Manifesto: 12 principles and 4 value statements about how to approach software development. These are the 4 statements from the manifesto:

➤ Individuals and interactions over processes and tools

➤ Working software over comprehensive documentation

➤ Customer collaboration over contract negotiation

➤ Responding to change over following a plan

Scrum does not address these statements directly, but it is easy to see how the Scrum framework supports the Agile Manifesto:

➤ **Individuals and interactions over processes and tools** — The team is ultimately responsible for the success of the project. Traditional software projects put great stock in planning, process, and tools. Such projects invest heavily in studying, researching, planning, testing, documenting, and analyzing before a single line of code is written. Scrum places its bet on the team and trusts that the team will learn more from building software than it will learn from extensive planning.

➤ **Working software over comprehensive documentation** — Scrum prescribes that the team is ready to ship working software at the end of each sprint. With each sprint, the team produces an increment of the product that could deliver value to customers. Working software at the end of every sprint demonstrates that a team is capable of delivering software end-to-end.

➤ **Customer collaboration over contract negotiation** — The product owner in Scrum, the individual responsible for the requirements, typically spends 50% of his or her time with customers. The product owner is the customer advocate and looks for ways to involve customers at every stage of the process.

➤ **Responding to change over following a plan** — Learning happens throughout the process. After each sprint, the team learns more about what it will take to deliver the product. The learning provides valuable information that can be used in the next sprint. Waterfall attempts to manage change with formal processes and long-range planning. On the other hand, Scrum embraces change and expects that it will lead to a better product in the end. Each new sprint gives the team a chance to respond and adapt to changing business needs and requirements.

The following sections of this chapter look more closely at the artifacts and activities of a Scrum project. Then it digs into how to enact Scrum on a team by using the Microsoft Visual Studio Scrum 1.0 process template for TFS 2010.

SCRUM ARTIFACTS

An *artifact* is an object created for a practical purpose. Scrum has four artifacts: the product backlog, sprint backlog, sprint burndown, and release burndown. A team uses these artifacts during the Scrum process to manage the production of working software. They are certainly not the only ones that a Scrum team can or should use, but they represent the main artifacts in Scrum:

➤ **Product backlog** — A prioritized list of requirements for the product being developed

➤ **Sprint backlog** — A list of tasks created by the team to turn a set of items from the product backlog into an increment of potentially shippable product

➤ **Sprint burndown** — A graph that measures the remaining sprint backlog items over the duration of a sprint

➤ **Release burndown** — A graph that measures the remaining product backlog over time

The following sections look more closely at these artifacts.

The Product Backlog

Every software project has requirements. A *requirement* describes something a stakeholder expects from a product. For example, if your project requires security, you might have a requirement which states that every user must log in with a username and password. Another requirement might state that a valid password must be six of more characters and must contain at least one letter and one number. A team needs to define requirements to ensure that the project achieves the business goals.

Scrum prescribes that requirements be captured and prioritized on the product backlog. The product backlog, in simple terms, is the list of things that the team needs to complete to deliver the product. Each item on the product backlog is called a *product backlog item (PBI)* and represents a single requirement for the product.

In the sections that follow, you will examine how to ensure that value is delivered from the product backlog using acceptance criteria, how to manage dependencies between items on the product backlog, and how to minimize the impact of changing requirements.

Delivering Customer Value

You describe each item on the product backlog in words that reflect the value the item will bring to a customer. Delivering value, early and often, is the first key concept of Scrum. Without understanding the value to the customer that implementing an item on the product backlog can bring, the team cannot properly prioritize. Every item on the backlog must clearly articulate the value it brings to the customer. If an item does not bring value to the customer, it does not belong on the product backlog.

What do you do with things that need to be done but do not relate to the customer? These types of tasks belong on the product backlog. However, you must justify each task in terms of customer value. For each task, ask yourself questions such as "Why are we doing this particular task?" "Do we really need to refactor the entire login class?" and "What value does the customer get if we do?"

Thinking about each task in terms of business value is extremely important. Teams often find themselves spending lots of time working on tasks that don't ultimately deliver any value to the customer. Scrum aims to minimize these distractions by insisting that items on the backlog are described in terms of customer value.

Defining Acceptance Criteria

Acceptance criteria are conditions that must be met in order for a PBI to be considered done. A product owner has no greater tool for communicating with the team than well-thought-out and detailed acceptance criteria. Ask 10 mature Agile teams "How do you know when you're 'done' with an item from your backlog?" and you will get the same answer from each one: by defining and using well-written acceptance criteria.

Acceptance criteria are the handshake between the product owner and the team on what *done* means. Until the acceptance criteria are met, the team is not finished. However, the value of acceptance criteria only starts here. Acceptance criteria set the stage for some of most meaningful conversations and interactions on the team.

Some of the best interactions on a team can occur as members dig into the acceptance criteria for each item on the backlog. As they begin to discuss the acceptance criteria, team members are likely to have a number of "a-ha!" moments and develop a shared understanding of the story.

Regardless of who is being enlightened, the power of acceptance criteria lies in the fact that the product owner and the team are building a shared understanding of what *done* means. And this is happening before the team has written a single line of code, before any work has been done, before commitments have been made, and before the sprint has started. By collaborating on acceptance criteria, the team minimizes risk and greatly increases the chance of delivering successfully.

Dependencies

A team manages dependencies between items on the product backlog by priority. If item A depends on item B, the team should move item B up on the product backlog. And if item C depends on item B, it should move item C up on the backlog. Instead of creating a complex dependency management system that requires a Ph.D. and full-time job to understand and manage, Scrum keeps things simple. The priority of the items on the backlog should closely reflect their execution order and account for dependencies between backlog items.

Changing Requirements

It is a basic unpleasant fact that requirements change. Scrum assumes that the list of requirements for a product is always incomplete; this is a big difference between Scrum and traditional software development processes. Don't mistake this for meaning that Scrum doesn't prescribe planning or that Scrum projects aren't well thought out ahead of time. In fact, in many ways, Scrum prescribes more planning than traditional processes. The difference is *when* the planning takes place.

Bringing Requirements to the Team

A team adds to the product backlog each item needed to both develop and deliver the product. Imagine that the team is a house; in this case, the product backlog is the front door. All work the team takes on and commits to must come through the front door (the product backlog). If a team is assigned work from too many sources — through side doors or even the garage — the team is bound to become confused, conflicted, and distracted from achieving its goal. This simple concept is fundamental to the success of a Scrum team.

LEARNING TO USE THE FRONT DOOR

On a recent project, a team was halfway through the third sprint when one of its team members, Phil, reported at the daily standup that he would not be able to work on tasks in the sprint for the next few days. Phil's manager had given him a new task that needed to be completed right away. This new task was unrelated to the sprint and would require a minimum of three days of Phil's time. Phil, along with most of the rest of the team, was fairly new to Scrum. This new work didn't alarm any of them; in fact, most seemed just fine with it. Distractions and randomizations like this one had become commonplace for the team. This was nothing new.

The ScrumMaster felt differently, however. The team had not made a commitment to this new work, and the work was being thrust upon a single member of the team through a side door. There was no way the team would be able to meet the commitment to the sprint without Phil's involvement.

The ScrumMaster asked Phil's manager if there was any way to postpone this work until the next sprint. In the end, the ScrumMaster negotiated most of Phil's time back and got the remaining work added to the product backlog and prioritized against other work on the backlog. Despite the small distraction, the team was able to successfully complete the sprint and deliver the items it had committed to.

The team also eventually delivered the new work that Phil's manager had asked him to do — after two more sprints. It turned out that the work wasn't quite as important as initially thought.

For team members new to Scrum, it's natural to want to say "yes" to requests from superiors. Most people want to please others and be viewed as helpful. If your team is new to Scrum, pay close attention to any work not entering through the front door. Such work can quickly lead to a situation where your team is not meeting its commitments, despite the fact that team members are trying to do the right thing. The following are some suggestions to help your team create a healthy environment for building its product backlog:

➤ Establish a culture where everyone understands that new work is brought to the team through the product backlog.

➤ Establish an agreement with management and other stakeholders that they will neither bypass the process nor engage team members directly with new work.

➤ Ensure that the team's ScrumMaster understands that he or she is responsible for protecting the team from distractions.

The Sprint Backlog

The sprint backlog consists of the items selected from the product backlog for a sprint plus the tasks the team will perform to turn those items into working functionality. During a sprint, the team's focus turns to the sprint backlog.

The team and product owner create the sprint backlog during the sprint planning meeting. In sprint planning, the team breaks down PBIs into a series of tasks for the team to complete. The team estimates the number of hours each task will take. Each day, team members select and work on tasks from the sprint backlog; they report on their progress during the daily standup.

The ScrumMaster owns the sprint backlog. His or her job is to ensure that the backlog is updated daily and that the sprint backlog always represents the remaining work the team has committed to. The sprint backlog should be kept simple and should be readily available to everyone on the team.

Remaining Effort

In Scrum, the remaining effort for all tasks must be tracked on the sprint backlog. Project managers often have a difficult time understanding this concept. It is common to hear traditional project managers ask, "If the team is only tracking remaining effort, how do I know how much work was completed?" With Scrum, completed work does not matter. Most teams have an initial problem with letting go of completed work. They have tracked it closely for years. However, there are a number of compelling reasons for not caring about completed work:

➤ **Estimates of completed work are rarely accurate** — Team members can always tell how much work remains. But work completed is a bit of a gray area.

➤ **Focusing on completed work distracts the team from what is important** — It makes no difference that a team completed 100 hours of work if 150 hours are needed to meet its commitment. The remaining 50 hours are what is important.

➤ **Focusing on completed work quickly pollutes a team atmosphere** — It puts team members into a competitive situation where everyone wants to have completed the most work.

New Work

A team should quickly deal with new work found during a sprint. After starting implementation, it is not uncommon for a team to uncover additional work that was not known or visible during sprint planning. There are two choices for new work:

➤ The team may decide to add the new work to the existing sprint. This decision must be made by the entire team and not by a single team member or the ScrumMaster.

➤ The team may decide, with the product owner, to add the new work to the product backlog.

When making any decisions about new work, it is important that a team understand whether the new work is necessary to complete the items from the product backlog that it has already committed to. If the work is absolutely necessary for a PBI to be considered done, the new work should be included in the sprint.

It's never okay to partially implement a PBI with the idea that the team will complete the work in the next sprint. Becoming comfortable with partially implemented PBIs can quickly lead to the team being comfortable not meeting its commitment. As soon as this pattern develops, the team loses its ability to accurately estimate future work. The entire process starts to unravel.

The most important rule regarding new work is that only the team can change the sprint backlog. It's not okay for the product owner to change the requirements of a PBI after the team has started work. The ScrumMaster is responsible for protecting the team from any changing requirements during a sprint and ensuring that the team is in control of its commitment.

The Sprint Burndown

The sprint burndown is a graph that shows the daily amount of work remaining (hours) in the sprint. The data for the graph is pulled directly from the sprint backlog. Work remaining for the sprint is a simple sum of all the hours remaining on all tasks in the sprint. The team reports its progress daily, in hours, so it can accurately understand exactly how much work remains in the sprint.

The sprint burndown chart shows the team how much work remains in the sprint as well as how much work is currently in progress. By tracking both of these pieces of data, the team can answer the following questions:

➤   Is the team on track to complete the remaining work before the end of the sprint?

➤   Does the team have too much work in progress relative to the amount of work remaining?

Figure 3-5 shows the sprint burndown chart for a Scrum team nearing the end of a sprint.

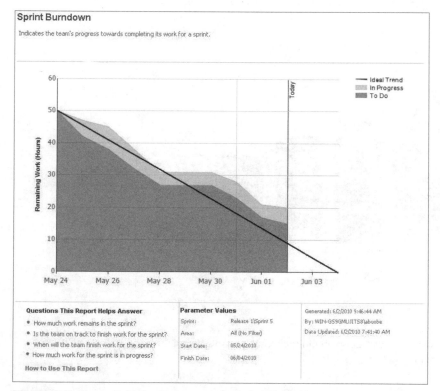

FIGURE 3-5: The sprint burndown report included in the Microsoft Visual Studio Scrum 1.0 process template.

Ken Schwaber, one of the founders of Scrum, has an interesting thought on sprint burndown charts becoming signatures of the team:

> *As a team works together, it develops its own style of creating and maintaining the sprint backlog. It also demonstrates unique work patterns, some working consistently, some in bursts, some at the end of a sprint. Some seek pressure, while others seek regularity. Across time, the backlog charts of each team develop predictable patterns. They stabilize as the team learns the technology, the business or product domain, and each other. These chart patterns are called sprint signatures.*

The Release Burndown

As you can see in Figure 3-6, the release burndown report shows the sum of the remaining effort on the product backlog over time (that is, across sprints). The effort is summed in whatever unit the team has decided to use.

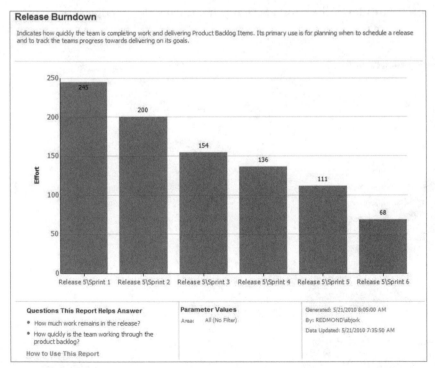

FIGURE 3-6: The release burndown report included in the Microsoft Visual Studio Scrum 1.0 process template.

The product owner and team use the release burndown report to gauge how much effort remains in the release before and after each sprint.

SCRUM ACTIVITIES

A Scrum team performs key activities during the life cycle of a Scrum project. Each activity is time-boxed to create certainty and regularity. By time-boxing its activities, a team learns to expect what is next and develop a rhythm. The following are some of the key activities of a Scrum team:

➤ **Release planning meeting** — This is an optional meeting where the team establishes the goal for the release.

➤ **Backlog grooming** — This is an ongoing activity of the product owner to keep the backlog prioritized and sufficiently detailed.

➤ **Sprint** — This is a 30-day (or less) time-boxed iteration during which the team turns items from the product backlog into working software.

➤ **Sprint planning meeting** — This is a time-boxed meeting in which the team selects and plans the work for the next sprint. In general, a sprint planning meeting should not be longer than eight hours. It's important that the meeting be confined to a single day to minimize the interruption to the team.

➤ **Daily Scrum** — This is a 15-minute meeting where the team gathers to report on progress.

➤ **Sprint review** — This is a time-boxed meeting during which the team and stakeholders review the work completed in the sprint. In general, the sprint review is no longer than four hours. Keeping this meeting under four hours helps ensure that the team's time is used efficiently.

➤ **Sprint retrospective** — This is a three-hour time-boxed meeting where the team examines its sprint to determine how it can improve.

The following sections look at these activities in more detail.

The Release Planning Meeting

The release planning meeting is an optional meeting that aims to establish a plan and goal for the team and organization. In release planning, the organization answers several questions:

➤ What are we going to build?

➤ Why are we building it?

➤ When do we hope to deliver it?

Release planning is not prescribed by Scrum, but most organizations do some level of release planning. Because release planning is not prescribed by Scrum, this book doesn't cover release planning in detail.

Backlog Grooming

Before the team gathers for the sprint planning meeting, the product owner must groom and prioritize the product backlog. Grooming the backlog simply means ensuring that items on the product backlog are in priority order and that items in the top portion of the product backlog are sufficiently detailed.

One of the first and often most difficult lessons that new Scrum teams learn is that it's impossible to have a successful sprint planning meeting (or a successful sprint for that matter) without a well-groomed backlog.

Your Scrum team may decide to hold regular product backlog grooming meetings. The team and the product owner attend each backlog grooming meeting. During the meeting, the product owner seeks input from everyone on the team to help prepare the backlog for the next sprint planning meeting. This might include adding new items to the backlog or splitting items that the team thinks are too large. It might also include doing some very rough estimating for items already on the backlog to help prevent the official sprint planning meeting from lasting an unnecessarily long time. In most cases, the estimates will change when they are officially estimated, but the product backlog grooming meeting plants seeds for the team about what is coming.

> It is always difficult for a team to pull away from its work mid-sprint so that it can attend a backlog grooming meeting. However, the value gained from doing so will lead to more effective sprint planning meetings and eventually more effective sprints. Although backlog grooming meetings are not a formal part of the Scrum process, Ken Schwaber advises that teams dedicate 5% of their time, per sprint, to this activity.

The Sprint

A team's real work occurs during a sprint itself. During a sprint, the team turns its plan into working software. The outcome of each sprint is something that is potentially shippable, no matter how simple or complex the end result. Delivering working software at the end of each sprint is fundamental to Scrum. It motivates the product owner to prioritize value to the customer first, it encourages the team to have short-term goals that have tangible results, and it puts the team in a position to ship at any time.

The following are some keys to the success of a sprint:

➤ **Keep team composition constant** — If the team composition is constantly changing in size or in terms of membership, the team can't understand what it is capable of accomplishing. Make sure the members of your team are committed to just the one team.

➤ **Choose a consistent duration for sprints** — Scrum recommends a 30-day sprint but doesn't mandate the duration. Find the duration that works for your teams and stick with it. Changing the sprint length for any reason will lead to inconsistencies in understanding the team's velocity, and it hinders the team from finding a rhythm to its work. The one exception to this rule is new teams. New teams should start with 1-week sprints so they have a chance to exercise their Scrum muscles. A new Scrum team operating in 30-day sprints will need a few months before it truly understands the flow of Scrum. By initially using week-long sprints, the team has an opportunity to quickly go through the process and develop a stronger set of Scrum muscles.

➤ **Don't end sprints on Fridays** — People don't tend to like Friday deadlines. Most people have plans for Friday nights that involve friends, family, and some level of up-front planning. People need weekends to recharge and re-energize. When sprints end on Fridays, team members are caught between their weekends and the team. Ending sprints midweek (Tuesday or Wednesday) gives team members more freedom with their weekends. This can do a lot for team morale.

Every sprint starts with a sprint planning meeting and ends with a sprint review meeting. These two meetings, described in the following sections, are the bookends of every sprint.

The Sprint Planning Meeting

At the sprint planning meeting, the product owner and the team negotiate which items from the product backlog the team will complete during the upcoming sprint. The entire meeting should be completed within one calendar day to ensure that that team's time is used efficiently. The product owner is ultimately responsible for determining which items are of the highest priority, but the team has a voice in the process and should be listened to as it gives input.

The sprint planning meeting has two distinct parts:

➤ **Part 1** — Part 1 is devoted to selecting work from the product backlog. This is done with the product owner and the team present.

➤ **Part 2** — During part 2 of the meeting, the team builds a sprint backlog from the work selected during part 1. The product owner often attends part 2 of the meeting but isn't required to be present.

A successful sprint planning meeting realizes a number of results, including the following:

➤ **Sprint goal** — The sprint goal is a clear agreement between the product owner and the team on what the team will complete by the end of the sprint.

➤ **Acceptance criteria** — The product owner and the team must have a clear understanding of the definition of *done* for each item. This is known as the acceptance criteria for each item.

➤ **Sprint backlog** — The team needs to create a clear set of tasks that detail the work needed to implement each item selected from the product backlog. The set of tasks together form the sprint backlog.

The sprint planning meeting is a critical component of a successful sprint. It requires involvement and a commitment from each member of the team.

Sprint Planning, Part 1

The goal of part 1 of the sprint planning meeting is for the team and the product owner to agree on which items will be completed in the sprint. The team and the product owner do this by describing, discussing, and estimating items from the product backlog.

Part 1 of the sprint planning meeting sets the tone for the entire sprint. If the product owner shows up and takes an hour or more to describe, discuss, and estimate the first few items on the backlog, the team members will feel that their time isn't valued. In this case, the sprint is unlikely to be successful.

Running a Sprint Planning Meeting

While there is no specific format for a sprint planning meeting, a typical meeting might look something like this:

1. The product owner and the team arrive at the meeting on time. Getting started on time sets the tone for the entire meeting.

2. The ScrumMaster writes on a whiteboard the amount of effort the team completed in the last sprint. This is known as *yesterday's weather* and represents the team's velocity. Yesterday's weather is usually a good predictor of upcoming weather. For example, if the team completed 20 units of effort in the last sprint, given that the conditions are the same for this sprint (time/team), the team can expect to complete 20 units of effort in this sprint.

3. Each member of the team announces any planned interruptions (vacations, appointments, holidays, and so on) that will impact how much work the team can commit to.

4. The ScrumMaster reviews the agreed-upon definition of *done* so that everyone is aware of what activities are included when the team declares an item done. Reviewing the done criteria during each retrospective is also a good practice.

5. The product owner presents the product backlog to the team by reading the title for each item on the top of the backlog. These are the items that that are likely to be completed in this sprint. This first pass of the product backlog gives the team context around what they're likely to commit to.

6. After any high-level clarifying questions are answered, the product owner returns to the top of the backlog and describes the backlog items in detail, including the acceptance criteria for the items.

7. New acceptance criteria are added to each item, based on new details uncovered during discussion.

8. The team estimates the time it will take to complete each item discussed.

Estimating PBIs

The team determines how much work it can complete in the sprint based on the estimates created for each PBI. There are many different acceptable methods for arriving at an estimate, but many teams today use a simple technique known as Planning Poker. Mike Cohn, who originated the idea of Planning Poker, is a founding member of the Scrum Alliance and an experienced Agile practitioner and coach. Planning Poker is an easy and fun tool for estimating work. In this process, each team member provides an estimate before deciding as a team on a value.

In Planning Poker, each team member has a deck of cards with a set of values. The values represent an estimate of the amount of effort needed to complete each backlog item. Most Planning Poker cards use the Fibonacci sequence (1, 2, 3, 5, 8, 13, and so on), as it reflects the fact that the team doesn't expect perfect estimates, particularly as PBI sizes grow. For example, what is the difference between estimates of 11 and 12 when discussing something on the backlog? In truth, there isn't much difference. Estimating at this level is nothing more than guessing, and the relative difference between the numbers is so small, it's not worth discussing. By using the Fibonacci sequence, teams are forced to choose between a set of known values.

The team members simultaneously reveal their estimates. Those who presented high or low estimates then explain their position. The goal of the exercise is not to arrive at a precise estimate. Rather, it's to spark conversations that lead to a shared understanding of what *done* means for each item being discussed. After discussion, the team plays another round of Planning Poker, until it arrives at a value that everyone agrees with.

After estimating the first item, the product owner presents the next item on the backlog, and the team repeats this process until it has accumulated enough effort to match its velocity. At this point, part 1 of the sprint planning meeting concludes. Together, the product owner and the team have selected items from the backlog that the team will complete in the upcoming sprint. Now, the team is ready to dig into the details of each of the items selected during part 1 before it makes a commitment.

> *It is not a coincidence that the first bullet in the Agile Manifesto states "We have come to value individual and interactions over processes and tools." Agile teams work together. By working together, they create better software. Start learning to love acceptance criteria and see if your team isn't more successful at delivering software.*

Sprint Planning, Part 2

During part 2 of the sprint planning meeting, the team makes a plan for how it will implement the items selected and decides which of those items it can commit to.

It is not necessary for the product owner to participate in this part of the sprint planning meeting. However, it's good practice for the product owner to be present to help answer questions that arise. The likelihood of success increases greatly when the product owner has time and energy to commit to the team.

Determining Tasks

In part 2 of the sprint planning meeting, the team decomposes each of the items selected in part 1, in priority order, into a set of tasks that represent all the work necessary to implement the PBI. The team estimates the time it will take to complete each task and adds it to the sprint backlog.

It is critical that everyone on the team be involved in task breakdown and estimation. A common trap that new and inexperienced teams fall into is to have one or two people on the team (leads, senior developers, and so on) do the task breakdown without input from the rest of the team. Falling into this trap kills morale on the team and often leads to very inaccurate estimates. It also prevents all the shared learning that occurs when the team estimates together. It isn't realistic to assume that one or two team members have the power to accurately discover, describe, and estimate all the work for a Scrum team.

The tasks that the team creates will include the traditional steps in a software development life cycle and should include all the work necessary to call an item from the backlog done. This often includes designing, developing, unit testing, exploratory testing, user acceptance testing (UAT), and documenting tasks. A common misconception about Scrum is that it does not include traditional software development activities. This could not be further from the truth. Where Scrum differs from the Waterfall method is that a Scrum team tackles these activities just-in-time rather than in long periods of time.

In a traditional software development project, the development and testing teams might be on very different schedules. The development team could be coding for weeks on end, without ever delivering anything for testing. Meanwhile, the test team is often far behind the development team, finding bugs in code that was checked weeks, or even months, earlier. This creates a vicious cycle that can be very difficult for a team to get out of.

On a Scrum team, coding and testing happen together and with minimal transition time. For example, when a developer on the team completes a task, he or she immediately hands it off to a tester on the team for testing. Bugs found during testing are dealt with immediately instead of being placed on the shelf to be tackled later. Bug debt is unacceptable to a Scrum team, and the team takes steps to ensure that debt is not accrued. A team should include all tasks necessary so that a PBI can be declared done at the end of the sprint.

After the team breaks an item down into tasks, it should review the estimate determined for the item during part 1 of the sprint planning meeting. Was new work found as the team discussed the details of implementation? Is the PBI bigger than initially suspected? Having the product owner present during part 2 of the meeting can be extremely beneficial, as additional negotiation may be necessary after the team has dug into the details of the item.

Making a Commitment

When all PBIs are decomposed into tasks, the team is ready to make a commitment to the work for the sprint. Before making a commitment, the team should review any planned interruptions to the sprint and be sure that everyone feels good about what the team is taking on.

The team should never commit to work that it does not think it can complete during a sprint. It is common for team members to want to overcommit. However, it is critical that the team learn to commit only to work that it collectively feels it can complete.

 If your team is new to Scrum, do not panic if the first few sprints result in drastic overcommitments by the team. This happens to most teams. As the team matures, it learns to understand how much work is involved to complete work from the backlog and begins to develop a better understanding of its capabilities.

The Daily Scrum

The team gathers daily for a 15-minute meeting known as the *daily Scrum* (or *daily standup*). At the daily Scrum, each team member answers the following questions:

➤   What did I accomplish yesterday?

➤   What am I planning to accomplish today?

➤   What obstacles are impeding progress?

The daily Scrum is the heartbeat of a Scrum team. Without it, the entire process falls apart. The daily Scrum is important because it provides a stage for communication across the entire team. It also helps the team identify and remove impediments that stand in the way of team members. In addition, it promotes a culture of information sharing from everyone involved. During sprint planning, the entire team made a commitment to the work in the sprint. It wasn't an individual commitment, and it wasn't a vote; it was a commitment that the team made together. By committing together, the team makes a statement that it will also achieve success together.

As team members are sharing what they accomplished and plan to accomplish during the daily Scrum, other team members become aware of how that work might affect what they were planning to tackle. The ScrumMaster records any obstacles (that is, impediments) identified during the meeting. The ScrumMaster must help the team remove impediments so that it can continue to make progress toward its goal.

The daily standup should be self-managed: Team members should want to be there, there should be an energy in the room, and the team should quickly and succinctly share information. One of the biggest drains on a Scrum team is unproductive daily Scrums. The following tips can help make your standup meetings as effective as possible:

➤ **Be timely** — Late-starting meetings waste everyone's time. When someone on the team is chronically late, that person is subtly telling everyone else in the meeting that their time is not a priority. To make it clear that everyone's time is important, ensure that standup meetings start on time.

➤ **Stand up** — Many teams hold daily standups in conference rooms with everyone sitting in chairs around a table. These meetings feel like meetings. When you're standing up, you're engaged and are part of what's happening. Standing up for the daily Scrum might feel strange at first, but it will quickly become very natural and lead to crisper, more effective standups. There's a reason many teams call this gathering the daily standup instead of the daily Scrum.

➤ **Be concise** — The standup should take 15 minutes, but it will take 45 minutes if team members aren't in the habit of sharing the right amount of data. This isn't a meeting where you recount *everything* you did in the past 24 hours. Rather, it's a meeting where you share what you did and how what you did impacts the team's commitment.

➤ **Don't allow laptops or cell phones** — Face it, we live in a culture where we want to be connected at all times. We're all tempted to check something on our devices, whether our favorite stock, our voice mail, or our e-mail. We're slowly becoming a very distracted culture. Next time you're out to eat, look at the tables around you. How many people are talking to each other? And how many are staring at handheld devices? Remember that the daily standup is about communicating, and it's next to impossible to communicate with someone who has his or her head buried in a laptop or cell phone.

➤ **Make standups fun** — Teams can come up with creative ways to make their standups fun. When people are having fun, they're producing better work. Look for ways to make your standup fun. The following sidebar provides some suggestions.

DAILY SCRUM SUGGESTIONS FROM THE REAL WORLD

The following are a few ideas from successful Scrum teams about how to make the daily standup more fun and effective:

➤ **Brainstorm team rules** — Team rules should enforce the culture your team is trying to create. Anyone can suggest a rule. Take a simple yes/no vote to determine whether to accept a new rule. Then follow your rules strictly. For example, your team might decide that for every minute someone is late to a standup, he or she has to put $1 into the team fund. At the end of the sprint, the money is used to buy food/drink for the sprint retrospective.

➤ **Gong people** — If someone is rambling on and on about the minutia of their tasks, and it's wasting the team's time, ring a bell to get the person to stop. People report on their daily progress much more efficiently after being gonged a few times.

➤ **Choose a good location** — Hold your standups in a common area in your office that doesn't feel formal. Standing around a conference room is awkward. Standing together in a common area feels natural and is generally a lot more fun.

➤ **Encourage collaboration** — Standups become tedious if the team isn't working together. Team members often drift into their *own* work space and do their *own* work. When this happens, they lose interest in what other team members are doing. Finding ways to get your team to collaborate and work together in as many ways as possible will make standups more meaningful and not just verbal status reports.

The ScrumMaster is responsible for ensuring that the team has a daily standup, but the team is responsible for conducting the meeting. Remember that the daily standup is *not* a status meeting for anyone to attend. The daily standup is a gathering of the team that made a commitment to the sprint, and the purpose is to communicate and inspect progress toward achieving the sprint goal.

The Sprint Review

At the end of the sprint — the last day of the sprint or the first day after the sprint has ended — the team holds a review meeting to discuss and demonstrate to stakeholders what was accomplished during the sprint. Even though this meeting should be informal, it's important that the team prepare so that it can effectively demonstrate what it achieved.

During the sprint review, the team reads each of the PBIs that it committed to and accomplished during the sprint. The team then demonstrates the functionality built for each.

During the sprint review meeting, the product owner accepts each PBI demonstrated. While the team may have completed the work, the product owner needs to accept the PBI as meeting the requirements outlined. In many cases, the product owner will identify additional requirements after seeing the PBIs demonstrated. This is natural and should be encouraged. A team should add new requirements to the product backlog as they arise and prioritize them appropriately.

The following are suggested rules for the sprint review meeting:

➤ **Only team members, the product owner, and stakeholders attend the meeting** — The sprint review is not a presentation. Do not let it turn into one. Inviting people who are unfamiliar with the sprint itself can be a distraction and a waste of time for the team. If work for the sprint needs to be demonstrated more broadly, ask your product owner to schedule a separate meeting and make it optional for the team to attend.

➤ **The team presents only items that are done** — If an item from the backlog was committed to during sprint planning but not completed during the sprint, it is left out of the sprint review. Make sure the definition of *done* is presented before the meeting starts to ensure that everyone is on the same page.

The Sprint Retrospective

The Scrum method is all about finding new and better ways to execute and operate as a team. The sprint retrospective is the team's opportunity to reflect on ways it can improve to work more effectively together. The sprint retrospective happens immediately after the sprint ends to ensure that the activities from the sprint are fresh in everyone's mind.

Everyone on the team should participate in the retrospective, including the product owner. However, the retrospective should not include people outside the team who might intimidate team members or discourage a team member from sharing openly and honestly about his or her experiences during the sprint.

The goal of the retrospective is to identify what the team is going to do differently during the next sprint. This is achieved by letting everyone on the team have a chance to share what worked, what didn't work, and what the team should do differently in the next sprint. No topic should be off-limits during the retrospective, and it's critical that everyone on the team have a chance to participate.

The following are some basic rules for the sprint retrospective:

➤ **Allow only affirming comments** — Abrupt and aggressive disagreement causes problems among team members. It is important for all team members to feel that they can participate. The retrospective must be a safe place for everyone to voice opinions.

➤ **Ask people to think about what they want to say before they start saying it** — Some people think and then speak, and others speak to think. The think-and-then-speak types usually have insightful observations to share but are often crowded out by those who speak to think. Ask everyone on the team to spend time before the meeting thinking about what to share. This doesn't mean that spontaneous ideas or observations are discouraged, just that everyone on the team will get more out of the meeting if the participants show up prepared.

➤ **Make sure that items identified to be done differently in the next sprint are actionable** — You don't want to end up with a list of items such as "We should make sure nobody gets sick during the next sprint." Instead, turn this into something actionable, such as "Let's plan for unplanned interruptions to the sprint before we commit." The latter is actionable — it's something that the team can actually change in the next sprint.

➤ **Ensure that the team follows through on changes to its process** — Team members are likely to get discouraged if they sit through an energized retrospective meeting and emerge with a list of changes that is never acted upon. Such retrospectives kill morale. Don't let this happen on your team. If the team comes up with ideas to improve its process, act on them.

The sprint retrospective is one of the most energizing and fun parts of the Scrum process. The team is empowered to control its own destiny during this meeting, and each member has a chance to affect the team's process. By the end of the sprint retrospective, the team should have a reasonable list of actionable items that it wants to implement in the next sprint. Chapter 10 describes in more detail how you can run an effective sprint retrospective meeting.

SUMMARY

TFS and Scrum can help teams minimize risk, improve predictability, and maximize their ROI. TFS is a platform for storing and tracking your team's data, and Scrum is a framework for implementing and executing a project successfully. In this chapter, you learned how TFS stores project data, examined the various artifacts that make up the Scrum process, and explored the key activities involved in running a successful Scrum team. In Chapter 4, you will learn how to install and get started with the Microsoft Visual Studio Scrum 1.0 process template.

Getting Started with the TFS Scrum Template

WHAT'S IN THIS CHAPTER?

➤ How to get started with the Microsoft Visual Studio Scrum 1.0 template.

➤ How to create a release.

➤ Understanding the importance of shipping.

➤ Understanding the importance of quality.

➤ Understanding the importance of repeatability.

➤ Understanding sprints.

In Chapter 3, you learned how your project data is stored in Team Foundation Server (TFS) and how the members of your team can use that data. You also learned about the Scrum process and the key activities and artifacts that a Scrum team uses.

This chapter is a gentle introduction to getting a Scrum project started with TFS. In this chapter, you will learn how to install the Microsoft Visual Studio Scrum 1.0 template. You will also learn how to launch a new Scrum project, using this Scrum template.

This chapter also discusses the importance of three aspects of producing software: building in quality, shipping the product, and ensuring repeatability. The chapter also introduces the concept of sprints. In the rest of this book, we cover the material explored in this chapter in much greater detail.

GETTING STARTED WITH THE SCRUM TEMPLATE

Installing the Microsoft Visual Studio Scrum 1.0 template involves downloading and installing the template and then importing the template into TFS. The following sections walk through these processes, as well as how to begin using the template by creating a new product backlog item (PBI).

Downloading and Installing the Scrum Template

To download the Microsoft Visual Studio Scrum 1.0 template, follow these steps:

1. Go to `http://msdn.microsoft.com/en-us/vstudio/aa718795.aspx` (see Figure 4-1) and click the Microsoft Visual Studio Scrum 1.0 link. The template downloads to your machine.

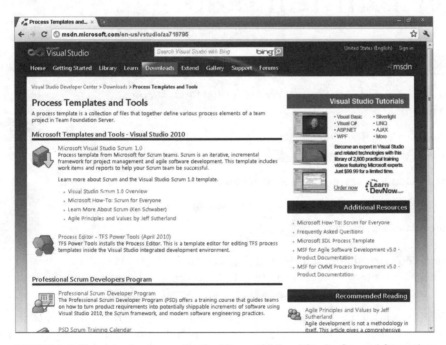

FIGURE 4-1: The download page for the Microsoft Visual Studio Scrum 1.0 template.

2. Install the template by double-clicking the `.msi` file and following the instructions that appear. Take note of where you install it. The Microsoft Visual Studio Scrum 1.0 Setup Wizard appears, ready to guide you through the setup process (see Figure 4-2).

After you've installed the template, you're ready to import it into TFS.

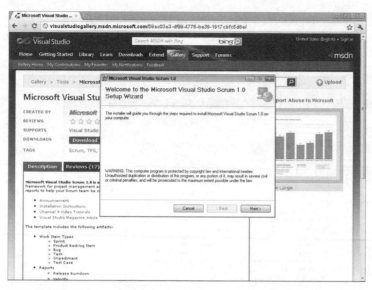

FIGURE 4-2: The opening screen of the Microsoft Visual Studio Scrum 1.0 Setup Wizard.

Importing the Scrum Template into TFS

To import the Microsoft Visual Studio Scrum 1.0 template into TFS, follow these steps:

1. In Visual Studio, open the Process Template Manager by selecting Team ➪ Team Project Collection Settings ➪ Process Template Manager, as shown in Figure 4-3. The Process Template Manager appears.

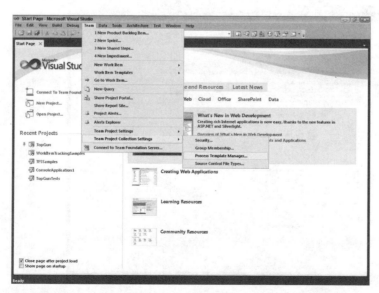

FIGURE 4-3: Opening the Process Template Manager to import the Scrum 1.0 template into TFS.

2. In the Process Template Manager, click the Upload button and select the directory where you installed the template, as shown in Figure 4-4. Visual Studio installs the Scrum 1.0 template, as shown in Figure 4-5.

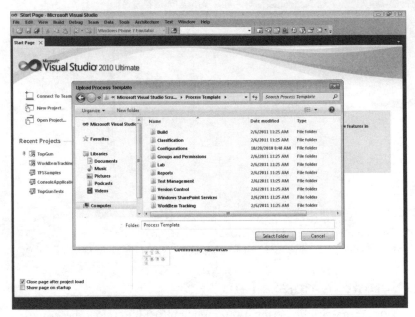

FIGURE 4-4: Selecting the main Scrum 1.0 template directory in the Process Template Manager.

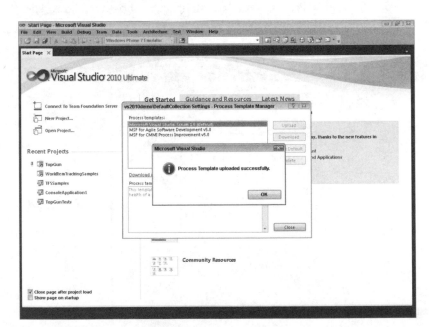

FIGURE 4-5: TFS installing the Scrum 1.0 template from the Process Template Manager.

Keep in mind that a team project is not the same as a Visual Studio project.

3. To test that the template has been installed correctly, create a new team project, based on the Scrum 1.0 template. To do this, select File ➪ New Team Project, as shown in Figure 4-6.

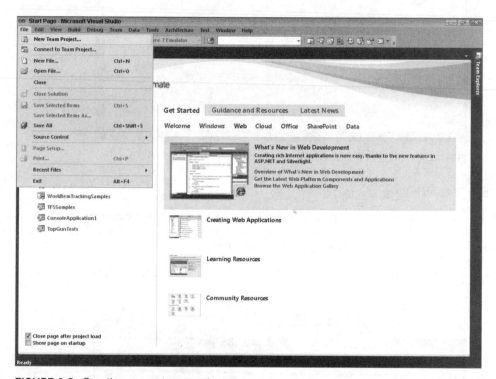

FIGURE 4-6: Creating a new team project.

4. When the New Project Wizard asks for the name of the project and its description, enter this information and then click Next.

5. When the wizard asks you to select the process template, click the down arrow and verify that the Microsoft Visual Studio Scrum 1.0 template has been installed, as shown in Figure 4-7.

Congratulations! You have successfully installed the Scrum 1.0 template. This template gives you access to a wealth of Scrum-related features. Next, you'll learn how to move ahead in Visual Studio and create a new PBI.

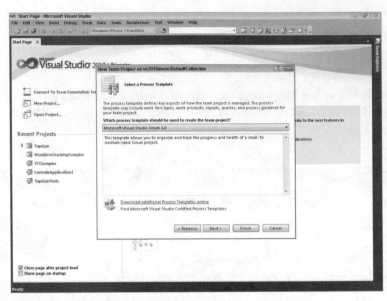

FIGURE 4-7: Verifying that the Scrum 1.0 template has been installed.

Creating a New PBI

You start a new Scrum project by creating PBIs. A TFS PBI is a rich structure that can store many details. Exactly which fields you need to complete is typically determined by your Scrum team's charter. The following steps show how to create a PBI:

1. In Visual Studio, select Team ⇨ New Work Item ⇨ Product Backlog Item, as shown in Figure 4-8.

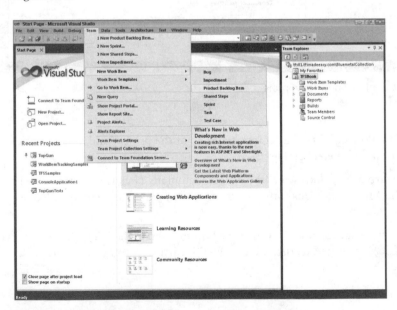

FIGURE 4-8: Creating a new PBI.

Note that the menu entries at the top of the Team menu vary, depending on how frequently you select each menu item. As a result, the top items on your menu may be different than the items in this figure.

2. Complete the Title, Iteration, Assigned To, and Description fields as shown in Figure 4-9. This information will be saved for future reference.

TFS uses the term iteration *to refer to sprints. These two words are often used interchangeably in the Agile community.*

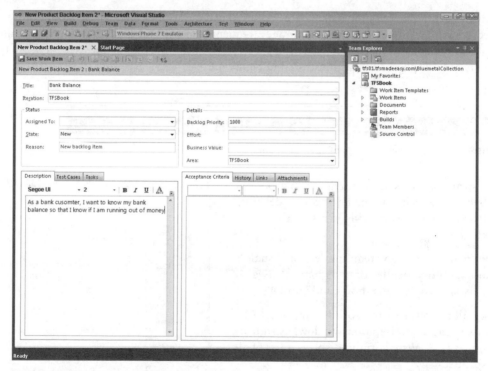

FIGURE 4-9: Creating a minimal PBI.

This short example illustrates just one of the many features of the Scrum template. PBIs are the building blocks of sprint and product backlogs. You link tasks to PBIs and track the completion of those tasks by using a burndown chart.

You will now learn about releases.

UNDERSTANDING RELEASES

Once you have installed the Scrum template and started to create PBIs, you need to group the PBIs into releases. Releases are a core part of Scrum. Several meetings and artifacts are associated with releases:

➤ The release planning meeting

➤ The release backlog burndown chart

➤ The release goal

> *For more information on releases, see the* Scrum Guide, *at* www.scrum.org/scrumguideenglish/.

Many companies already have release processes in place. Scrum replaces or modifies those processes with a framework that encourages frequent inspection and adaptation. Scrum also defines simple-to-understand metrics to chart the progress of a team during the release. A release typically consists of multiple sprints, as illustrated in Figure 4-10.

FIGURE 4-10: A release consists of several sprints.

Each sprint provides an opportunity to groom the backlog, which may include adding, deleting, modifying, and reprioritizing items on the backlog.

When you create a new team project in Visual Studio, it automatically contains four releases with six sprints each, as shown in Figure 4-11.

To see all the releases and sprints, you select All Sprints in the Team Explorer window, as shown in Figure 4-12. Visual Studio displays a list of all the sprints.

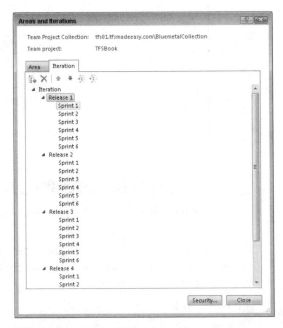

FIGURE 4-11: A new team project by default contains four releases with six sprints per release.

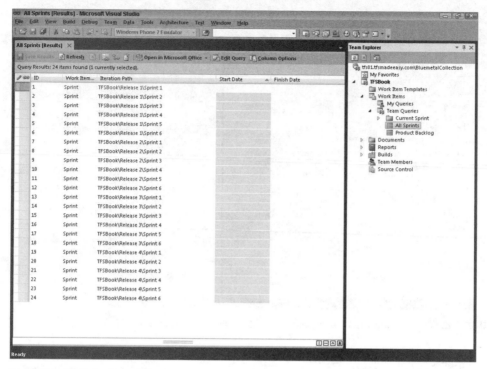

FIGURE 4-12: Selecting All Sprints.

The Release Planning Meeting

The release planning meeting is an optional meeting in which a Scrum team sets goals and expectations for the next release and also identifies risks for the release. All the artifacts produced during the release planning meeting are subject to refinement during the sprints that occur during the release period.

If the product owner has not already entered all PBIs into TFS, you should do this during the release planning meeting. To do so, follow these steps:

1. Select Team ➪ New Work Item ➪ Product Backlog Item, as shown earlier in this chapter, in Figure 4-8.

 You can also load PBIs by using Excel. This is discussed in Chapter 8.

2. Complete the Title, Iteration, and Description fields for the PBI as shown in Figure 4-13.

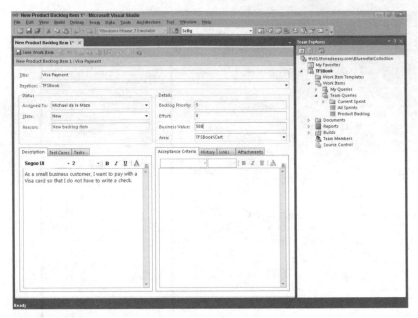

FIGURE 4-13: Completing the Title, Iteration, and Description fields for the PBI.

3. Ensure that the Backlog Priority field is set.

The team will set the Effort field after it has gone through Planning Poker. Planning Poker is discussed in Chapter 3 and later in this section.

4. To assign an individual to a PBI, select one from the Assigned To pull-down menu. Most teams do not assign a PBI to an individual on the technical team. Typically, the entire Scrum team takes responsibility for completing a user story, and only tasks are assigned to individuals. The PBI can be assigned to the product owner.

5. Select an item from the Area pull-down menu.

The term area *is not defined within Scrum, so the team should feel free to use this field as it desires. For a website,* area *might refer to sets of web pages. See Chapter 5 for more information on areas.*

6. To create a new task, click the Tasks tab in the PBI and then click New. The Add New Linked Work Item dialog appears, as shown in Figure 4-14.

Before you create a new task, the PBI must first be saved. If it is not, the New button will be disabled.

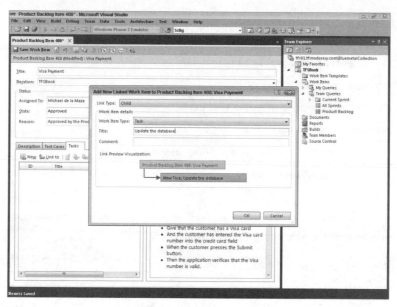

FIGURE 4-14: The Add New Linked Work Item dialog.

7. In the Add New Linked Work Item dialog, type in the title for the task and, if you choose, a comment. Then click OK. You now see the new task screen, as shown in Figure 4-15.

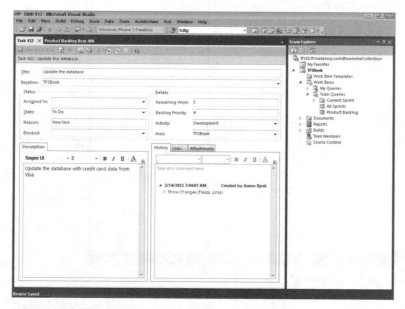

FIGURE 4-15: The new task screen.

At the end of the release planning meeting, the technical team has a high-level understanding of what end user–visible features it will be delivering over the next few sprints. In addition, the product owner has a sense of when these features will be ready.

Acceptance Criteria

Each user story typically has acceptance criteria, often written using the Gherkin language. Here is a simple example of an acceptance test written in the Gherkin language:

> Scenario: Withdraw money
>
> > Given a bank account with a negative balance
> >
> > When the customer withdraws funds
> >
> > Then the customer is told that funds are not available

In this example, *Scenario*, *Given*, *When*, and *Then* are all keywords in the Gherkin language, and the rest is free text.

 You can learn more about Gherkin at `http://specflow.org`.

The product owner typically provides acceptance tests when entering the PBI into TFS. Figure 4-16 illustrates acceptance criteria with Gherkin-style acceptance tests.

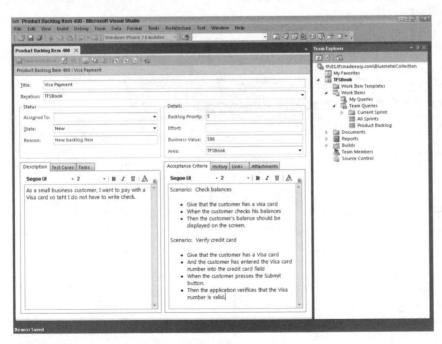

FIGURE 4-16: Gherkin-style acceptance tests.

Other PBI-Related Information

A number of other tabs in TFS hold further information on PBIs. The History tab, for example, keeps track of all changes to the PBI. The information provided in this tab is very detailed (see Figure 4-17).

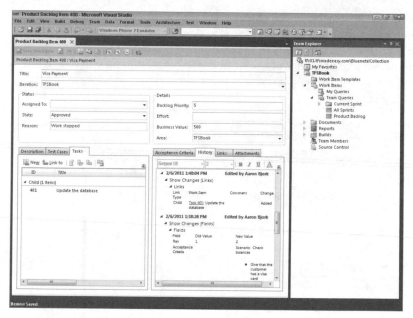

FIGURE 4-17: The History tab.

The Links tab lets you connect a PBI to other work items. The two items that are most commonly linked to a PBI are tasks and tests. These are typically linked to the PBI through other means, but you can use the Links tab to link them manually. As shown in Figure 4-18, you can also link a number of other types of items to the PBI.

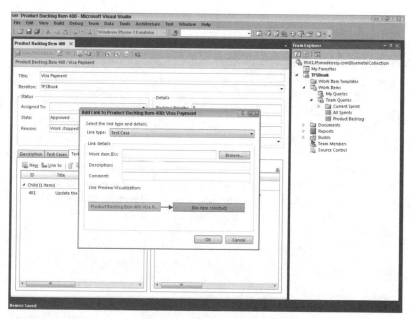

FIGURE 4-18: The Add Link to Product Backlog Item dialog.

The Attachments tab allows you to attach any document to a PBI. Its use is illustrated in Figure 4-19. For teams that have not automated user interface development by using Microsoft Expression, one common use for the Attachments tab is to attach a sketch of the user interface. Another common use is to attach a photograph of the whiteboard diagramming what the team did to understand the technical requirements behind the user story.

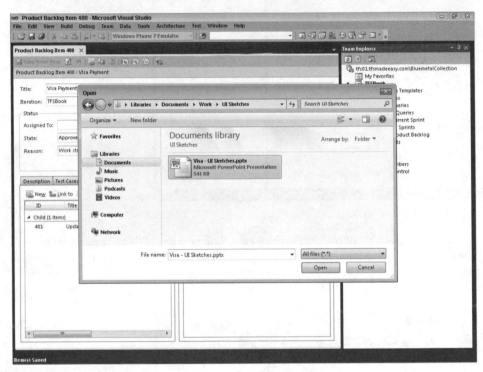

FIGURE 4-19: A dialog that lets you select the attachment.

Planning Poker

The release planning meeting involves estimating the amount of effort that PBIs will require and subsequently prioritizing them. A common way to estimate effort is to use Planning Poker, as discussed in Chapter 3. The team enters the final estimate produced by Planning Poker in the Effort field of the PBI, as shown in Figure 4-20. In this example, 13 has been entered in that field.

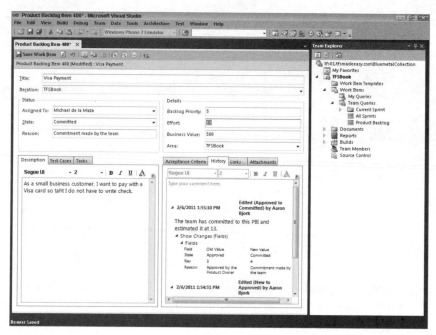

FIGURE 4-20: Entering the effort for a PBI.

The Release Burndown Chart

The release burndown chart measures the amount of work remaining to be done on the release backlog. It is identical in concept to the sprint burndown chart except for the important difference that it burns down over the course of the entire release instead of burning down during the course of a single sprint.

Because the release backlog might be modified during sprint planning meetings, there is a possibility that it will take on an appearance quite different from that of a sprint backlog. For example, suppose that the product backlog begins with the effort estimates shown in Table 4-1.

TABLE 4-1: Story Point Estimates

USER STORY	EFFORT ESTIMATE
1	8
2	13
3	5
4	20
5	8

The total amount of work to be burned down is 8 + 13 + 5 + 20 + 8 = 54 story points. Suppose that the team completes user story 1 and user story 2 during the first sprint. This leaves 5 + 20 + 8 = 33 story points at the end of sprint 1. The release burndown chart now looks like the one in Figure 4-21.

The problem with this chart is that it does not account for any new stories that the product owner has added during the sprint. This is a serious shortcoming. Suppose that the product owner added three more user stories to the release during this sprint, as shown in Table 4-2.

TABLE 4-2: Revised Story Point Estimates

USER STORY	EFFORT ESTIMATE
6	40
7	20
8	3

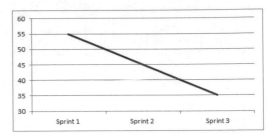

FIGURE 4-21: A simple implementation of a release burndown chart.

At the start of the second sprint, there are $33 + 40 + 20 + 3 = 96$ story points remaining in the release. There are at least three useful ways to display this information:

➤ **A chart that distinguishes between the end of the sprint and the start of the sprint** — One type of release burndown chart looks like the one shown in Figure 4-22. This release burndown chart contains information about both the user stories that the team has burned down (the difference between Sprint 1 Start and Sprint 1 End) and information about how many story points the product owner added during the sprint (the difference between Sprint 1 End and Sprint 2 Start).

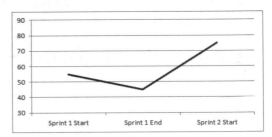

FIGURE 4-22: A release burndown chart that distinguishes between the end of the sprint and the start of the sprint.

➤ **A burnup/burndown chart** — Another way to visualize the number of story points the team has completed and the number of story points that the product owner has added is to plot two separate lines — one for each of these data series — and a third line that shows how many story points are remaining. This is sometimes called a burnup/burndown chart because the remaining story points burn down while the story points added and completed burn up. Figure 4-23 shows an example of this type of chart.

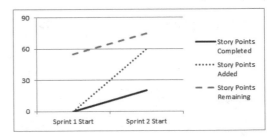

FIGURE 4-23: An example of a burnup/burndown chart.

➤ **A chart that shows how much work is remaining at the beginning of each sprint** — Yet another way to create a release burndown chart is to show how much work is remaining at the beginning of each sprint. This is analogous to the sprint burndown chart and is how the standard release burndown report in TFS works. This type of burndown chart looks like the one shown in Figure 4-24.

To see the release burndown chart in TFS, you navigate to the Team Explorer window and select Release Burndown, as shown in Figure 4-25.

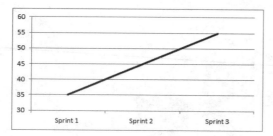

FIGURE 4-24: A release burndown chart that shows the amount of work remaining at the beginning of each sprint in the release.

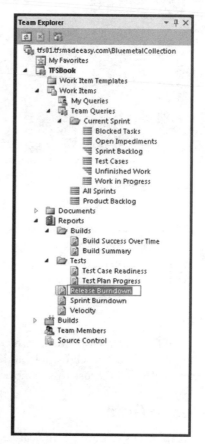

FIGURE 4-25: Selecting the release burndown report from the Team Explorer window.

Figure 4-26 shows an example of a release burndown chart in TFS. This release burndown chart shows the amount of work remaining at the beginning of each sprint.

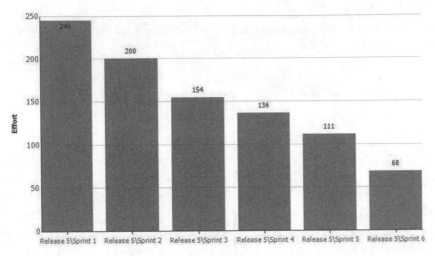

FIGURE 4-26: A release burndown chart in TFS.

 In the release burndown chart, the Y axis can measure any type of effort that the team chooses. Most teams choose to track their progress in terms of story points or hours.

In order for TFS to create the burndown chart, the team must assign PBIs to releases and sprints and update the Effort field in each task. In addition, the team must regularly update the State field of the PBI. Chapters 8 and 9 discuss this in more detail.

The Release Goal

A Scrum team needs to develop a *release goal* — a high-level statement that provides a simple, succinct statement of what the team plans to do. The purpose of the release goal is to promote shared understanding across the team and the larger business. An example of a release goal might be "Implement an online payment system."

TFS does not have a special field for a release goal. To create a place for the release goal, you can create a special sprint that contains information such as the release goal that pertains to the release.

If you create a sprint to contain a release goal, take care not to misuse this special sprint by, for example, assigning PBIs to it. Doing so would cause all related reports to be incorrect.

To create a sprint specifically to store the release goal, follow these steps:

1. Create a new sprint in Visual Studio by selecting Team ➪ New Work Item ➪ Sprint, as shown in Figure 4-27. Visual Studio creates the sprint.

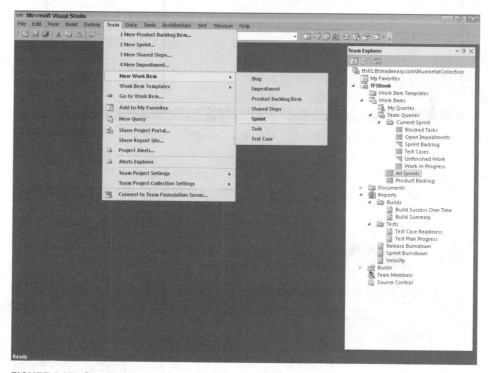

FIGURE 4-27: Creating a new sprint.

2. Set Iteration to <Project Name>\<Release #>, as shown in Figure 4-28. Normally the iteration name is <Project Name>\<Release #>\<Sprint #>. The fact that there is no sprint number in the Iteration field indicates that this sprint will hold information about the release.

3. Change both the Start Date and Finish Date fields to the date immediately before the sprint start date. This causes the release to be listed in the correct order, before all the sprints in the release. In the example in Figure 4-28, the sprint starts on November 1, 2010, so the Start Date and the Finish Date are set to October 31, 2010.

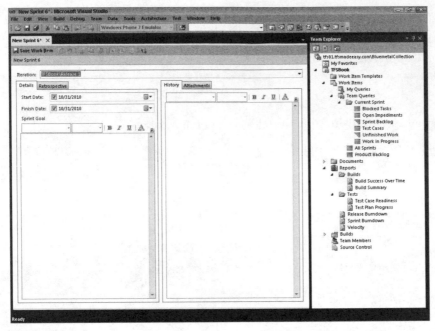

FIGURE 4-28: Changing the Iteration, Start Date, and Finish Date fields for the sprint.

4.   Enter the release goal in the Details tab, as shown in Figure 4-29. Note that the special release sprint that you have just created is listed before the sprints in the release.

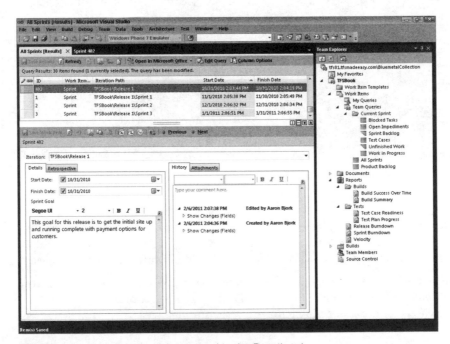

FIGURE 4-29: Entering the release goal in the Details tab.

Some teams also have a prerelease hardening sprint to perform regression, integration, and performance tests. To support a prerelease sprint, you can create a new sprint and include the term *Prerelease* in the name of this sprint, as shown in Figure 4-30.

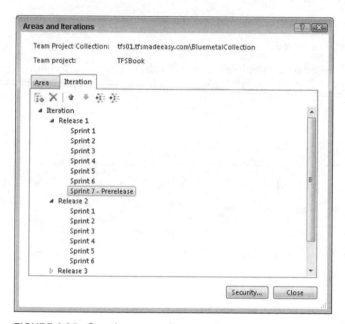

FIGURE 4-30: Creating a prerelease sprint.

To create this sprint, you right-click the project in the Team Explorer window and navigate to Areas and Settings. From there, you add a new sprint to the release.

THE IMPORTANCE OF SHIPPING SOFTWARE

A pretty good solution that ships is better than a great solution that does not ship. An overemphasis on technical beauty or on getting the product right before shipping violates the key Scrum principles of empiricism and feedback.

One of the key practices of Scrum is to create potentially shippable software by the end of every sprint. On the best Scrum teams, the product owner is able to press a single button and release the software that the team shows during the demonstration meeting at the end of the sprint.

To that end, a Scrum team needs to define what *done* means and make sure that every PBI can be completed in one sprint. At a minimum, *done* means that the coding and testing are complete and that the product owner has indicated that the software meets the acceptance criteria for the user story. Code being *complete* might mean all of the following:

➤ The code has been reviewed by at least one other team member.

➤ The code has been documented.

➤ The code has been refactored.

A test being *complete* might mean all of the following:

➤ Unit tests have been written and executed for every method.

➤ The unit test coverage is at least 90%.

➤ The software has been integration tested.

➤ The software has been performance tested.

Exactly what code being complete and tests being complete mean will differ from team to team. The definition of *done* will often be encapsulated in the team's charter, which is typically revised and updated during the retrospective.

DEFINING *DONE*

Here is an example of one team's definition of *done*:

➤ All public methods have been unit tested.

➤ Coded user interface tests have been created for every user story.

➤ Code has been reviewed with Bill or Sandra.

THE IMPORTANCE OF QUALITY

As discussed in Chapter 1, there are three commonly discussed constraints in software development: cost, time, and features. Quality is not explicitly mentioned but, presumably, when customers ask for a feature, what they mean is that they want a bug-free feature. And yet teams regularly adjust their feature set by adjusting the amount of effort — as measured by time and cost — they invest in quality.

It is commonly thought that the cost of fixing a bug increases by a factor of 10 between the requirements stage and coding and then increases by more than a factor of 10 from coding to production. That is to say, fixing a bug in production costs over 100 times as much as fixing the bug in the requirements stage. Hence, most teams adopt a "no bugs" rule during a sprint. Killing bugs takes precedence over developing or extending features.

For bugs in stories the team is working on for the sprint, the team should simply not consider the user story done until all known bugs are resolved. For bugs discovered during the sprint for user stories that were completed during previous sprints, the product owner should create bug items and prioritize them higher than any of the PBIs.

ENSURING REPEATABILITY

Because each sprint is a microcosm of the entire development process, everything that a Scrum team does becomes highly polished and repeatable in a very short period of time. This is one of the great advantages of Scrum.

Consider the experience that a Scrum team with 2-week sprints has over the course of a year. It has the opportunity to go through its entire software development cycle 26 times. In contrast, a team that has a 6-month software development cycle will go through its entire cycle only twice in a year. As a result, the Scrum team will have 13 times as much experience as the team with the longer cycle. The team with the 6-month cycle will have difficulty claiming that anything that it has done is repeatable, while the Scrum team will have demonstrated the repeatability of almost everything that it does.

At the end of the year, a Scrum team will have developed a great sense of confidence in its ability to frequently ship high-quality software. After all, it has already been successful 26 times, and so the likelihood that it will be successful the 27th time is very high.

UNDERSTANDING SPRINTS

Sprints, sometimes called *iterations*, are a critical concept in Scrum. A sprint begins with a planning meeting and ends with a demo meeting and retrospective meeting. The length of a sprint typically ranges from one to four weeks. This length is fixed by the team and does not depend on scope.

This section covers prioritizing the backlog for the sprint planning meeting, determining release schedules, and understanding spikes. Chapter 9 discusses the details of running a sprint.

Prioritizing PBIs

As discussed previously, teams prioritize PBIs across sprints and within sprints. The product owner is responsible for prioritizing PBIs.

PBIs are prioritized to maximize business value. The product owner is also responsible for defining *business value*. The meaning of *business value* will change from product to product and company to company. Sometimes it will change from release to release. What might *business value* mean? It might be measured by revenue, profits, visits to a website, or new customer registrations. Often, business value is a combination of several of these factors.

A team should make the definition of *business value* clearly visible and enter it into each PBI, in the Business Value field.

Determining Release Schedules

Should Scrum teams agree to fixed release time lines? If they agree to release on a certain date, does this mean that no change can occur over that period of time? And if no change can occur, is the team still agile? These are some of the questions that an organization must ask when it requires its Scrum teams to create release schedules. In practice, there is no such thing as a date that cannot slip. But if an organization believes that it must ship software on a certain date, then it must allow the scope to float unless it is able to predict the future with perfect accuracy.

Creating a release schedule must begin with an understanding of the team's velocity and estimation of the PBIs. When those two items are combined, they naturally lead to the best possible estimate of the release schedule. Say that a team's velocity is 100 story points per sprint and that its release backlog contains a total of 450 story points. The team can estimate that completing the release backlog will take four or five sprints (that is, 450 / 100 = 4.5).

Release dates are often driven by the business, not by a Scrum team. If a team finds that it cannot meet a release date, it has several options, including reducing the feature set or increasing the amount of effort.

Understanding Spikes

A *spike* is a technical exploration designed to inform a team about how to best make a technical decision. For example, say that a team is thinking about whether to use Silverlight out-of-the-browser or to instead use Windows Presentation Foundation. It might want to implement functionality in both and then decide which technical solution is best. Spikes are entered into the product backlog as new PBIs. It is a good idea to add the word *Spike* to the PBI, as shown in the Title field in Figure 4-31.

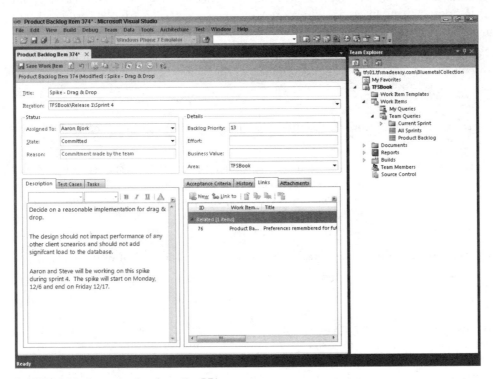

FIGURE 4-31: An example of a spike PBI.

Spikes are different from typical user stories because they do not deliver end user functionality. They do not result in potentially shippable software. Hence, they are often called out in the product backlog.

Note that spikes do not refer to explorations in which the technical approach is not in question. For example, say that a team is exploring various user interfaces. It does this by first developing the user interfaces and then presenting them to end users. While the team is experimenting with user interfaces and does not know which one is the best, this activity does not constitute a spike because the team understands the technical approach — the method of determining which user interface is best. (Chapter 11 covers spikes in more detail.)

SUMMARY

In this chapter, you have learned the basics of the Scrum template. You know how to install the Scrum template and how to enter PBIs. This chapter also introduces a simple way to manage the release and product backlogs.

The key concepts of shipping, quality, and repeatability are introduced in this chapter. The chapter provides descriptions of the role that these concepts play in Scrum and how the TFS Scrum template supports these activities. Finally, this chapter discusses the key role that sprints play in Scrum.

In Chapter 5, you will learn about tracking items in TFS.

5

Work Items, Queries, and Reports

WHAT'S IN THIS CHAPTER?

➤ Understanding how to use work items in the Scrum template.

➤ Using the queries in the Scrum template.

➤ How to use the reports in the Scrum template.

In Chapter 3, you saw how to store project data in Team Foundation Server (TFS) and how the Scrum framework works in the context of a team project. In this chapter, you will examine the specifics of each artifact in the Microsoft Visual Studio Scrum 1.0 process template and see how each one contributes to tracking a project. This chapter focuses on three aspects of the Scrum process template:

➤ Work items

➤ Work item queries

➤ Reports

Together, these artifacts provide the tools needed to successfully manage and track a Scrum project. The following sections discuss them in detail.

WORK ITEMS

Project data in TFS is stored in artifacts known as *work items*. As noted in Chapter 3, work items are database records that track the definition, assignment, priority, and state of work for your team. The Microsoft Visual Studio Scrum 1.0 process template includes seven work item types:

➤ Product backlog items

➤ Tasks

➤ Sprints

➤ Impediments

➤ Bugs

➤ Test cases

➤ Shared steps

To create a new work item, you right-click the Work Items node in your team project and select a work item type from the New Work Item menu. A blank work item form appears. After you enter all the necessary data, you click the Save Work Item button on the form. Then you can query the work item and its data by using a work item query, as described later in this chapter.

Each work item type includes a set of fields to store and track information about the work item. Some fields are consistent across all work item types, while others are defined only on a specific type. All changes made to fields during the life cycle of a work item are stored in the work item's History field. When any change is made, the old and new values, the individual making the change, and the date/time stamp are stored. The following sections examine how to use the Scrum process template work item types.

Before digging into each work item type, you will see how you can use two system fields in TFS, Area Path and Iteration Path, to group and categorize the work items in the Scrum template.

The Area Path and Iteration Path Fields

The Area Path and Iteration Path fields support the grouping of work items into categories. These two fields are system fields in TFS. *System fields* are shared across all work item types and cannot be modified or customized in your process template. The Area Path field delineates either product components or teams. The Iteration Path field delineates iterations of work. Both fields are hierarchical, meaning they support parent and child nodes.

Areas

The Microsoft Visual Studio Scrum 1.0 process template does not prescribe a specific use for the Area Path field. Most teams, however, use area paths to separate work into product components or to separate work by teams. The Area Path field exists on all work item types and all reports included in the template. You can add areas to a team project from the Areas and Iterations dialog. Figure 5-1 shows the Area tab of this dialog, populated with sample areas.

FIGURE 5-1: The Area tab of the Areas and Iterations dialog, populated with sample areas.

Iterations

The Iteration Path field stores the iteration schedule for a project. In Scrum, a *sprint* is an iteration of work. Many sprints together make up a *release*. You assign work items to iterations to identify the sprint in which a team will complete the work. All reports included in the Scrum template display the Iteration Path field, making it easy to track work across sprints.

By default, a team project started from the Microsoft Visual Studio Scrum 1.0 process template has 24 predefined sprints across four releases. One of the first activities after project creation is to create iterations to match the team's release schedule, as described in Chapter 4.

 Why are we talking about iterations *for what Scrum refers to as* sprints? *TFS defines the Iteration Path field as a system field, which means it is always present, and its definition is constant across all team projects. Although the field is named Iteration Path, the actual iteration nodes are sprints.*

You use the Areas and Iterations dialog box to configure the iterations for a team project. From within Team Explorer, right-click your team project and select Team Project Settings ⇨ Areas and Iterations. Switch to the Iteration tab and use the buttons on the toolbar to add new iterations, delete existing iterations, and adjust the iteration hierarchy. To rename an existing iteration, right-click the iteration and select Rename. Figure 5-2 shows the default iterations created for a new team project.

FIGURE 5-2: The Iteration tab of the Areas and Iterations dialog, populated with 24 default iterations.

Product Backlog Items

A *product backlog item (PBI)* is the central work item in a Scrum project. A PBI describes a requirement for the product and the value that implementing the requirement produces. A team works with the product owner to define, estimate, and implement each PBI. When the product owner defines a PBI, he or she should focus on customer value and avoid details about the implementation. A team should prioritize PBIs based on business value, effort, and relative dependency on other backlog items. To minimize duplicating work, a team should focus only on the highest-priority PBIs. Spending too much time on PBIs with lower priorities often results in waste. Figure 5-3 shows a PBI form.

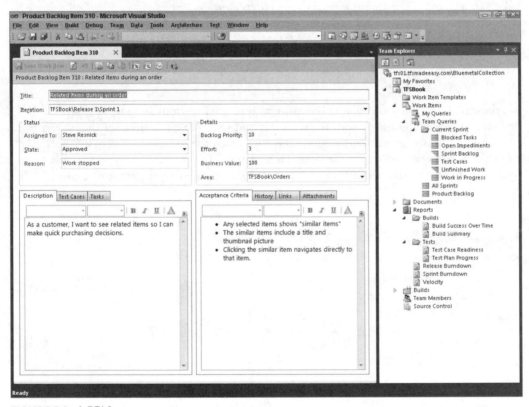

FIGURE 5-3: A PBI form.

PBI Form Fields

Table 5-1 lists the fields on a PBI form. You use the fields described here to track a PBI throughout its life cycle.

TABLE 5-1: PBI Form Fields

FIELD	DESCRIPTION
Title	A brief description of the PBI.
Iteration	The sprint in which the PBI is implemented.
Assigned To	The owner of the PBI (typically the product owner).
State	The current state of the PBI.
Reason	The reason a product backlog is in its current state. The Reason field contains predefined values that guide the team through appropriate state transitions during the life cycle of the PBI.
Backlog Priority	The position of a PBI on the product backlog. New PBIs default to a backlog priority of 1,000.
Effort	The amount of effort required to implement a PBI. The Scrum template does not prescribe a unit of effort. Common units include story points, ideal days, and hours.
Business Value	The amount of customer value delivered by a PBI. You should choose a number between 1 and 100 to represent the amount of business value that implementing the PBI will deliver to your customers.
Area	The team implementing a PBI or the product component the PBI belongs to.
Description	A detailed description of a PBI.
Acceptance Criteria	A bulleted list of criteria a PBI must meet before the team will accept it as done.

THE DEFAULT BACKLOG PRIORITY VALUE

Why does a new PBI default to a backlog priority value of 1,000? Why not a value of 1? Or why not a blank value? In TFS, query results always sort by a field included in the query definition. By default, the product backlog sorts by backlog priority, in ascending order (that is, smaller numbers on top, larger numbers on the bottom). This works quite well. But it gets tricky when blank values are present. TFS sorts items that don't have backlog priority values to the top of the result list. Therefore, new PBIs that don't have backlog priority values automatically float to the top of the product backlog. This is not the ideal behavior, as items not assigned backlog priority values are likely lower in priority. To prevent this from happening, the PBI form defaults the priority to a value of 1,000. This default ensures that an item without an explicitly assigned priority does not float to the top of the backlog.

PBI States

Like all other work items, PBIs move through a series of state transitions. The current state is always stored and displayed in the State field. All state transitions appear as records in the History field. Figure 5-4 shows a state transition from approved to committed.

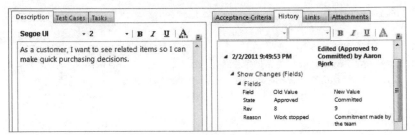

FIGURE 5-4: A PBI whose state has transitioned from approved to committed.

A PBI moves through the following states:

➤ **New** — The PBI exists on the product backlog but lacks detail the team would need to implement it. Low-priority PBIs often remain in the new state for an extended period, while high-priority items move quickly to the next state.

➤ **Approved** — The PBI is sufficiently detailed and ready to present to the team for implementation. All PBIs discussed during sprint planning are in the approved state.

➤ **Committed** — The team has committed to implement the PBI in the next sprint. PBIs in the committed state have been estimated and decomposed into task work items.

➤ **Done** — The PBI has been implemented, tested, and demonstrated. Ideally, this state transition happens immediately after the sprint review meeting.

➤ **Removed** — The PBI is no longer needed or is out of scope. A PBI can move to the removed state from the new or approved state. Only the product owner can mark a PBI as removed.

Tasks

A team uses task work items to track all the work needed to implement a PBI. The team creates tasks during sprint planning for each PBI. Each day, the team updates tasks for the sprint, indicating the current state of the task and the amount of remaining work. Together, the set of tasks for a sprint is known as the *sprint backlog*. See the section "The Sprint Backlog Query," later in this chapter, for more details. Figure 5-5 shows a task work item form.

Task Form Fields

Table 5-2 lists the fields on the task form. You use the fields described here to track a task throughout its life cycle.

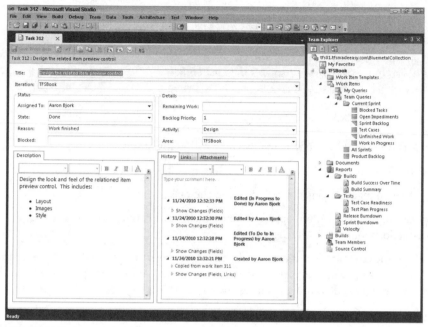

FIGURE 5-5: A task work item form.

TABLE 5-2: Task Form Fields

FIELD	DESCRIPTION
Title	A concise description of the work tracked by the task.
Iteration	The sprint in which the task is implemented.
Assigned To	The team member responsible for completing the task.
State	The current state of the task.
Reason	The reason the task is in its current state.
Blocked	Whether the team is blocked from making progress on the task.
Remaining Work	The amount of remaining work (in hours) to complete the task.
Backlog Priority	The priority of the task on the sprint backlog.
Activity	The type of activity of the task. Activity is an optional field.
Area	The team implementing the task or the product component the task belongs to.
Description	Implementation details of the task.

It is interesting to note that the Blocked field has a Yes value but not a corresponding No value. This is intentional, to draw attention to blocked tasks in query results and on the work item form. To mark a task as blocked, you set the Blocked field to Yes. To clear the Blocked field, you ensure that this field is blank.

Task States

A task work item moves though a life cycle that involves the following states:

➤ **To do** — The task is awaiting implementation. A new task starts in the to do state.

➤ **In progress** — A team member has started work on the task.

➤ **Done** — All work on the task is completed. When a task transitions to this state, the remaining work field is automatically set to zero.

➤ **Removed** — The removed state is not a normal part of the task life cycle. It exists to mark a task as unwanted or out of scope. Removed tasks are filtered out of the sprint backlog. A task can move to the removed state from either the to do or in progress states.

The current state is stored in the State field. All state transitions and changes to state are recorded in the History field. Figure 5-6 shows a state transition from in progress to done.

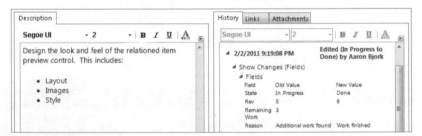

FIGURE 5-6: Task state transition from in progress to done.

Sprints

You use a sprint work item to record information about each sprint on your team's schedule. This information includes the following:

➤ Sprint goal

➤ Sprint start date

➤ Sprint end date

➤ Sprint retrospective

The sprint work item form is unique in that it does not include the Title field or the State field found on other work item forms. Sprints do not have titles that differ from the iteration path. Because of this, a sprint work item does not display a Title field. The State field is absent because sprints do not have an explicit state model, as do traditional work items. For example, the task work item moves through three distinct states: to do, in progress, and done. The sprint work item instead has start and end dates that define the state of the sprint. Unlike a task, a sprint is in the to do state when today's date precedes the start date. A sprint is considered in progress when today's date is within the sprint start and end dates. And a sprint is considered done when today's date succeeds the end date. Figure 5-7 shows a sprint work item form.

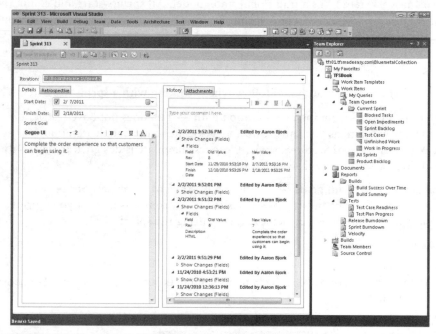

FIGURE 5-7: A sprint work item form.

Sprint Form Fields

Table 5-3 lists the fields on a sprint form. You use the fields described here to track a sprint throughout its life cycle.

TABLE 5-3: Sprint Form Fields

FIELD	DESCRIPTION
Iteration	The iteration path associated with the sprint.
Start Date	The first day of the sprint.
Finish Date	The last day of the sprint.
Sprint Goal	The goal of the sprint, as described by the team and the product owner. A sprint goal describes what the team will achieve during the sprint.
Retrospective	Notes from the team's retrospective meeting.

Retrospectives are critical to the success of a Scrum team. For more information on how your team can execute successful retrospectives, jump ahead to Chapter 10.

Sprint States

As noted earlier, the sprint work item lacks a traditional state model. All sprints start and end in the created state, which indicates the creation of a new sprint. Because only one state and no transitions exist, the State field is not present on the sprint work item form.

Sprint Best Practices

The following is a list of best practices you should follow when working with a sprint work item:

> **Create only one sprint work item for each iteration path** — TFS does not have restrictions on how many sprint work items you can create and associate with a single iteration. However, the Microsoft Visual Studio Scrum 1.0 process template is designed to have only one sprint work item associated with each iteration.

> **Set simple and achievable sprint goals** — A common mistake of many new Scrum practitioners is setting complex and unrealistic goals for a sprint. Ensure that your sprint goals are simple and that the team can achieve them during the sprint.

Impediments

An impediment work item tracks anything blocking a team from making progress. Figure 5-8 shows an impediment work item form.

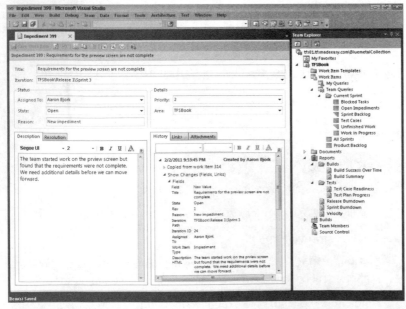

FIGURE 5-8: An impediment work item form.

Impediment Form Fields

Table 5-4 lists the fields on an impediment work item form. You use the fields described here to track an impediment throughout its life cycle.

TABLE 5-4: Impediment Form Fields

FIELD	DESCRIPTION
Title	A short description of the impediment.
Iteration	The sprint the impediment is blocking.
Assigned To	The team member responsible for removing the impediment, typically the ScrumMaster.
State	The current state of the impediment.
Reason	The reason the impediment is in its current state.
Area	The team dealing with the impediment or the product component the impediment belongs to.
Description	The details of the impediment.
Resolution	The steps taken to remove the impediment.

Impediment States

An impediment work item moves though a life cycle that involves two states:

➤ **Open** — A new impediment always starts in the open state. This state indicates that the impediment is blocking the team from making progress.

➤ **Closed** — An impediment moves from the open state to the closed state when the impediment has been removed and is no longer blocking the team.

Figure 5-9 shows a state transition from open to closed.

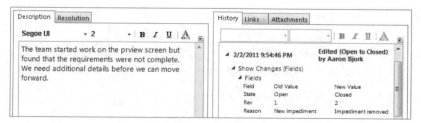

FIGURE 5-9: An impediment state transition from open to closed.

Bugs

A bug work item tracks defects found in the product. Bugs surface on the product backlog and are prioritized against other bugs and PBIs. Bugs appearing directly on the product backlog is a major difference between Scrum and traditional software processes. Figure 5-10 shows a bug work item form.

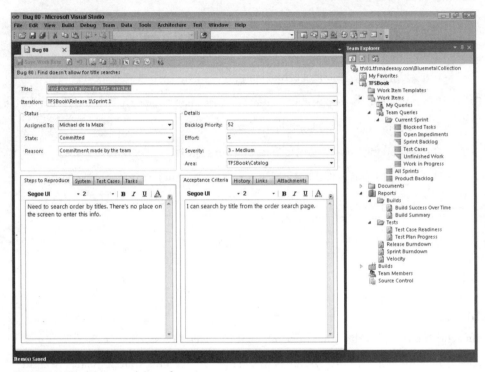

FIGURE 5-10: A bug work item form.

Bug Form Fields

Table 5-5 lists the fields on a bug work item form. You use the fields described here to track a bug throughout its life cycle.

TABLE 5-5: Bug Form Fields

FIELD	DESCRIPTION
Title	A short description of the bug.
Iteration	The sprint in which the bug will be fixed.

FIELD	DESCRIPTION
Assigned To	The team member responsible for prioritizing the bug against other items on the product backlog—typically the product owner.
State	The current state of the bug.
Reason	The reason the bug is in its current state.
Area	The team dealing with the bug or the product component the bug belongs to.
Steps to Reproduce	A detailed account of the steps taken when the bug was found. It's important to write these steps clearly so others can easily reproduce the behavior.
Acceptance Criteria	The set of criteria used to verify whether the team has fixed the bug.
Test Cases	A list of test case work items linked to the bug.
Tasks	A list of task work items created by the team tracking the necessary work to fix the bug.

Bug States

A bug moves through the same set of states as a PBI:

➤ **New** — The bug has been discovered, reproduced, and entered on the product backlog for the product owner to prioritize.

➤ **Approved** — After a decision has been made about the priority of the bug, the product owner works with team members to understand the steps needed to fix the bug. The bug is moved to the approved state when it is sufficiently detailed and ready to bring to the team for implementation.

➤ **Committed** — The team has committed to implement the bug in the next sprint. Bugs in the committed state have been estimated and decomposed into task work items.

➤ **Done** — The bug has been fixed, tested, and regressed. This transition happens immediately after the bug is fixed and verified.

➤ **Removed** — The bug will not be fixed by the team, or the bug is out of scope or no longer needed.

Figure 5-11 shows a state transition from approved to committed.

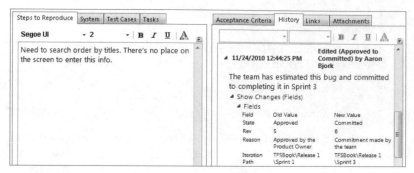

FIGURE 5-11: A bug state transition from approved to committed.

Test Cases

A test case work item tracks testing efforts on PBIs and bugs. The majority of the data of a test case is the test steps. These steps represent the actions a team member will take to execute a test. See Chapter 7 for more on linking test cases to PBIs and bugs. Figure 5-12 shows a test case work item form.

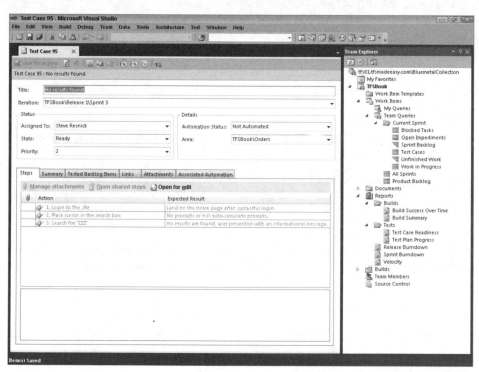

FIGURE 5-12: A test case work item form.

Test Case Form Fields

Table 5-6 shows the fields present on a test case work item form. You use the fields described here to track a test case throughout its life cycle.

TABLE 5-6: Test Case Form Fields

FIELD	DESCRIPTION
Title	A short description of the goal of the test.
Iteration	The sprint tracking the test case.
Assigned To	The team member responsible for executing the test case.
State	The current state of the test case.
Priority	The relative priority of the test case.
Automation Status	Whether the test case is automated.
Area	The team involved in the test case or the product component the test case belongs to.
Steps	A list of steps defining the action, validation steps, and parameters that are a part of the test.
Tested Backlog Items	A list of PBIs and/or bugs tested by the test case.

Test Case States

A test case has three states associated with its life cycle:

➤ **Design** — The test case is being authored but is not ready to be executed.

➤ **Ready** — The test case is ready to be executed. A test case in this state has a complete set of steps associated with it and is ready for a team member to execute.

➤ **Closed** — The test case moves to the closed state when its life cycle is complete. This transition typically occurs after the PBI or bug the test case is testing is verified as done.

Figure 5-13 shows a state transition from design to ready.

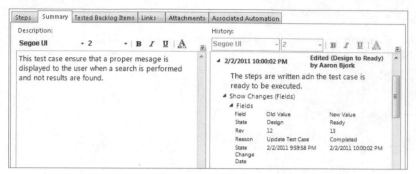

FIGURE 5-13: A test case transition from design to ready.

Shared Steps

Shared steps allow you to streamline the definition and management of manual test cases. You can create shared step work items when you encounter a set of steps that are the same across multiple test cases. Figure 5-14 shows a shared steps work item form.

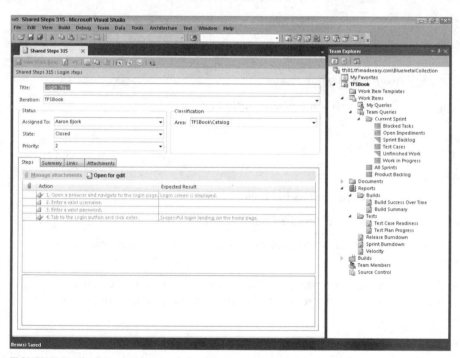

FIGURE 5-14: A shared steps work item form.

Shared Steps Form Fields

Table 5-7 shows a list of fields present on a shared steps work item form. You use the fields described here to track a shared steps work item throughout its life cycle.

TABLE 5-7: Shared Steps Form Fields

FIELD	DESCRIPTION
Title	A short description of reusable steps.
Iteration	The sprint tracking the shared steps.
Assigned To	The team member authoring the set of shared steps.
State	The current state of the set of shared steps.
Priority	The relative priority of the shared steps.
Area	The team involved in the shared steps or the product component the shared steps belong to.
Steps	A list of steps defining the action, validation steps, and parameters that will be shared across multiple test cases.

Shared Steps States

A shared steps work item has two states associated with its life cycle:

➤ **Active** — The shared steps work item is ready to be used across test cases.

➤ **Closed** — The shared steps work item is no longer used in any test cases.

Figure 5-15 shows a state transition from active to closed on a shared steps work item.

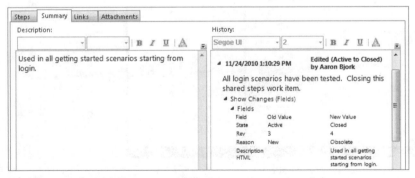

FIGURE 5-15: A shared steps transition from active to closed.

WORK ITEM QUERIES

By default, the Microsoft Visual Studio Scrum 1.0 process template provisions eight work item queries. These queries help you track and manage a Scrum project. The following sections examine the three query types you can record in TFS as well as the eight work item queries.

Query Types

TFS provides three query types for you to use when querying project data:

➤ Flat list

➤ Work items and direct links

➤ Tree of work items

The following sections examine these three query types.

Flat List Queries

The flat list query type is the most basic and most widely used of the three work item query types. A flat list query works as you might expect: It returns query results in a list, sorted by the field specified in the query options. Flat list query results do not reflect relationships between work items. Figure 5-16 shows an example. By default, all new work item queries are flat list queries.

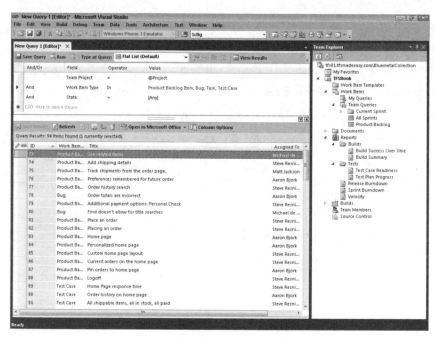

FIGURE 5-16: Query options of a flat list work item query.

Work Items and Direct Links Queries

Work items and direct links queries display work items and associated linked work items based on the criteria specified in the query definition. The Microsoft Visual Studio Scrum 1.0 process template does not include a work items and directed links query, but this query type is still a valuable tool for a team, a ScrumMaster, and a product owner to use to track a team project. As shown in Figure 5-17, a work items and directed links query has three sets of filter criteria.

Each set of criteria plays an important role in the selection of the work items returned in the result. The top portion limits the first tier of work items returned in the result. This portion works identically to a flat list work item query.

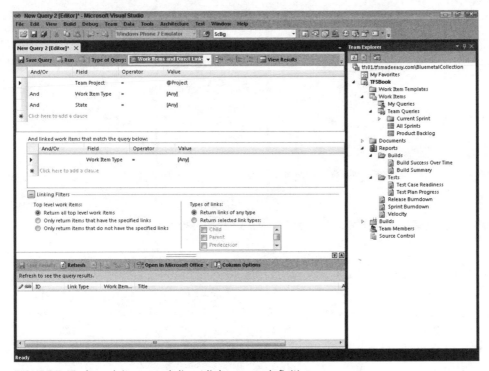

FIGURE 5-17: A work items and direct links query definition.

The middle portion, labeled Linking Filters, identifies the type of linked work items to return and additional criteria that will filter both the first-tier and second-tier work items results. These are the choices:

> **Return All Top Level Work Items** — All first-tier work items matching the criteria specified in the top portion of the query definition are included in the result.

> **Only Return Items That Have the Specified Links** — This option limits the items in the first-tier result set to work items with the specified link type. If no link type is specified, all work items matching the criteria in the top portion are returned.

> **Only Return Work Items That Do Not Have the Specified Links** — This option limits the first-tier result set to work items that do not have the specified link type.

The bottom portion of the query defines additional criteria used to filter the work item results.

Because work item and direct links queries can be difficult to understand, Figure 5-18 shows an example of how to use this query type. In this example, the query definition is showing all PBIs and bugs in a sprint that do not have associated test cases.

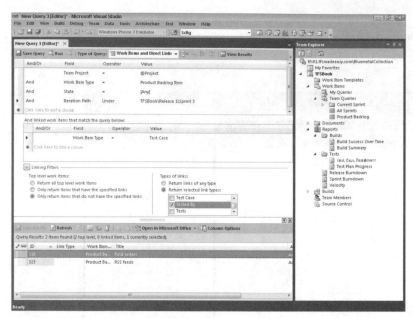

FIGURE 5-18: A query showing PBIs and bugs without test cases.

Tree of Work Items Queries

A tree of work items query displays work item results in a hierarchy. All nodes returned in the hierarchy link to a parent work item with a parent/child link type. As with the work items and direct links query type, you can add filter criteria for multiple areas of a tree of work items query. Figure 5-19 shows the query definition of a tree of work items query.

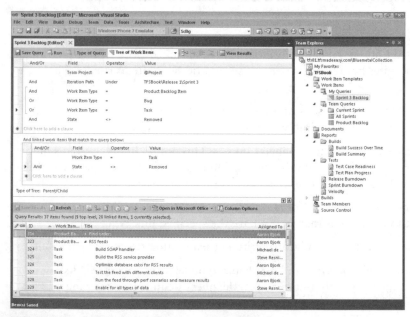

FIGURE 5-19: A tree of work items query definition.

The top portion of the definition limits the first tier of work items returned in the query result. The bottom portion limits work items returned in the hierarchy.

As you will see later in this chapter, the tree of work items query type plays an important role in the Microsoft Visual Studio Scrum 1.0 process template.

Work Item Queries

The Microsoft Visual Studio Scrum 1.0 process template includes eight work item queries:

- ➤ All sprints
- ➤ Product backlog
- ➤ Sprint backlog
- ➤ Unfinished work
- ➤ Work in progress
- ➤ Open impediments
- ➤ Blocked tasks
- ➤ Test cases

The following sections examine the definition, results, and uses for each of these queries.

The All Sprints Query

The all sprints query tracks all sprint work items created in a team project. The default sort order is by start date, in descending order (that is, future dates on top). Figure 5-20 shows an example.

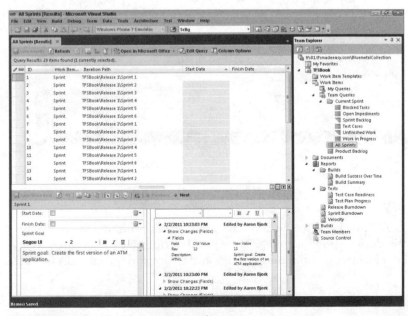

FIGURE 5-20: An all sprints query result.

You use an all sprints query to keep track of upcoming sprints as well as to see past sprint dates. You can double-click any of the results to view details such as the sprint goal and retrospective notes.

The Product Backlog Query

A product owner and Scrum team can use a product backlog query to manage and track requirements for a project. The query results contain both PBIs and bug work items. The results of the product backlog query sort by the Backlog Priority field, in ascending order. Figure 5-21 shows the results from a product backlog query.

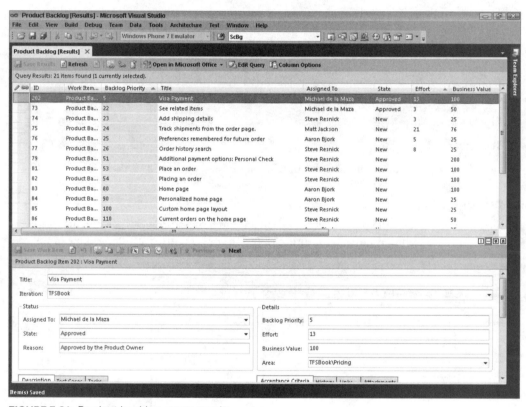

FIGURE 5-21: Product backlog query results.

The Sprint Backlog Query

A sprint backlog query lists all PBIs, bugs, and linked tasks for a single sprint. It is based on the sprint backlog a team creates during sprint planning. The sprint backlog query is a tree query: Work item results display as a hierarchy, with PBIs and bugs at the root and linked tasks beneath. Figure 5-22 shows an example.

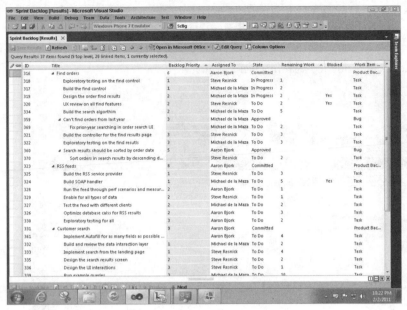

FIGURE 5-22: Sprint backlog query results.

Work item results are sorted on the Backlog Priority field, in ascending order. Parents are sorted before children. Because the query results display as a hierarchy, you can expand and collapse different nodes of the tree to find the data you want. Figure 5-23 shows sprint backlog query results with some collapsed nodes.

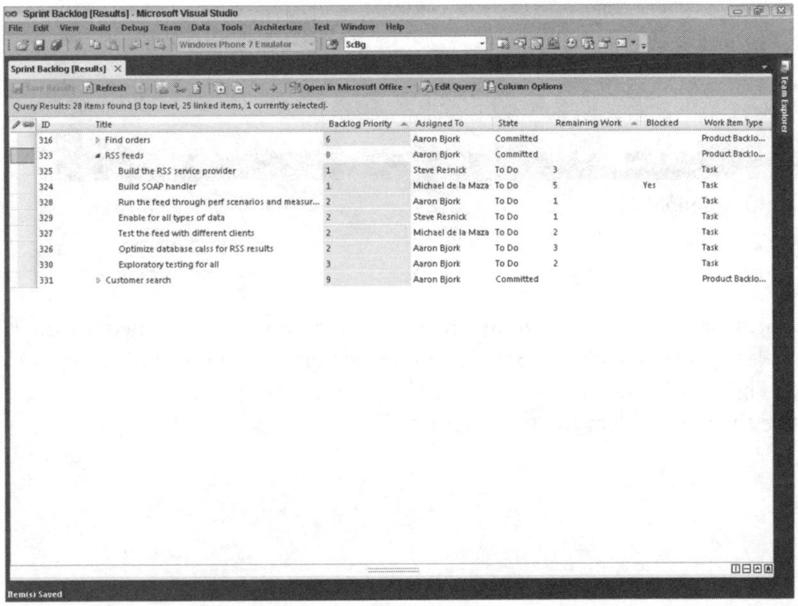

FIGURE 5-23: Two collapsed nodes for sprint backlog query results.

The query results include the Remaining Work field from the task work item, which makes it easy to track how much work remains for the team. All queries in the Current Sprint folder are scoped to a single sprint.

Figure 5-24 shows the query definition for a sprint backlog query.

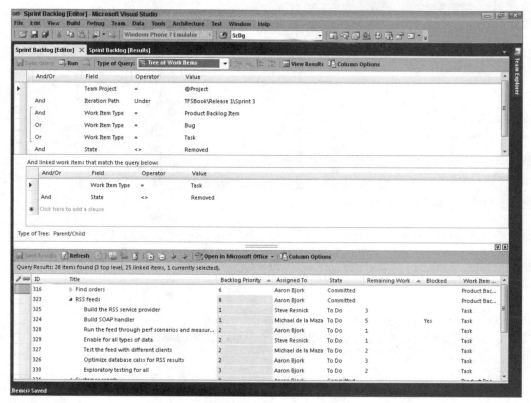

FIGURE 5-24: Sprint backlog query definition.

At the end of your first sprint, you copy the Current Sprint folder to a new folder named Sprint 1. Then you modify the query definition of each query in the Current Sprint folder to point to your team's next sprint, sprint 2. Figure 5-25 shows the query folders for a team project at the beginning of sprint 3. Notice the new folders for sprints 1 and 2.

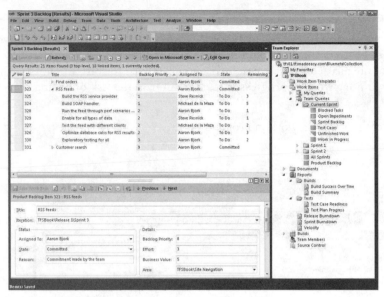

FIGURE 5-25: Query folders at the start of sprint 3.

The Unfinished Work Query

A team uses an unfinished work query to track all work that is not marked as done in the sprint. The unfinished work query is almost identical to the sprint backlog query, except that the results of this query exclude completed work. This behavior makes the query a valuable tool for tracking the remaining work in the current sprint. As work is completed, it is removed from the query results.

Figure 5-26 shows the query definition for an unfinished work query.

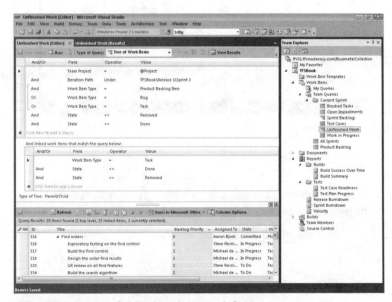

FIGURE 5-26: An unfinished work query definition.

The Work in Progress Query

A work in progress query tracks all the in-progress tasks for the current sprint. This query helps you ensure that your team does not have too much work in progress. One of the principles of Scrum is starting and finishing work at a regular cadence. Scrum asks team members to start and finish tasks before starting new tasks. By limiting work in progress, a team minimizes the risk of ending the sprint with unfinished work.

Figure 5-27 shows the query definition for a work in progress query.

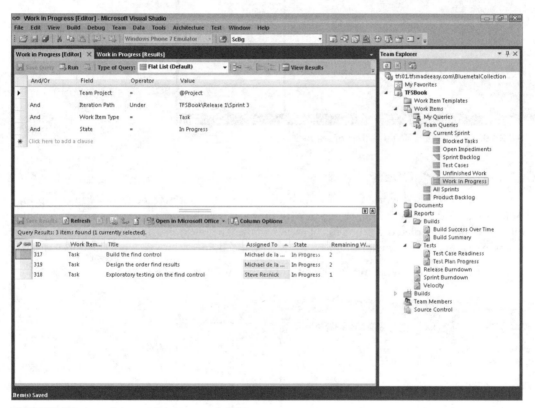

FIGURE 5-27: A work in progress query definition.

The Open Impediments Query

Impediments in Scrum are items that are blocking the team from making progress. An open impediments query lists all impediments in the open state for the current sprint.

Figure 5-28 shows the query definition for an open impediments query.

FIGURE 5-28: An open impediments query definition.

The Blocked Tasks Query

A blocked tasks query returns a list of all tasks in the current sprint marked as blocked. Blocked tasks often result in impediment work items opened and surfaced in the open impediments query.

Figure 5-29 shows the query definition for a blocked tasks query.

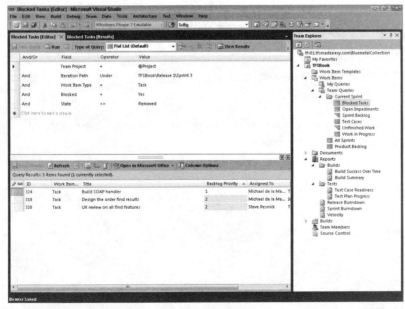

FIGURE 5-29: A blocked tasks query definition.

The Test Cases Query

A test cases query returns a list of all test case work items assigned to the current iteration. A team can use this query to track the testing efforts in its current sprint.

Figure 5-30 shows a test cases query definition and results.

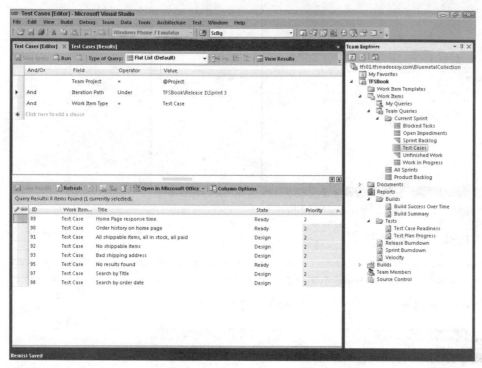

FIGURE 5-30: A test cases query definition.

REPORTS

The Microsoft Visual Studio Scrum 1.0 process template includes seven reports to track project progress. These reports can be grouped into categories:

➤ Scrum reports:

   ➤ Sprint burndown

   ➤ Velocity

   ➤ Release burndown

➤ Engineering reports:

   ➤ Test case readiness

   ➤ Test plan progress

> ➤ Build success over time
>
> ➤ Build summary

Each of these reports answers key questions about the team's progress during different stages of the product cycle.

The following sections examine each report in detail and show how to use the reports to track your team's work. You'll also learn how to build custom reports with the help of Excel.

Scrum Reports

While teams use many different metrics to track the progress of a software development project, Scrum prescribes three project management reports: sprint burndown, release burndown, and velocity.

Sprint Burndown Reports

A team uses a sprint burndown report to track daily progress toward completing a sprint. The sprint burndown report provides four important pieces of information about a sprint:

> ➤ How much work remains in the sprint
>
> ➤ How much work for the sprint is in progress
>
> ➤ The ideal trend toward completing all work in the sprint
>
> ➤ Whether the team is on track to complete all work in the sprint

The remaining work for the sprint is represented as a series on the report. The value for each day in the series is determined by summing the Remaining Work field for each task assigned to the sprint in the to do state. As team members report completed work, the series changes to reflect the team's progress. This is known as *burning down work*, hence the name *sprint burndown report*. See Figure 5-31.

Sprint Burndown

Indicates the team's progress towards completing its work for a sprint.

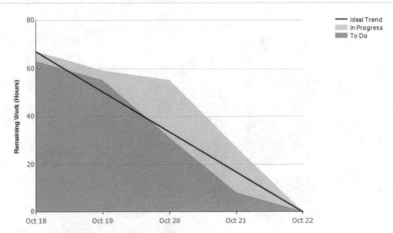

FIGURE 5-31: A sprint burndown report.

Work in progress is the second series on a sprint burndown report. This series is calculated daily by summing the Remaining Work field for each task assigned to the sprint whose State field is set to In Progress. Work in progress is a critical measurement throughout a sprint to ensure that the team is not starting work without finishing it. The work in progress series should remain relatively constant during the life of the sprint. If the work in progress series begins to grow over time, the team should stop all new work and figure out why work is not being completed.

A sprint burndown report displays an ideal trend line from the first day of the sprint to the last day of the sprint. This trend line represents the team's burndown if the same amount of effort were burned down each day across the entire life cycle of the sprint. If the team's trend is above the ideal trend, the team is not on track to meet its goal for the sprint. Likewise, if the team's trend is below the ideal trend, the team is on track to meet its goal for the sprint. A team should inspect the sprint burndown report daily to ensure that it is on track to meet its commitments.

Velocity Reports

A velocity report tells the team the amount of effort it can complete in a sprint. The report displays a column for each sprint that shows the amount of effort completed by the team. Effort is calculated by summing the value of the Effort field for each PBI or bug marked as done and assigned to the sprint.

A velocity report provides a team with three critical pieces of information:

➤ How much effort the team is completing during each sprint

➤ The average amount of effort the team is completing across all selected sprints

➤ The velocity trend across all selected sprints — whether the velocity is going up or down over time

Figure 5-32 shows a velocity report for a team averaging 20 units of effort per sprint.

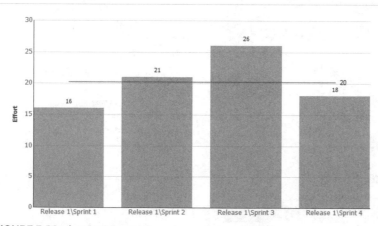

FIGURE 5-32: A velocity report.

Release Burndown Reports

A release burndown report provides understanding about how much work remains in the release and how much work is being burned during each sprint. The report is calculated by summing the total amount of effort remaining on the product backlog on the first day of each sprint. The height of each column on the report indicates how much effort was on the product backlog (across all bugs and PBIs) at the start of each sprint.

During the life cycle of a release, items are continually added to the product backlog. Bugs are found after work is completed. New requirements emerge as the team gains a deeper understanding of the implemented functionality. Priorities change as the product owner learns from the customer. As discussed in Chapter 4, Scrum expects and embraces change. Because of this, it is not possible to draw an exact correlation between the velocity report and the release burndown report.

WHERE IS THE FINISH LINE?

If you started with 100 units of effort, and the team is burning through 20 units of effort per sprint, the release burndown is not telling you anything you don't already know, right? You will be done in five sprints, right? This calculation is correct, but this line of thinking assumes that the 100 units of effort the team started with remains constant. It also assumes that the team's velocity will remain constant over the five sprints. If you were estimating the number of miles between two cities, you could assume with high certainty that the estimate would be correct. The start and finish lines would remain constant during the trip. However, in software production, the finish line often looks much different after starting than it looked in the planning stages.

Figure 5-33 shows a release burndown report for a team that has completed four sprints.

Release Burndown

Indicates how quickly the team is completing work and delivering Product Backlog Items. Its primary use is for planning when to schedule a release and to track the team's progress towards delivering on its goals.

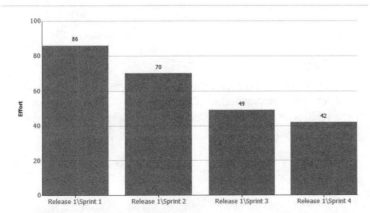

FIGURE 5-33: A release burndown report.

Engineering Reports

The reports described in this section are not core to the Scrum framework but instead represent common reports that software engineering teams rely on.

Test Case Readiness Reports

A test case readiness report provides a team with a view of progress toward designing test cases and making them ready for testing. Because test cases can be reused across sprints, a test case readiness report is not limited to sprint boundaries. Parameters on the report let you set custom start and end dates for the report. Figure 5-34 shows a test case readiness report.

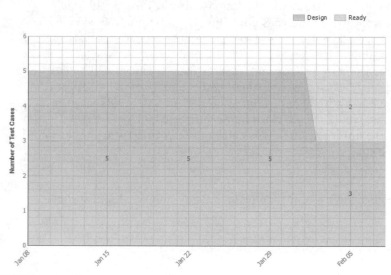

FIGURE 5-34: A test case readiness report.

Test Plan Progress Reports

A test plan progress report tracks a team's overall progress in testing a product. Like a test case readiness report, a test plan progress report is not limited to the sprint boundaries. A test plan progress report shows, over time, the results of executing tests for the project. Each result falls into one of the following categories:

➤ **Passed** — The number of test cases that passed

➤ **Failed** — The number of test cases that failed

➤ **Blocked** — The number of test cases marked as blocked

➤ **Never Run** — The number of test cases that have never been run

➤ **Other** — The number of test cases that were run and assigned a result different from passed or failed

By monitoring the test plan progress report during a sprint and over the life cycle of a release, a team can gain a better understanding of the quality of the product and how the team is progressing toward ensuring that the product is thoroughly tested.

Figure 5-35 shows a test plan progress report.

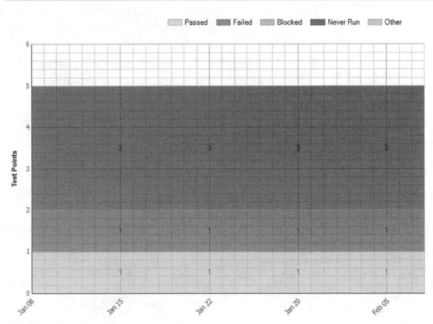

FIGURE 5-35: A test plan progress report.

Build Success over Time Reports

A build success over time report displays the status of the last build for each build category run for each day. You can use this report to help track the quality of the code that the team is checking in. Figure 5-36 shows a build success over time report.

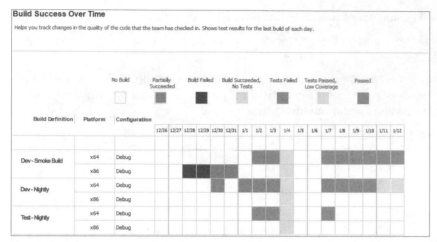

FIGURE 5-36: A build success over time report.

Build Summary Reports

A build summary report lists information about the test results, test coverage, code churn, and quality for each build run. Figure 5-37 shows a build summary report.

Build Summary

Helps you determine the status of each build. Shows a list of builds with test results, test coverage, code churn, and quality notes.

| | | | | | Passed | Covered | |
| | | | | | Failed | Not Covered | Code Churn |

Date	Build Name	Platform	Progress	Build Quality	% Tests Passed	% Code Coverage	Code Churn (lines)
1/4/2011 10:11 AM	Dev - Nightly_20110104.1	x64	Succeeded	Passed			
1/5/2011 10:11 AM	Dev - Nightly_20110105.1	x86	Succeeded	Passed			
1/6/2011 8:14 AM	Dev - Smoke_20110106.1	x86	Succeeded	Passed			
1/7/2011 9:15 AM	Dev - Nightly_20110107.1	x86	Succeeded	Failed			
1/7/2011 11:17 AM	Test - Nightly_20110107.1	x86	Succeeded	Passed			
1/4/2011 10:11 AM	Dev - Smoke_20110108.1	x86	Succeeded	Passed			
1/8/2011 11:03 AM	Dev - Nightly_20110108.1	x86	Succeeded	Failed			

FIGURE 5-37: A build summary report.

Building Custom Reports

In the previous sections, you learned about the reports included in the Scrum process template for TFS. These reports help you track and manage your team's work throughout the Scrum process. However, they do not reflect everything that your team may want or need to track. In the following sections, you will learn how to use Excel to generate rich custom charts to track and manage your team's work.

Getting Starting with Excel Reporting

As mentioned in Chapter 3, TFS provides a SQL Server Analysis cube for tracking and reporting on your project data. The cube is a data structure that allows for fast analysis of large amounts of data. At regular intervals, the cube is updated with your current project data. By default, the cube is set to update every two hours. There are many different ways of accessing the data in the cube, but the easiest way, as described in this section, is to use Excel.

TFS 2010 includes a new feature that allows you to create reports in Excel directly from a work item query. To access this feature, you simply right-click a work item query and select Create Report in Microsoft Excel, as shown in Figure 5-38. You can also click Create Report in Excel from the Query Results menu on all flat list queries, as shown in Figure 5-39. This convenient feature allows members to start a report from a familiar artifact — a work item query.

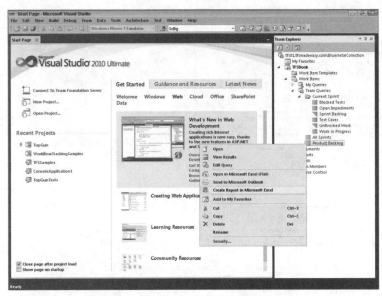

FIGURE 5-38: Using Excel to create a report from a query.

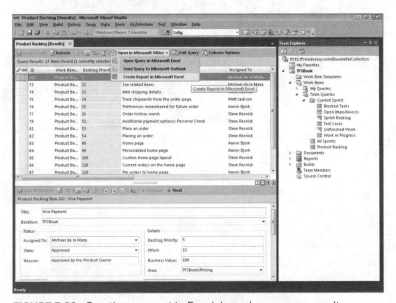

FIGURE 5-39: Creating a report in Excel, based on a query result.

In the following example, you will create a series of reports from the product backlog query:

1.   In TFS, select the Team Queries node. Double-click Product Backlog. TFS generates results for the product backlog query.

2.   From the menu above the query results, click the Open in Microsoft Office button and select Create Report in Microsoft Excel, as shown in Figure 5-39. Excel opens a dialog similar to the one shown in Figure 5-40.

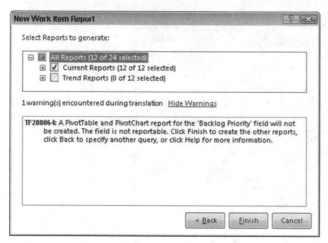

FIGURE 5-40: The New Work Item Report dialog.

 Figure 5-40 displays an error that the Backlog Priority field is not reportable. This is expected. Excel builds a report for each column in your query result. In this example, the product backlog query is sorted by the Backlog Priority field. However, the Backlog Priority field is not marked as a reportable field in the process template.

3.   In the New Work Item Report dialog, select the reports you want Excel to generate. For this example, select all 24 available reports, as shown in Figure 5-41. Click Finish. Excel begins to generate the reports selected, as shown in Figure 5-42. This step may take a few minutes to complete.

After all the reports are generated, a table of contents page is displayed on the first worksheet in Excel, with hyperlinks to each report generated (see Figure 5-43). Each report is created on a separate worksheet.

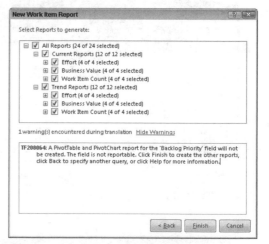

FIGURE 5-41: Selecting reports in the New Work Item Report dialog.

Notice that the reports available for you to create coincide with the columns displayed in the product backlog query from which you started.

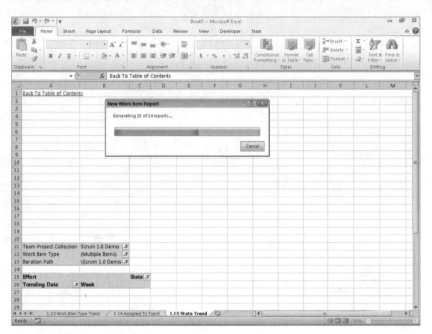

FIGURE 5-42: Excel generating your reports.

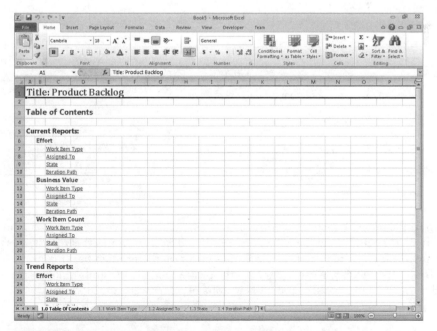

FIGURE 5-43: An Excel report table of contents page.

4. Browse through the worksheets to examine each report and click hyperlinks from the landing page to jump directly to specific reports. Click the first worksheet, titled Work Item Type under the Current Reports heading or click the first hyperlinked report from the table of contents. Figure 5-44 shows the report that Excel generates; it shows the amount of effort from the product backlog, broken down by work item type. In this example, you can see that 18 units of effort on the product backlog are categorized as bugs, and 34 units of effort on the product backlog are categorized as PBIs.

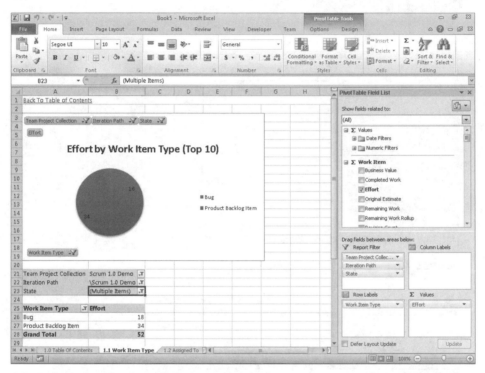

FIGURE 5-44: An effort by work item type Excel report.

 Each report generated is built from a PivotTable connected to the TFS cube.

5. Return to the table of contents worksheet and select the first trend report by clicking Work Item Type under the Trend Reports heading. Excel generates this report, as shown in Figure 5-45; it is a report of the amount of effort on the product backlog over time. In this example, you can see that in the past week, 18 new units of effort were added to the backlog as bugs, and 15 new units of effort were added as PBIs.

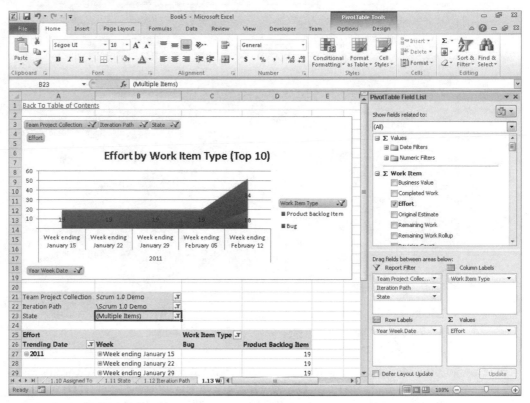

FIGURE 5-45: An Excel effort by work item type over time report.

In this example, you saw the power of using Excel to build reports directly from work item queries in a team project. Because the reports are built in Excel, you can customize and modify them to include data that is important to your team and to your software project. In the next section, you will learn another way to modify the reports you create in Excel.

Saving Reports Built in Excel

After you build an Excel report, it's likely you'll want to save the report so that it is accessible to everyone on your team. The Microsoft Visual Studio Scrum 1.0 process template includes a SharePoint portal for each new project, and you can save reports generated in Excel directly to the portal. (Chapter 8 discusses the SharePoint portal in more detail.)

To save a report generated in Excel to the SharePoint portal, follow these steps:

1. From the Excel report, select File ⇨ Save As, as shown in Figure 5-46. Excel opens the Save As dialog.

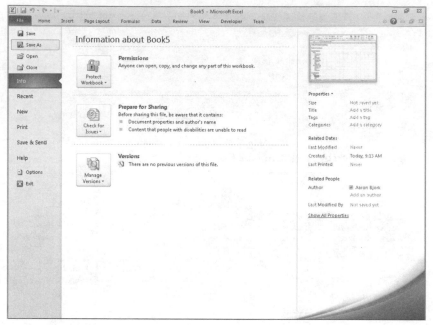

FIGURE 5-46: Saving an Excel report to the SharePoint portal.

2. In the Save As dialog, enter the URL of your SharePoint portal into the address bar, as shown in Figure 5-47. Double-click the Shared Documents folder, enter a name for your report, and click Save. Close Excel and go back to Visual Studio.

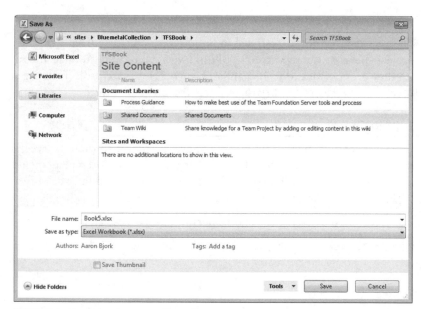

FIGURE 5-47: Selecting your SharePoint portal.

3. Open Visual Studio, and in the Team Explorer, expand the Shared Documents folder for your team project. As shown in Figure 5-48, the Team Explorer displays the report you just created.

FIGURE 5-48: An Excel report displayed in Team Explorer.

 You can store reports like this locally as well as on other network resources to which your team has permissions.

Modifying Reports Built in Excel

When you create Excel reports from work item queries, Excel generates them using PivotTables and PivotCharts. A *PivotTable* is a data summarization tool that provides automatic sorting, counting, and totaling based on specific parameters. PivotTables are powerful tools for analyzing project data. In this section, you will learn how to manipulate a PivotTable and PivotChart to create charts that help you track your team's progress.

After you create an initial set of reports from a work item query, you can use PivotTable features in Excel to further analyze and study your data. The structure of the fields in the PivotTable field list comes directly from the TFS cube. For example, in the PivotTable Field List box shown in Figure 5-49, each field represents a reportable field in TFS.

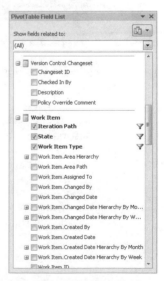

FIGURE 5-49: A PivotTable field list.

You can toggle these fields on and off in each PivotTable. In the following steps, you'll manipulate a report you created earlier (refer to Figure 5-44). In this example, you will change a pie chart showing effort by work item type to a column chart that shows effort by work item type broken down based on the Assigned To field:

1. Open the effort by work item type Excel report you created in the previous section. Then open the report's first worksheet, titled 1.1 Work Item Type. Select the pie chart in the report. Excel displays the PivotTable Field List box on the right side of the screen.

2. Scroll through the PivotTable Field List box until you find the Assigned To field under Work Item, as shown in Figure 5-50.

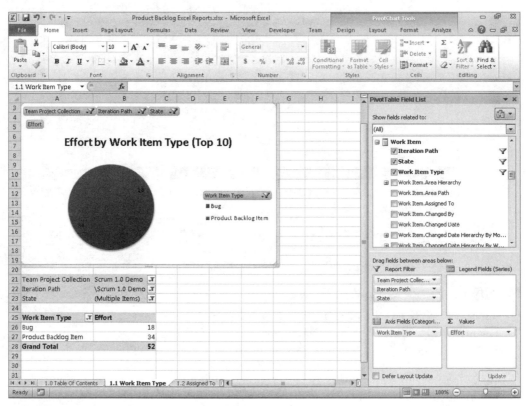

FIGURE 5-50: The PivotTable Field List box for a report.

3. Select the Assigned To field under Work Item. The chart changes, and the Assigned To field is added to the Axis Fields list, as shown in Figure 5-51.

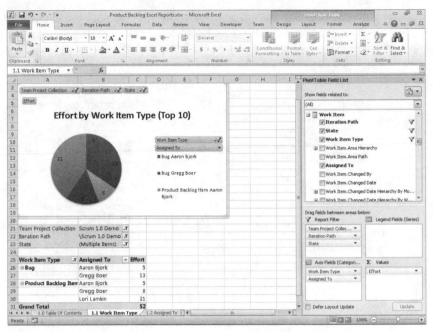

FIGURE 5-51: Adding the Assigned To field to the Axis Fields area.

4. Click the Assigned To field in the Axis Fields area and drag it to the Legend Fields area. Notice again the changes to the PivotChart, as shown in Figure 5-52.

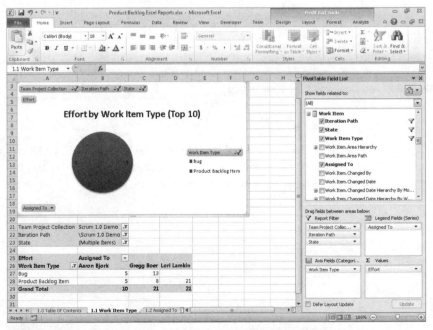

FIGURE 5-52: Adding the Assigned To field to the Legend Fields area.

5. On the Excel Ribbon, switch to the PivotChart Tools tab and click the Change Chart Type button in the top left of the tab. The Change Chart Type dialog appears, as shown in Figure 5-53.

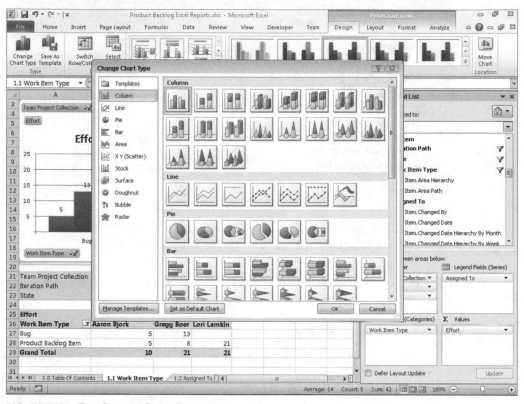

FIGURE 5-53: The Change Chart Type dialog.

6. In the Change Chart Type dialog, select the Column chart type and click OK. As shown in Figure 5-54, the PivotChart is updated as a column chart, showing the amount of effort across work item types, pivoted by who the work items are assigned to.

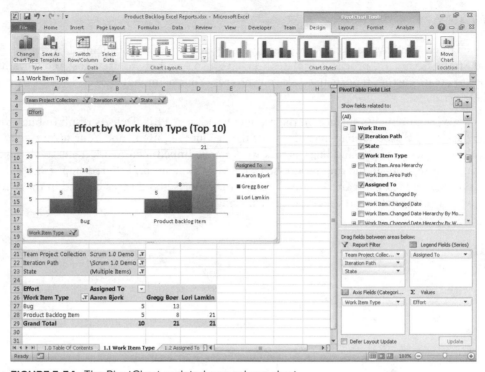

FIGURE 5-54: The PivotChart updated as a column chart.

This is just one example of using PivotCharts and PivotTables to build data-rich reports. You can use the steps listed here to create additional reports to assist in tracking your team's work. The following are some examples:

➤ Task assignments during a sprint

➤ Blocking tasks over time

➤ Impediment trends across sprints

➤ Business value on the product backlog

➤ Remaining work by team member

➤ Remaining work by team activity

SUMMARY

In this chapter, you have seen the work item types, queries, and reports defined by the Microsoft Visual Studio Scrum 1.0 process template. You have also seen how to use Excel and work item queries to create custom reports to track your project. Your team manages and tracks a project with all these artifacts.

In summary, requirements surface on the product backlog as PBIs. Defects result in bug work items and surface on the product backlog, alongside the product requirements. Your team tracks all its work to implement PBIs and bugs as task work items. Impediment work items track anything blocking your team from making progress. Test case work items and shared steps track the quality of the progress made by a team. Finally, by using the reports and queries defined in the template, a team can stay aware of its progress toward achieving its goals.

The Product Backlog

WHAT'S IN THIS CHAPTER?

➤   Managing the product backlog.

➤   Creating and prioritizing PBIs.

➤   Linking artifacts: PBIs, tasks, and bugs.

➤   Understanding impediments.

In Chapter 5, you examined the specifics of the artifacts in the Microsoft Visual Studio Scrum 1.0 process template: work items, queries, and reports. You saw how each one contributes to tracking a project. This chapter focuses on the product backlog, which is the list of requirements for a system. The product backlog is a dynamic list that grows and shrinks over the course of a project.

This chapter discusses a number of topics related to the product backlog: managing the product backlog; creating and prioritizing product backlog items (PBIs); linking PBIs, tasks, and bugs; and understanding impediments. Understanding these concepts will help your team control its product backlog.

MANAGING THE PRODUCT BACKLOG

Before learning how to create PBIs in TFS, it's important to consider the goal of the product backlog as a whole. The *product backlog* is the list of features that the product owner believes will make a great product.

While the product backlog defines the full product, the PBIs define the individual features. A larger product has more features than a smaller product, so it has more PBIs. How many PBIs should define a product? How many is too many? How many is too few? How do you write good PBIs? The product owner must answer all these questions before writing the PBIs.

 Chapter 8 has a section titled "Considering the INVEST Characteristics" that describes the essential characteristics of PBIs.

Before the project begins, and before the team is assembled, the product owner meets with customers to develop a deep understanding of their needs. Once the product is in a demonstrable form and is shown to customers, the product owner will learn more about their likes, dislikes, and tolerances. The product backlog, just like the product itself, is built iteratively.

The product backlog is never static and is never complete. It has one set of items before the first sprint, and it has a very different set with every sprint afterward. It grows as customers see the product and have more suggestions. It grows as project sponsors see the product as well. It shrinks as the team builds features — taking PBIs off the product backlog, putting them on the sprint backlog, and marking them as complete.

The product backlog is the sole input queue for the team. If a feature isn't on the product backlog, it won't be scheduled and committed for a sprint, and it won't be built. Therefore, bugs that exist at the end of one sprint are put onto the product backlog for attention in subsequent sprints. The product owner, who sets the priority for all items on the product backlog, determines whether the bugs should be sorted above other PBIs or below. In most cases, some bugs sort higher than features while others sort lower.

Figure 6-1 shows the flow of new features into a product. It begins with the product manager translating customer needs and desires into a list of product features that can be built by the team. This list is called the product backlog. A Scrum team is organized to efficiently build a product in small sprints of activity. The product owner prioritizes the product backlog and identifies a subset of related features that can be implemented in a sprint. Each sprint has its own list, called a sprint backlog.

Each sprint begins with a list of features to build. Each sprint ends with most, but not all, of the features complete. The incomplete items are added back to the product backlog for inclusion in another sprint. After a few sprints — typically between 3 and 10 — the team is ready to release a version of the product. It releases the bits, distributes the product to customers, gets feedback, and begins building the next version.

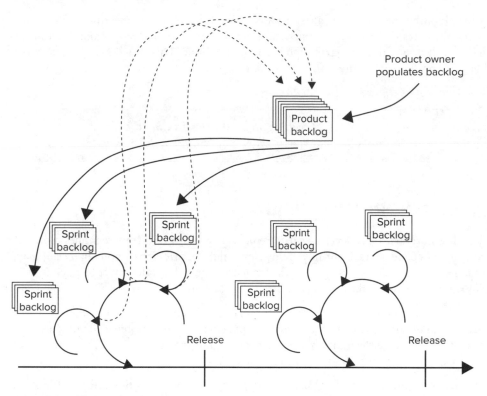

FIGURE 6-1: The product backlog cycle.

The product backlog is an effective tool for managing feature creep in the iterative sprints and release of Scrum. A team can add features to the product without limits; it's just a matter of prioritization and resources. If a customer or sponsor tells the product owner "we must have feature X," the response can be accurate and very supportive, such as "That sounds great; let's put it on the product backlog and schedule it into a future sprint." With the new PBI, the product owner can then evaluate the return on investment (ROI) of the feature and compare it to other competing PBIs for subsequent sprints.

FEATURE CREEP

Everyone has good ideas. When someone sees a partially built product, he or she invariably has ideas about how to make it better. As new ideas are added to the current release, the number of features creeps up, requiring additional resources (time, people, and money) that may not be available. Managing (read: eliminating) feature creep is essential to shipping a product.

With each sprint, PBIs are removed from the backlog and bugs are added. With every customer demo, PBIs are added, and the list is prioritized. The product backlog is most manageable if it is pruned regularly. The product owner should periodically review the backlog to find PBIs that continually get overlooked for selection in a sprint. At some point, those PBIs should be removed from the list.

With each sprint planning meeting — or at least with each release planning meeting — the team should review its estimates of PBIs. This is important because an estimate may change significantly as the team gains skill or as different parts of the product are built. This process may make feasible some PBIs that were previously written off.

 By pruning the product backlog at regular intervals, the product owner can keep it efficient. Remember that the backlog is the sole input queue for the team.

CREATING AND PRIORITIZING PBIS

The product backlog starts with high-level user requirements and grows as a team identifies more subtle user needs and system dependencies. It shrinks as the team builds features into a potentially shippable product with each sprint. The list grows again as the team encounters bugs that must be fixed in successive sprints. It also grows as the team demonstrates the system to users who suggest more features.

The product backlog consists of *product backlog items (PBIs)*. Each PBI is an individual requirement that is small enough to build and test within a sprint. PBIs are generally user-centric requirements, such as "manage the online shopping basket," but they can also be IT-centric, as in "verify that credit card data is not persisted in the database."

The product owner is responsible for the PBIs, from defining them in enough detail that the team can build them to including acceptance criteria so the team knows when the PBIs are done.

The product owner needs to prioritize the PBIs on the product backlog so that the team works on the items that are most import to the business. The items are sorted by priority number, with lower priority numbers showing up higher on the list and higher priority numbers floating down to the bottom.

The product owner needs to determine the scope of each release and verify that the PBIs are prioritized properly. At the beginning of each sprint, the team should inspect the highest-priority PBIs to determine which ones it can commit to finishing within that sprint. This list becomes the sprint backlog. Sprint by sprint, the team finishes the PBIs for each release of the product.

The following sections discuss how to choose a tool for creating PBIs, the PBI workflow, and how to prioritize PBIs.

Choosing a Tool for Creating PBIs

You can create PBIs by using Visual Studio, Excel, or SharePoint. Regardless of which tool you choose, Team Foundation Server (TFS) manages the PBIs and stores them in SQL Server. The central nature of TFS and SQL Server means that different people can use different tools, or one person can use many tools, without loss of fidelity from tool to tool. Visual Studio is generally the best tool for everyone on a Scrum team to use, as it's tuned for development teams and most people probably already have it installed. Visual Studio enables you to access more features than Excel or SharePoint, so for this reason, all team members should install Visual Studio.

> **VISUAL STUDIO VERSIONS**
>
> You can use any version of Visual Studio 2010: Professional, Premium, Ultimate, or Test. However, Visual Studio 2010 Professional has a limitation: If you purchase it without a full MSDN subscription, then you'll need to purchase TFS licenses from Microsoft.
>
> If a team member doesn't need or want the full development tool, he or she can just install Visual Studio Team Explorer. Team Explorer loads into the Visual Studio shell as a stand-alone tool that provides full access to Team Foundation Server. The *Visual Studio shell* is the container in which Visual Studio features, such as the code editor and debugger, reside, so Team Explorer will look natural in the Visual Studio shell. The Team Explorer install bits are located on the Team Foundation Server 2010 installation kit, which ships with each version of Visual Studio. In other words, if you have Visual Studio, you have TFS. And if you have TFS, you have Team Explorer. The stand-alone Team Explorer is a viable option for the product owner or someone who needs flexible access to the PBIs and other TFS artifacts but who won't be doing any actual development.

People outside the Scrum team who need access to the PBIs, tasks, and other items can use an Internet browser and the SharePoint site that's associated with the team project, or they can use Excel. Using an Internet browser enables access to the product backlog without requiring any special tools to be installed on the desktop. Security is controlled via TFS and Active Directory groups, so someone either on the Scrum team or in IT needs to set that up.

 If someone outside the team needs quick access to the backlog but won't be updating any information, you can easily create a snapshot of the backlog in Excel. Once in Excel, you can e-mail this snapshot to someone or copy it and then paste it into PowerPoint for status meetings.

The PBI Workflow

The product owner creates PBIs. Initially, the product owner creates each item with just enough information and context to describe the feature or user requirement. It's common for the product owner to enter dozens of PBIs early in the project definition phase, in order to capture the full scope of a release or product. When entering PBIs en masse, it's easier to use Excel than Visual Studio, as you'll see later in this chapter.

With the initial set of PBIs defined, the product owner goes back through the list to revise it, paying special attention to the following:

➤ **Refining the list** — The product owner refines the PBIs by adding crucial details such as business value, acceptance criteria, and priority.

➤ **Pruning the list** — The product owner removes duplicates or poorly defined PBIs.

➤ **Changing the status** — For each item that is complete, the product owner sets the status to approved, meaning that it's approved to be scheduled for a later sprint in the release.

At the sprint planning meeting, the team reviews the PBIs at the top of the backlog priority list. For each item, the team determines whether it can complete the PBI within the current sprint. It then sets the state of any such PBIs to committed, meaning that the team is committed to completing those items in the sprint.

PBIs are sorted in ascending order, where items with lower backlog priority sort higher in the list than items with higher backlog priority. TFS defaults backlog priority to 1,000, forcing new PBIs to the bottom of the list when they are initially entered.

During the sprint — when the actual work gets done — the team works on building and testing the PBIs. The team codes and unit tests each PBI, ensuring that it meets the acceptance criteria defined for that PBI. When the team feels that a PBI is fully functional and in shippable condition, it sets the state to done.

Figure 6-2 shows the overall PBI workflow.

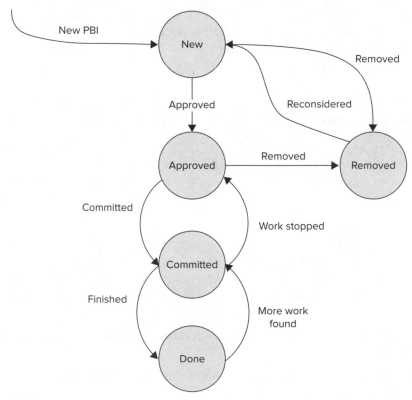

FIGURE 6-2: PBI workflow.

Prioritizing PBIs

A product grows and shrinks throughout the duration of a project. You may have dozens of PBIs, or you may have hundreds. With thousands of PBIs or more, though, it becomes very difficult for the product owner to organize the PBIs in a coherent way. And with a small number of PBIs, such as a dozen or so, any one PBI is probably too large to complete in a single sprint. Therefore, most projects have hundreds of PBIs.

Not all PBIs have the same benefit to the business. Some may be very important, and others may be just nice to have. On one end of the spectrum are PBIs that are critical; the team won't even think of shipping a release without those features. At the other end are features that are somewhat frivolous; someone could be fired for holding up a release for any of these features.

Similarly, not all PBIs have the same cost. Some are quite easy to build and are largely independent of the rest of the system. Other PBIs require significant engineering and testing, and they have dependencies on other components or teams.

By looking at the benefit and the cost of a PBI, a team can determine its ROI. The ROI is simply the benefit of a PBI divided by its cost. With financial assets (stock, bonds, and so on), ROI is measured in dollars or other currency. You divide the return (selling price – purchase price) by the investment (purchase price) to get the ROI. A greater ROI is a better investment, and a lower ROI is a worse investment. If you control the variables, you can increase ROI by increasing the return or decreasing the investment. If you don't control the variables, you're seeking opportunities with greater return in proportion to the investment.

As part of the planning process, the product owner defines the benefit and the team defines the cost of each PBI. The business value is generally not defined in dollars, and the effort is generally not estimated in hours, so the ROI is not measured in dollars; it's simply benefit divided by effort (or cost).

ROI PRECISION

ROI is often used as a measure with good precision. If you invest in a machine that costs X, and it reduces your labor cost by Y, and Y > X, then the ROI > 1, and it's a potentially good investment. Once you factor in the cost of money and the risk of realizing the benefit, you make a decision.

In Scrum, ROI is only a relative term. You can compare the ROI of one PBI with that of another to inform your decision about which PBI to implement first.

Chances are that the product owner doesn't have solid metrics to define the real return of implementing each PBI. In addition, the team probably doesn't have a real cost estimate. As a result, the ROI of a PBI isn't precise. But ROI is useful as a relative measure and is one factor to consider when prioritizing the backlog. As the team scans the backlog for items to include in a sprint, it can choose to include or exclude some PBIs based on their ROI. Figure 6-3 shows some obvious choices.

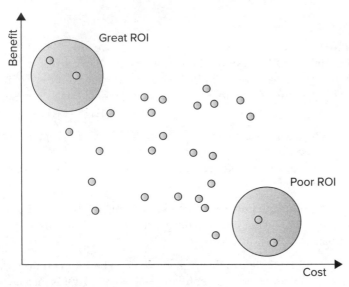

FIGURE 6-3: Plotting PBIs to determine ROI.

For example, say that you're working on a retail website, and the current sprint focuses on the checkout process. The backlog has an item titled "save the cart" that enables a shopper to save his cart and come back later to finish the purchase. The product owner assigns it a business value of 70 on a scale from 1 to 100. When the team considers how difficult this system is to build, assuming that it already has basic security and login features in place, it decides that the effort required is worth 5 points. So the ROI of the "save the cart" PBI is 70 / 5, or 14.

Continuing on with this example, say that there's another item on the backlog titled "e-mail the cart" that enables a shopper to e-mail her cart to a friend as a recommendation. The product owner assigns it a business value of 45 because fewer people will use this feature than the "save the cart" feature. The team feels that this feature is somewhat more difficult to implement because it involves capturing and providing security around e-mail addresses. The team therefore assigns this PBI an effort of 21 points. The ROI of the "e-mail the cart" feature is 45 / 21, or about 2.

In this example, clearly the "save the cart" PBI — with an ROI of 14 — is a better use of time than the "e-mail the cart" PBI — with an ROI of 2. The ROI method enables the team to make smarter decisions about which features to include in the sprint during the sprint planning meeting.

Documenting PBIs

You can enter a PBI in Visual Studio, Excel, or SharePoint. Whichever tool you chose, the information is stored in TFS so it is accessible to other tools and reports.

To document a PBI in Visual Studio, you select Team ➪ New Item ➪ Backlog Item. Then you fill in the following fields:

➤ Title

➤ Iteration

➤ Assigned To

> State

> Reason

> Backlog Priority

> Effort

> Business Value

> Area

> Description

> Acceptance Criteria

These fields are not all required in Visual Studio, but throughout the flow and life cycle of a PBI, they are all used. The following sections describe them in more detail, and Figure 6-4 shows the Visual Studio screen where you enter PBIs.

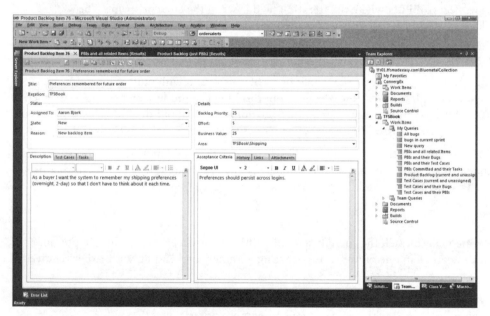

FIGURE 6-4: The screen for entering PBIs in Visual Studio.

Title

In the Title field you provide a brief description of the PBI. Remember that PBIs often start as user stories, and the genesis of a user story is a note card with one sentence on it. The title of a PBI should represent the intent of the PBI. After a sprint planning meeting, or anytime during a sprint, the team should be able to articulate what the PBI represents by just hearing its title.

Iteration

In the Iteration field you indicate the sprint in which a PBI is implemented. When you first enter a PBI into TFS, Iteration defaults to the current project, meaning that it's not yet scheduled for a sprint. During the sprint planning meeting, when the team commits to implementing a PBI, you set this field to the iteration representing the sprint.

> ### PRE-ASSIGNING SPRINTS TO ITERATIONS
>
> You can pre-assign PBIs to specific sprints ahead of time. To do so, you populate the Iteration field early in the project. This is helpful for planning which features will be implemented when. You don't want to go so far as to plan the whole release ahead of time, with features in one sprint being dependent on features in prior sprints. However, pre-assigning a few PBIs sporadically is okay.

When the Iteration field is set to the current sprint, the PBI goes from the product backlog to the sprint backlog. Two predefined queries in the Scrum 1.0 template use this field. The sprint backlog query selects all PBIs where the Iteration field is set to the current sprint. The product backlog query selects all PBIs where the Iteration field is set to the project.

Assigned To

In the Assigned To field you indicate the owner of a PBI. On a team with multiple product owners, you select the owner with the most knowledge about this PBI. The product owner who's assigned to the PBI is responsible for answering questions and providing detail about the PBI. This person is also responsible for verifying that the PBI meets acceptance criteria before the team finishes the sprint.

When a PBI is first created, the Assigned To field defaults to the user entering the PBI, so it's best to set it to the product owner at that point. You may change it, though, if or when another product owner is added to the project and PBIs are being split among the owners.

State

You use the State field to track the current state of a PBI. As shown earlier in this chapter, in Figure 6-2, a PBI can be in one of five states, starting with new and ending with either removed or done:

- ➤ **New** — The PBI is entered into TFS. It may be just be the initial text of a user story, or it may be fully defined with test cases and acceptance criteria.

- ➤ **Approved** — The PBI has been approved by the product owner and is a candidate to be assigned to a sprint at the sprint planning meeting.

- ➤ **Committed** — The PBI has been assigned to a sprint, and the team has committed to completing it.

- ➤ **Removed** — The PBI is no longer needed. This is useful when you're pruning the backlog to remove duplicates, to consolidate similar PBIs, or to simply remove the PBIs that are such low priority that they will never be built.

- ➤ **Done** — The PBI is complete, and the product owner has tested and verified it.

Reason

Reason is a read-only field that is predefined based on the state and transition of the PBI. It has the following definitions in the Scrum 1.0 template:

- ➤ New

    - ➤ **New Backlog Item** — The PBI was just entered but not yet prioritized or estimated.

    - ➤ **Reconsidering Backlog Item** — The item had been removed but was reconsidered and is now back in the backlog.

- ➤ Approved

    - ➤ **Approved by the Product Owner** — The PBI was approved by the product owner and is now ready to be included in a sprint.

    - ➤ **Work Stopped** — The PBI had been committed to a sprint, but the team decided to stop work on it and put it back in the backlog for a future sprint.

- ➤ Committed

    - ➤ **Commitment Made by the Team** — The team has committed to implement the PBI in a sprint.

    - ➤ **Additional Work Found** — The PBI was previously considered done, but more work was found, so it's back in the backlog.

- ➤ **Removed** — The PBI was removed from the backlog.

- ➤ **Done** — The work on the PBI is finished.

Backlog Priority

You use the Backlog Priority field to determine the position of the PBI on the product backlog. New PBIs default to a backlog priority of 1,000. This field represents an item's location in the backlog, not its business value. It indicates when the PBI should be scheduled, relative to other items on the list. The product owner adjusts this value when pruning the backlog throughout the release, moving items up and down on the list to reflect their relative importance to the product.

Effort

You use the Effort field to track the estimated effort required to implement a PBI, relative to other PBIs in the release. *Relative* is the operative word here, as the effort is not in terms of hours or days. Rather, it's a just a number used to compare the relative effort required for PBIs.

You can estimate effort in terms of story points, where 1 point can be an ideal day (no interruptions, coding in the zone, and so on) or an ideal week. Or you can estimate it in terms of complexity, where 1 point is 1 dependency. Regardless of the measure you choose, it's important to be consistent.

ESTIMATING IN CALORIES

On one project, where the early sprints were being planned during the holiday season, the team labeled the estimates as "calories," since good holiday food was on everyone's mind. This label stuck and was useful for two reasons. First, sentences such as "How many calories will that feature consume?" or "How many calories can the team expend in 1 week?" intuitively make sense and capture the real meaning of the estimation.

Second, when communicating with management, using calories as the estimate made it clear that the team was not speaking about days. Having 300 calories on the backlog didn't mean that the release would cost 300 times someone's daily wage. Nor did it mean that it would take 300 person-days to complete. It meant that the team could divide the calories by its velocity, add some time for stabilization and release sprints, and get a fairly accurate estimate of how much time was needed to complete the release.

In addition to choosing a measure, you should pick an upper bound and a lower bound for the range. The upper and lower bounds represent the minimum effort and maximum effort worth tracking. Any item outside those numbers should be combined or split into multiple items.

Finally, in addition to the range, you should choose valid steps in the range. The most obvious choice is inclusive integers. For example, you might estimate effort between 1 and 10 as 1, 2, 3, 4, 5, 6, 7, 8, 9, and 10. In such as system, one PBI may be 4 story points, while another PBI might be 7.

A less obvious but fairly common approach is to use the Fibonacci sequence for effort estimates. This works for two reasons. First, it forces you to use a known set of numbers and prevents you from squabbling over whether the effort is 19 or 15, since neither of those are valid choices in the series. Second, it forces more fine-grained estimates for smaller items and more coarse-grained estimates for larger items. This just is a function of the series (1, 2, 3, 5, 8, 13, 21, 34, 55, 89, and so on) because you can probably estimate the difference between 2, 3, and 5 more easily than you can between 21 and 34.

 Planning Poker is another technique for converging on an estimate. For more information, see the section "Estimating Product Backlog Items" in Chapter 3.

A team also uses the effort estimate retrospectively, to determine its velocity for future sprint planning. If, after three sprints, you know that the team can complete 500 effort points in a two-week sprint, you can confidently commit to PBIs that add up to that amount of effort in the fourth sprint. This makes sprints more predictable.

Business Value

You use the Business Value field to track the amount of business value delivered by a PBI. You should choose a number between 1 and 100 to represent the amount of business value that implementing the PBI will deliver to your customers. Higher numbers imply greater business value. A PBI with a low business value and a high effort estimate probably won't get scheduled into a sprint and will remain on the product backlog.

The product owner defines the business value when creating the PBI, and it generally doesn't change.

Area

You use the Area field to track the area or component of the product. This field is very helpful in managing a project because it naturally identifies compartmentalized sections of the product. For example, a retail website might have areas such as \Checkout, \HomePage, \Catalog, \Catalog\ Search, and \Catalog\Import.

The product owner defines the area when creating a PBI. The team may update it over time, as components and subsystems are decomposed or refactored.

TFS uses the Area field across all work items, so the area of a PBI should be carried across other items. For instance, a PBI in the \Catalog area would be linked to tasks, bugs, and test cases also defined in the \Catalog area.

TFS does not automatically copy the area of one work item to the next. For instance, if you create a bug or a task from a PBI, the bug or task will not inherit the PBI's area, so you should pay attention to classifying each bug or task properly.

Description

You use the Description field to provide a detailed description of a PBI. This is where the product owner describes what the feature does and who needs it. If you're defining PBIs via user stories, then this is the written record of the feature. It needs to convey enough information so that the product owner and team can speak intelligently about what's being requested and how it will be used.

Don't be tempted to put a full requirement spec here; it's just a proxy for a deeper dialogue among constituents who fully understand and will build the feature. The real spec is the discussions and shared understanding between the product owner and the team as well as formal documentation that exists elsewhere.

The product owner fills in the Description field when creating the PBI. He or she adds more content after the PBI is committed to a sprint because that's when the information is really needed.

Acceptance Criteria

You use the Acceptance Criteria field to provide a bulleted list of criteria a PBI must meet before it will be accepted as done. The product owner defines the acceptance criteria either when initially creating the PBI or when the PBI is added to a sprint.

It's critical to have sufficient information in this field for a PBI because these are the criteria against which the team will build the feature during the sprint.

LINKING ARTIFACTS: PBIS, TASKS, AND BUGS

The product backlog is the central list on which a team focuses its attention. This makes sense because it is defined by the product owner on behalf of the user. The product backlog therefore helps the team focus its attention on the user's top priorities. Using the items on the backlog as the hub, the team can create other work items that organize the release and sprints.

From a PBI, the team defines test cases and tasks. When a test case fails, the team creates bugs. When a task is blocked, the team creates an impediment. The team can either create secondary work items (bugs and impediments) against the items that they impact (the test case and task), or it can link the items back to the PBI, which is the real focus of the team. Figure 6-5 shows the high-level relationship among work items.

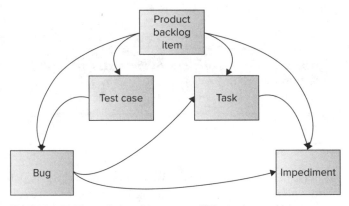

FIGURE 6-5: The relationship among PBIs, tasks, and bugs.

Linking PBIs to Test Cases

When creating PBIs, it's important to be very specific with the acceptance criteria. If the criteria are not specific enough, the team and product owner may have different views about when the PBI is really done. Even worse, they may have different views about how the feature will be used.

Verbal communication and follow-up e-mail between the product owner and team about product features will generally have the greatest detail about the PBI. This information should be captured and included in the acceptance criteria of the PBI.

Test cases are more specific than acceptance criteria, and they are also much more repeatable. You can create extensive unit tests in Visual Studio and have test tests run automatically. You can do this as part of the build process, or you can do it within Test Manager. Alternatively, you can define manual test cases in Test Manager and have the team run those test cases and verify results.

Test cases are linked to PBIs. Within TFS, a test case is different from acceptance criteria in that test cases are separate work items. They can be created, assigned, and tracked over time. Acceptance criteria, in contrast, are just stored in one field within the PBI. In terms of data relationships, a PBI "is tested by" a test case, and a test case "tests" a PBI. Figure 6-6 shows this relationship.

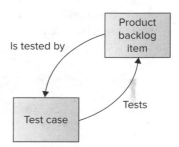

FIGURE 6-6: PBI and test case links.

You can create a test case in Visual Studio. To do so, you select the Team menu and create a new work item. Then you need to link the new item to the PBI by using a tests relationship. The dialog in Figure 6-7 shows linking from a new test case to an existing PBI. Notice that the Link Type setting is Tests.

You can also create a test case from a PBI. When you do this, the Link Type setting defaults to Tested By, rather than Tests, as shown in Figure 6-8.

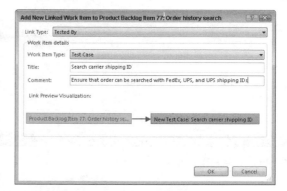

FIGURE 6-7: Linking from a test case to an existing PBI.

FIGURE 6-8: Linking from an existing PBI to a test case.

You can use Visual Studio to see all the test cases for all PBIs within a sprint or release. This is helpful in determining test coverage of the PBIs. This is different from the reports and queries that ship with the Scrum template, which are as follows:

➤ **Team Queries/Current Sprint/Test Cases** — This shows the test cases defined in the current sprint, but not their associated PBIs.

➤ **Reports/Tests/Test Case Readiness** — This shows a chart that indicates how many test cases are still being designed and how many are ready to be run.

➤ **Reports/Tests/Test Plan Progress** — This shows a chart that indicates how many test cases are passing and failing their tests.

Figure 6-9 shows the creation of a query that lists which PBIs have test cases defined and which don't. Creating this custom query takes only a minute or two. You can use this query to ensure that you have adequate test cases defined for the PBIs in a sprint or release.

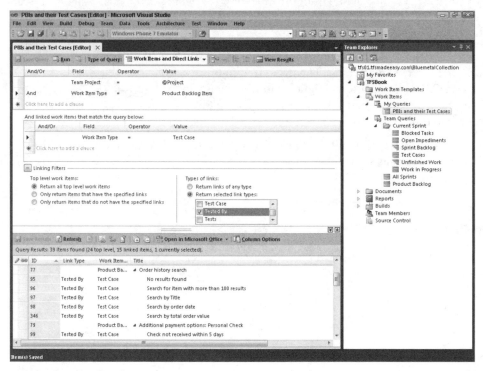

FIGURE 6-9: A PBI and test case query.

In Figure 6-9, notice that the Type of Query setting is Work Items and Direct Links. New queries default to Flat, but this figure shows the query type changed in this drop-down. A flat query executes a nested loop over the data, returning all PBIs and their related items. Also notice that in the Linking Filters section, you're returning all test cases that are top-level work items. This helps you see what's going well (that is, where a PBI has at least one test case) and what's not (that is, where a PBI doesn't have any test cases defined). Next, notice that Types of Links is set to Tested By. Because this query looks for all PBIs, you want the Tested By setting. Finally, notice that the results are sorted by PBI and then show all the associate test cases.

You could also query in the reverse direction. Rather than check which PBIs have associated tests, you could check which tests are not associated with a PBI. This is helpful because a test case that's not associated with a PBI may never get run as part of a sprint.

Figure 6-10 shows a query that presents the same information (PBIs and test cases) as Figure 6-9 but is oriented by test case rather than PBI. It returns all test cases and their related PBIs. In the Linking Filters section, you're still returning all top-level work items. This time, notice that Types of Links is set to Tests. Because this query looks for all PBIs, you want Tested By instead.

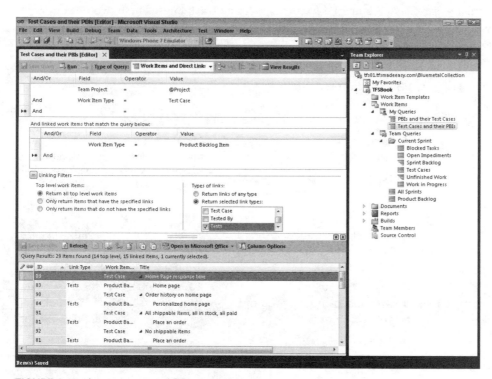

FIGURE 6-10: A test cases and PBIs query.

Linking PBIs to Bugs

As you develop software, you create bugs. It's just a fact of life. Using solid engineering practices can help you avoid common mistakes, and you can use tools to help track them. But if you're writing software, you're creating bugs.

Bugs are work items in TFS. You can therefore link them to any other work items by using the various link types. You can link bugs to PBIs, test cases, or other work items. Whether you link bugs to PBIs or test cases depends on how rigorous you are with respect to test-driven development (TDD).

If you're committed to TDD at both the unit and acceptance test levels, you will use test cases as your measure of quality. You will define test cases for each PBI and populate those test cases with automated and manual tests. You will use the test case readiness report to monitor how many of your test cases are fully defined and then use the test plan progress report to monitor the test case results to ensure that they're passing their tests. In this case, you can link bugs to test cases to easily see the bugs associated with each test case.

If you're using TDD but not necessarily defining all the artifacts for tracking and running tests within TFS, then linking bugs to PBIs is more appropriate. With this scheme, you can track the bugs and associated tasks for each PBI in one place. For each bug that you enter in TFS, you should link the bug to the PBI — not necessarily to a test case.

Linking bugs to PBIs and linking bugs to test cases both have pros and cons (see Table 6-1). In either case, you can use Visual Studio and Excel to enter and track bugs. These two options are not mutually exclusive. You can track bugs to both PBIs and test cases. Doing so will give you the benefits of both methods.

TABLE 6-1: Linking Bugs to PBIs and to Test Cases

WHERE TO LINK BUGS	WHEN TO DO THIS	WHY
PBIs	If you don't define test cases for all PBIs If you want to track bugs (status) and tasks (effort) together with a PBI	The PBI is the central focus area for the team. Linking bugs to a PBI is an easy way to track it all in one place.
Test cases	If you are rigorous about testing and define at least one (but probably many) test case for each PBI If you use the built-in reports for tracking test plan readiness and test plan progress	By associating bugs with test cases, your team will focus its effort on fixing bugs so the test cases pass. If you define test cases to properly cover the validation of the PBI, then reporting in this manner will be easier.

Linking Bugs to PBIs

Linking bugs to PBIs is straightforward. By associating a bug directly with a PBI, you can easily count and track quality at the PBI level. This way, you can bypass the test case and keep the team focused on the PBI itself. As shown in Figure 6-11, in terms of the data relationship between a bug and a PBI, a bug is a child of a PBI.

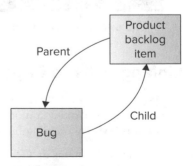

FIGURE 6-11: Data relationship between a PBI and a bug.

LINKING WORK ITEMS

You'll notice that the descriptions and figures shown in Figures 6-5, 6-6, 6-7, and 6-8 are very similar to those shown in Figures 6-10, 6-11, 6-12, 6-13 and 6-15, 6-16, 6-17, and 6-18. That is because they are all examples of linking work items in TFS. This common data structure, and the common tools and queries for manipulating it, makes TFS a powerful tracking tool.

You can create a new bug from Visual Studio as a new work item from the Team menu. After you create the bug, you need to link it to the PBI by using a child relationship. The dialog in Figure 6-12 shows how to link a new bug to a PBI. Notice that Link Type is set to Child.

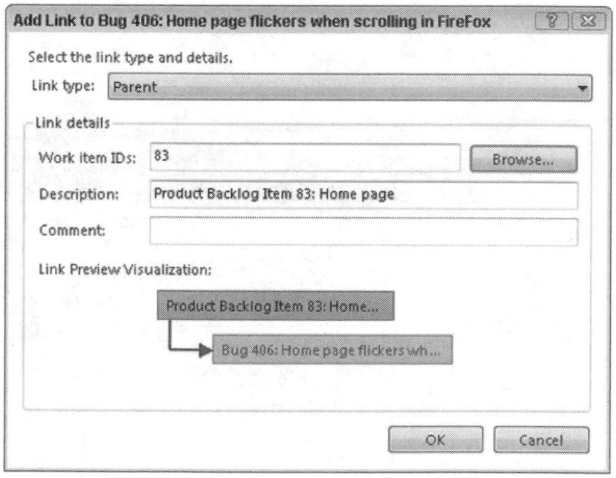

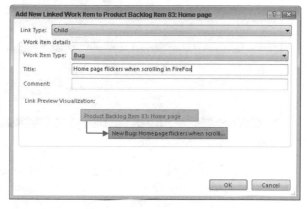

FIGURE 6-12: Linking from a PBI to a new bug.

Alternatively, you can create a new bug and then link it to the PBI that it relates to. In this case, the Link Type setting is Parent, from the bug to the PBI, as shown in Figure 6-13.

FIGURE 6-13: Linking from a new bug to a PBI.

You can use Visual Studio to see all the bugs for all the PBIs within a sprint or release. This is helpful for tracking bugs against PBIs. The query in Figure 6-14 shows all PBIs that have open bugs.

First, notice that the Type of Query setting is Work Items and Direct Links. Remember that new queries default to Flat, but you can change the query type in this drop-down. Also notice that you're only picking up related items of type Bug. Next, notice that in the Linking Filters section, you're returning only linked items of type Child. Finally, notice that the results are sorted by PBI and show all the associated bugs — and that every PBI has at least one bug. There may be many PBIs that have no bugs, but the intent of this query is to show only the problematic PBIs.

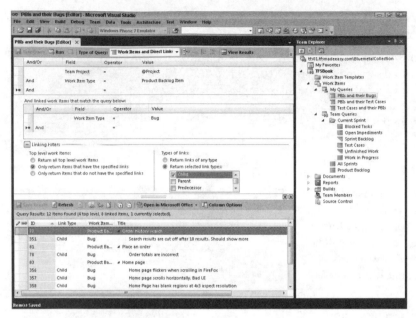

FIGURE 6-14: A PBI and bugs query.

During your daily Scrum meeting, it's helpful to review the bugs associated with PBIs in the sprint backlog. This keeps the team focused on the most critical work affecting the sprint. You can use Visual Studio to review the list, and you can even use Excel. The advantage of using Excel is that you can quickly update the state of bugs, from new to approved, to committed, to done. Figure 6-15 shows the preceding PBI and bugs query exported to Excel.

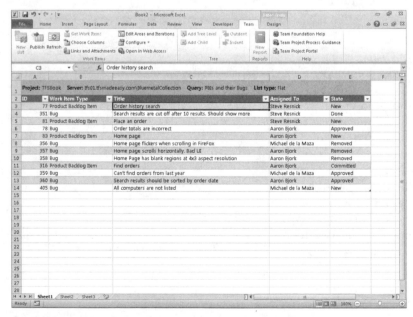

FIGURE 6-15: The PBI and bugs query in Excel.

Linking Bugs to Test Cases

You may discover bugs when manually running test cases or when running unit tests. The product owner may also discover them in his or her daily or weekly testing of product features. By linking bugs to test cases, you can ensure that your test cases are heavily exercised for validating the PBIs and that the team is fully involved in the test cases. This keeps testing focused on ensuring that PBIs pass their test cases and ensuring that bugs found during testing are resolved and retested.

As shown in Figure 6-16, PBIs are tested by test cases, which in turn may have associated bugs.

You can create a new bug from Visual Studio as a new work item from the Team menu. After you create it, you need to link it to the test case by using a child relationship. The dialog in Figure 6-17 shows linking from a new bug to an existing test case. Notice that the Link Type setting is Child.

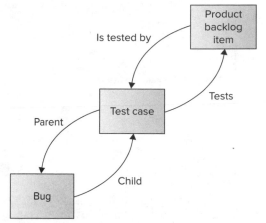

FIGURE 6-16: Data relationship of a PBI, a test case, and a bug.

Alternatively, you can create a new bug and then link it to the test case in which it was found. In that case, as shown in Figure 6-18, the Link Type setting is Parent, from the bug to the test case.

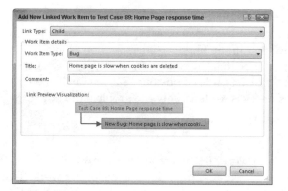

FIGURE 6-17: Linking from the test case to the new bug.

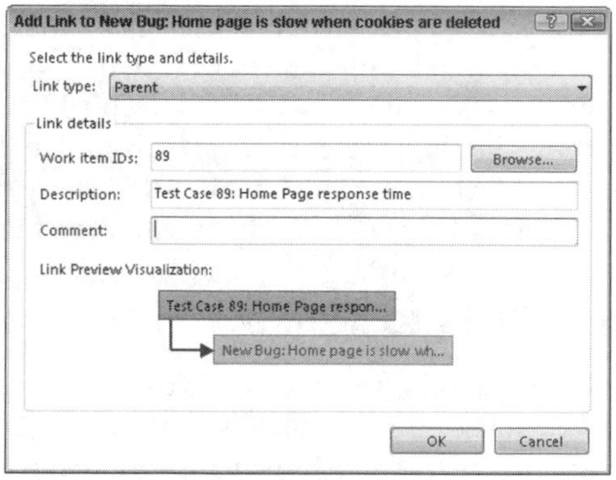

FIGURE 6-18: Linking from the new bug to the test case.

You can use Visual Studio to see all the bugs for all the test cases within a sprint or release. This is helpful for tracking bugs against test cases. The query being created in Figure 6-19 shows all test cases that have open bugs.

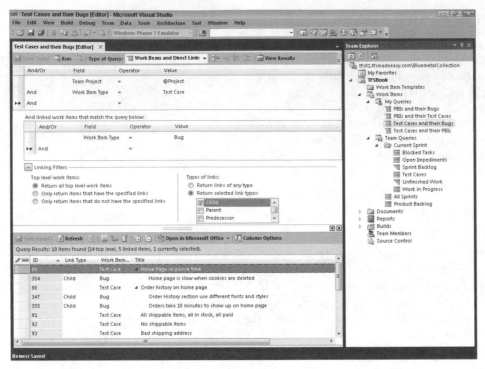

FIGURE 6-19: A test case and bugs query.

Notice that the Type of Query setting is Work Items and Direct Links. Remember that new queries default to Flat, but you can change the query type in this drop-down. Also, notice that you're only picking up related items of type Bug. Third, notice that in the Linking Filters section, you're only returning linked items of type Child. Finally, notice that the results are sorted by test case and show all the associated bugs — and every test case has at least one bug. There may be many test cases that have no bugs, but the intent of this query is to show only the problematic test cases.

Linking PBIs to Tasks

In software development, a *task* is the smallest unit of work. Each person on a software development team has a task list that he or she uses to organize and prioritize his or her work. This isn't unique to Scrum; it's the basis for most methodologies and is baked into most software project management tools.

In Scrum, you use tasks in two ways: to assign and track work associated with a PBI and to assign and track work associated with bugs. Tasks associated with PBIs represent things you have to build, while tasks associated with bugs represent things you have to fix. From a scheduling perspective, there's really not much difference between PBIs and bugs. The team is completing a potentially shippable product with each sprint, so the items need to be built and tested, and they need to have no critical bugs.

Figure 6-20 shows the relationships among a PBI, a task, and a bug. The PBI is the parent of both tasks and bugs, which are, by definition, children of PBIs. By defining a task from a PBI, you're defining the work to implement the PBI. By defining a task from a bug, you're defining the work to fix a bug.

The relationships among PBIs, bugs, and tasks are transitive. When you define the work related to a bug that's related to a PBI, you're indirectly assigning work to the PBI. That work, combined with work that's directly related to the PBI, is the total work defined for the PBI. The tree of work items query type in TFS models this relationship so that you can see direct and indirect items related to a PBI.

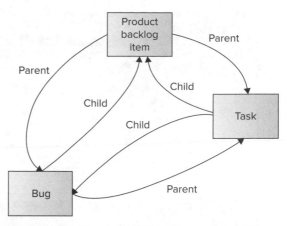

FIGURE 6-20: The data relationships among a PBI, a task, and a bug.

Linking Tasks to PBIs

Soon after creating PBIs and committing them to a sprint, you create new tasks in Visual Studio from each PBI. You can do this from the PBI itself or from the results of a query that lists a set of PBIs. The dialog in Figure 6-21 shows how to create a new task from an existing PBI and establish the relationship. Notice that the Link Type setting is Child.

Alternatively, you can create a task on its own and then link it to the PBI later. This is a very useful technique for capturing items as they come up. For instance, say you're in the daily Scrum or you're just thinking about the

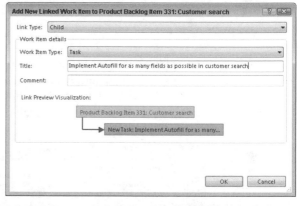

FIGURE 6-21: Linking from a PBI to a new task.

project and remember "oh, let's not forget to do X." If you must search through TFS and figure out which PBI should track that task and then gain agreement from that product owner, you may not have time to enter the task. If, however, you can just enter the task in Excel without linking it to a PBI, TFS will have a more complete and accurate record of all the work that needs to be done.

You can use Visual Studio to see all the tasks for all the PBIs within a sprint or release. This is helpful for tracking work against PBIs. The query in Figure 6-22 shows all committed PBIs and their associated tasks. In Figure 6-22, notice that the type of query is Work Items and Direct Links. Remember that new queries default to Flat, but you can change the query type in this drop-down. Also, notice that you're only picking up related items of type Task. Next, notice that in the Linking Filters section, you're returning all top-level work items. Notice that the results are sorted by PBI and show all the associated tasks; this list shows both PBIs that have tasks and those that don't. Any PBI that doesn't have tasks assigned is problematic because nobody is working on implementing that feature. Finally, notice that the Remaining Work field from the task item is displayed. This is critical information for the daily Scrum because it shows how much work remains to be done for a task and its PBI.

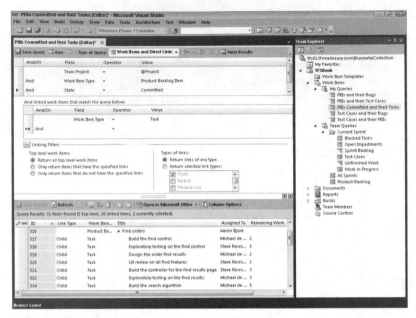

FIGURE 6-22: A PBI and tasks query.

By exporting the results of the Figure 6-22 query to Excel and focusing on the resulting Excel spreadsheet during the daily Scrum, you can quickly update the status and remaining work to keep a running total of effort needed to complete the PBI. Figure 6-23 shows data exported to Excel. You should be sure to use the Publish and Refresh buttons on the Team tab of the Ribbon in Excel to save changes back to TFS.

ID	Work Item Type	Title	Assigned To	Remaining Work	State
316	Product Backlog Item	Find orders	Aaron Bjork		Committed
317	Task	Build the find control	Michael de la Maza	2	In Progress
318	Task	Exploratory testing on the find control	Steve Resnick	3	In Progress
319	Task	Design the order find results	Michael de la Maza	2	In Progress
320	Task	UX review on all find features	Steve Resnick	2	To Do
321	Task	Build the controller for the find results page	Steve Resnick	3	To Do
322	Task	Exploratory testing on the find resutls	Michael de la Maza	3	To Do
334	Task	Build the search algorthim	Michael de la Maza	5	To Do
369	Task	Fix prior-year searching in order search UI	Michael de la Maza	2	To Do
370	Task	Sort orders in search results by descending date	Steve Resnick	2	To Do
323	Product Backlog Item	RSS feeds	Aaron Bjork		Committed
324	Task	Build SOAP handler	Michael de la Maza	5	To Do
325	Task	Build the RSS service provider	Steve Resnick	3	To Do
326	Task	Optimize database calss for RSS results	Aaron Bjork	3	To Do
327	Task	Test the feed with different clients	Michael de la Maza	2	To Do
328	Task	Run the feed through perf scenarios and measure r	Aaron Bjork	1	To Do
329	Task	Enable for all types of data	Steve Resnick	1	To Do
330	Task	Exploratory testing for all	Aaron Bjork	2	To Do
331	Product Backlog Item	Customer search	Aaron Bjork		Committed
332	Task	Build and review the data interaction layer	Michael de la Maza	2	To Do
333	Task	Implement search from the landing page	Steve Resnick	4	To Do
335	Task	Design the search results screen	Steve Resnick	2	To Do
336	Task	Design the UI interactions	Steve Resnick	1	To Do
339	Task	Run example queries	Michael de la Maza	10	To Do
340	Task	Verify page load speed	Aaron Bjork		Removed
361	Task	Implement Autofill for as many fields as possible	Aaron Bjork	4	To Do

FIGURE 6-23: PBIs and tasks in Excel.

Linking Tasks to Bugs

During each sprint, you create, find, and fix bugs in the software. In order to track the nature, severity, and impact of each software bug, you create bug items in TFS. Each bug item in TFS stores the essential criteria about the bug. This includes the steps to reproduce the bug and environmental data such as builds and server and desktop configurations. It also contains the acceptance criteria for fixing the bug.

Each bug item contains an Effort field. You should treat this field similarly to the Effort field for a PBI. Specifically, effort is not the actual time you estimate to fix the bug; it's a rough estimate of its complexity so you can make decisions about when to schedule it in a sprint. This is different from the Remaining Work field on a task, which is the team's estimate for completing a unit of work.

At a minimum, you should create one task for each bug. For simple bugs, the task will be assigned to the person who's responsible for fixing it, which is normally the same person assigned to the task. In order to track the work associated with the bug, you create a new task in Visual Studio from the bug. In the task item, you fill in the Remaining Work information. The dialog in Figure 6-24 shows how to create a new task from an existing bug and establish the relationship. Notice that the Link Type setting is Child.

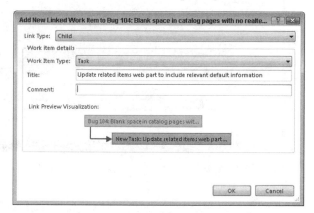

FIGURE 6-24: Linking from a bug to a new task.

You can use Visual Studio to see all the tasks for all the bugs within a sprint or release. This is helpful for tracking work against bugs. The query being created in Figure 6-25 shows all bugs and their tasks. Notice that the type of query is Work Items and Direct Links. Remember that new queries default to Flat, but you can change the query type in this drop-down. Also, notice that you're only picking up related items of type Task. Next, notice that in the Linking Filters section, you're returning all top-level work items. Finally, notice that the results are sorted by bug and show all the associated tasks; this list shows both bugs that have tasks and those that don't.

By exporting the results of the Figure 6-25 query to Excel and using the resulting Excel file during the daily Scrum, you can quickly update the status and remaining work to keep a running total of effort needed to complete the bug. You can also indicate whether an item is blocked. During the daily Scrum, blocked items will take high importance. Figure 6-26 shows the data exported to Excel. Remember to use the Publish and Refresh buttons on the Team tab of the Ribbon in Excel to save changes back to TFS.

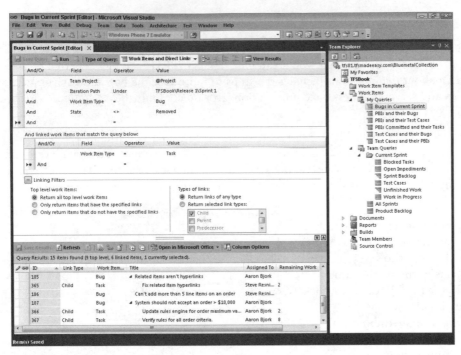

FIGURE 6-25: A bugs and tasks query.

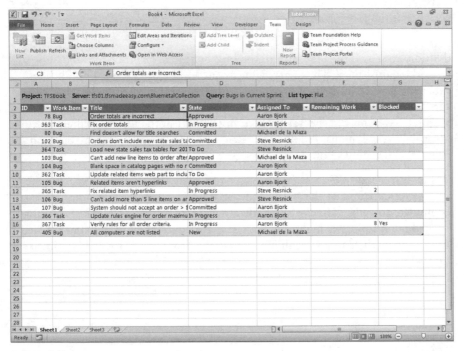

FIGURE 6-26: Bugs and tasks in Excel.

Using the Unfinished Work Query

The unfinished work query that is built into the Scrum template brings together the three work items types PBI, bug, and task. It first queries TFS for these three work items types by using the tree of work items list type. It links these items to their children of type Task but filters the tasks so it doesn't pick up those whose state is done or removed. The resulting list shows all tasks under each PBI. It also shows all bugs under each PBI and the tasks under them. Figure 6-27 shows the unfinished work query in Visual Studio.

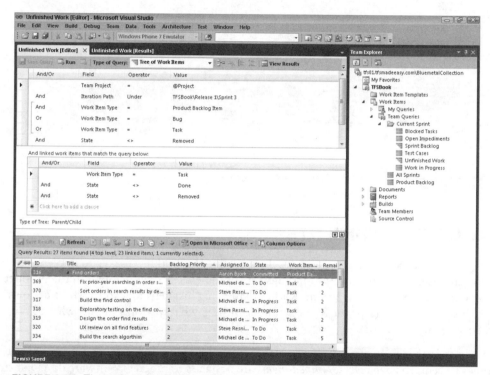

FIGURE 6-27: The unfinished work query.

When you export the results of the query in Figure 6-27 to Excel, you get the results shown in Figure 6-28, where you can see all tasks associated with a sprint. One particularly useful feature of Excel when working with this view — or any other tree of work items list — is the ability to add child items directly into the spreadsheet. Say, for instance, that during the daily Scrum, you're discussing a new bug that was encountered, named "home page is too slow." One of the testers already entered a bug into the system, tied to a PBI. A team member yells out, "Oh, I know how to fix that! We just need to edit the config file." Right then and there, you can add a new task in Excel and link it to the bug, which is linked to the PBI.

Figure 6-28 shows how you can select a row (in this example, the bug row; row 29 in the figure) and click Add Child to create an item under that row. This opens a row in Excel (row 30 in the figure), where you can fill in a task work item, allocate one hour of remaining work, and assign the task to the team member.

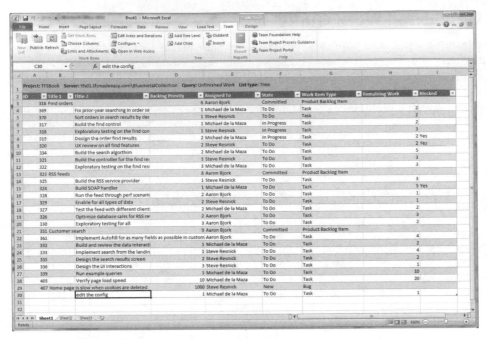

FIGURE 6-28: Results of the unfinished work query in Excel.

UNDERSTANDING IMPEDIMENTS

PBIs define the features to be built into a product. Tasks define the work necessary to implement them. Test cases are used to verify quality, and bugs track problems as they're found in the product. These tracking elements come alive in Scrum. Rather than being just cells in a spreadsheet or rows in a database, this information helps the Scrum team determine what to worry about, what to do next, and when something is done.

But of course things don't always go according to plan. Sometimes progress slows down. Sometimes it stops. Sometimes it seems to go in reverse. *Impediments* are obstacles to progress. Software development is rich with impediments. Dependencies among technical components, dependencies among team members, and unclear requirements are three of the most common impediments. Scrum recognizes impediments as significant elements to track in order to improve the overall quality of a product. The ScrumMaster's primary job is to remove impediments that are blocking or slowing down the team.

Any work item type can be affected by an impediment. For instance, a PBI may be blocked because the product owner needs to get information from someone external to the team and the team cannot complete that PBI until it has answers. Or, a task may be blocked by a bug in an underlining component or third-party control. Without that fixed, the bug cannot be resolved. Or, a bug may be blocked, maybe pending hardware resources required to adequately reproduce the bug in a lab. In each case, the ScrumMaster should own resolution of these impediments, often working with the product owner or team member.

Figure 6-29 shows the data relationship among impediments and other work items. Notice that an impediment is never a parent; rather, it's blocking some other parent item, whether a PBI, a bug, or a task.

You track impediment work items as you do other work items in TFS. You can enter them in Visual Studio, Excel, or SharePoint. Generally, the Scrum team uses Visual Studio. Figure 6-30 shows how to create a new impediment from an existing PBI.

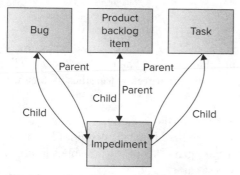

FIGURE 6-29: Data relationship of an impediment, a PBI, a bug, and a task.

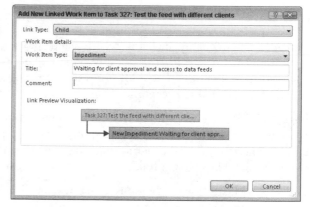

FIGURE 6-30: Linking from a PBI to a new impediment.

By creating an impediment item in TFS, you can track basic information, including a description and ultimately its resolution. Figure 6-31 shows a new impediment.

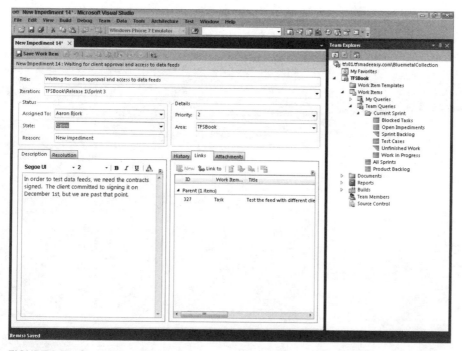

FIGURE 6-31: A new impediment.

Tracking impediments is an important aspect of Scrum that you should not overlook. The history of impediments can be helpful during the sprint retrospective and can offer clues about how to improve the team's velocity.

SUMMARY

The product backlog is the list of requirements for the system. It is the central focus of a Scrum team, representing the features that the team will build into the product. The product owner defines and prioritizes the PBIs. Each PBI stores the details of one product feature. It describes its business benefit, test cases, and acceptance criteria.

Bugs, like PBIs, are work items that the team must expend effort to fix. Like PBIs, bugs also have tasks associated with them. The remaining work of a sprint is defined by the tasks (not PBIs or bugs), so tasks become the central tracking element within the sprint. You can track bugs in one of two ways in TFS: You can link them to PBIs directly or to test cases.

The ScrumMaster's primary job is to remove impediments, so tracking them in TFS is an effective way to measure progress. Impediments serve as an early warning sign that progress is slowing down. You can link impediments to PBIs, bugs, or tasks.

In Chapter 7, you'll learn about tracking quality in a Scrum project.

7

Tracking Quality

WHAT'S IN THIS CHAPTER?

- ➤ Understanding what to measure.
- ➤ Tracking and resolving bugs and tasks.
- ➤ Creating and running test cases.
- ➤ Using Microsoft Test Manager.

Quality is generally easy to understand and observe. It's extremely subjective, but people can discern good quality from poor quality. A car that reliably starts and drives quietly down the road is good quality; one that requires a screw driver to start and sputters as you drive is clearly bad. Clean, fresh air is good quality; smog is bad.

Just as it's easy to understand quality, it's often easy to measure it. Measuring the loudness of engine noise is straightforward, using decibels as the metric. Measuring air pollution is also pretty simple, using parts per million as the metric. Both of these measurements involve sampling the system as its running, whether it's a combustion engine or the wind, and then counting the results. Samples can be taken under varying conditions, such as sampling engine noise at varying speeds and sampling air quality at different locations.

Once samples are measured, they can then be classified into something people care about. In the case of engine noise, quiet, average, and loud are simple categories. With air quality, good, average, and bad are well understood.

Finally, after quality is understood, measured, and classified, you can take action. You can choose to buy a quiet car or ignore the noise and go with a fast car. Knowing that the air quality is poor, you can choose to exercise indoors rather than go for a run outside.

In this chapter, you will learn how to measure and track quality, which is an important part of Scrum. You'll learn how to do this with test cases, bugs, and tasks in Visual Studio, Excel, and Team Foundation Server (TFS).

KNOWING WHAT TO MEASURE

Great software always has two common attributes: It's useful and predictable. Defining and running test cases for software ensures that the product is useful for its intended purpose; tracking and eliminating bugs during the construction phase ensures that it's predictable.

There are a variety of ways to measure software quality. You can measure data accuracy, system performance, reliability, or usability. Regardless of the measure, you will have a specific expectation of the result. Most software will have hundreds of such expectations that are ultimately codified into test cases. In aggregate, if the software meets the expectation, then it passes that quality metric. If not, it fails.

If software does not meet an expectation, you have a quality problem. It may be a very small problem, or it may be quite large — but either way, the problem exists. One way to measure software quality is to quantify the expectations that are not met. You can do this by counting the failed test cases. Another way is to quantify the technical items that must be fixed in order to meet expectations. You can do this by counting the number of open items, or *bugs*. If you're counting bugs, it's helpful to also count the estimated effort necessary to fix them. This is an indirect measure of quality, but it's crucial for planning.

 It's important for a team to estimate the effort required to fix a bug, just as it does with product backlog items (PBIs). Bugs ultimately get scheduled like PBIs in later sprints. During sprint planning, the team builds the sprint backlog by picking PBIs and bugs from the product backlog that add up to its velocity. If a team doesn't estimate bug effort, it cannot accurately commit to fixing the bugs in a sprint.

The combination of usefulness (passing test cases) and predictability (no bugs) is what defines quality. In other words, if the system does what the customer expects it to do and it does so predictably, then quality is high.

TRACKING AND RESOLVING BUGS AND TASKS

Fewer bugs equates to greater quality. Having 0 open bugs is ideal, but the bug count alone is an insufficient measure for managing quality. How do 10 open low-severity bugs compare to 3 open high-severity bugs? How do bugs in non-essential components compare with bugs in critical parts of the system?

The bug count has a subjective component and an objective component. Labeling a bug as low severity versus high severity is a subjective decision. On the other hand, counting the number of open bugs in each category is objective.

Of course, bugs don't fix themselves; people fix them. The fundamental way to assign work in TFS is to use tasks. For the bugs that will be fixed within the current sprint, you need to track tasks so people can allocate their time.

The Workflow for Resolving Bugs

Whether a bug is addressed during the sprint in which it is found or placed on the backlog for a future sprint, the team should have a workflow for tracking and resolving each bug. The Scrum 1.0 template for TFS implements a workflow for this.

When to Track and Resolve a Bug

You should track each bug from the moment you discover it until it is ultimately fixed. Certain bugs can be resolved within the current sprint, while others can be pushed to the product backlog and addressed in a later sprint. The product owner needs to make this determination, based on the product features that the bug affects.

If a bug relates to a PBI being addressed in the current sprint, then the bug should be fixed in the current sprint. You track a bug in three steps:

1. Enter a new bug as a new work item in the current sprint.

2. Create a new task or set of tasks to track the work required to fix the bug.

3. Link the task to the bug.

On the other hand, if a discovered bug relates to a feature that is not being worked on in the current sprint, you should add the new bug to the product backlog, but you should not assign any tasks to it. This way, the bug will not affect the current sprint, and it will not get lost.

For instance, assume that the goal of your current sprint is to implement an order entry screen in a web application. When testing the screen, you discover that date validation is not working. After 30 minutes of analysis, you determine that some business logic needs to change. You estimate that it will take four hours to fix and test the change. For this example, you would create a bug in the current sprint and create a task, linked to the bug, with an effort of 4.

If, however, your 30-minute analysis reveals that the date validation error is due to the user's time zone crossing the International Date Line from the server, and the system design doesn't address that scenario, you have a larger problem that may ripple through the system. In this case, it would be better to treat the bug as a new PBI. You would create the bug item but not assign it to a sprint and not create tasks.

Figure 7-1 shows the decision process for entering new bugs and their associated tasks into TFS and determining whether to track them on the product backlog or in the current sprint.

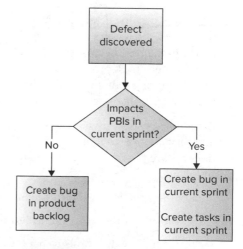

FIGURE 7-1: Determining when to track new bugs.

How to Track Bug State from New to Done

It is important to track progress from when a bug is first detected to when it is ultimately resolved. You capture this information in the State field of a bug item. Figure 7-2 shows the transitions built into the Scrum template.

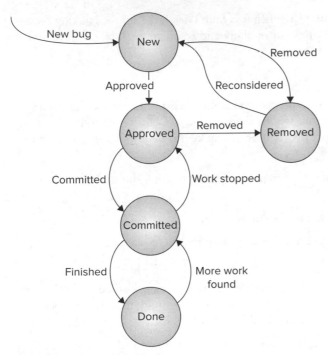

FIGURE 7-2: Bug state diagram.

When a bug is first detected, a new bug work item is created and assigned to a product owner. When the product owner reviews the bug, he or she changes its state to approved or removed. If the product owner approves the bug, he or she should set the Backlog Priority, Severity, and Area fields and should ensure that the Steps to Reproduce field is adequately detailed. The product owner can set the iteration to the project, putting it on the product backlog, or to the current sprint, placing it on the sprint backlog. If the product owner sets the state to removed, the bug will not be considered on any future sprint.

Before the product owner can put a new bug into the sprint backlog, the team must estimate the effort and then commit to fixing that bug. The team's commitment is necessary in order to mark the PBI as done before the end of the sprint. To put the bug on the sprint backlog, the product owner does the following:

➤ Sets the State field to Committed

➤ Updates the Iteration field to the current sprint

If the product owner wants to put the new bug in the product backlog rather than in the sprint backlog, the bug remains assigned to the product owner. It remains in the approved state but is not committed, and the iteration is the project. The bug will be considered in future sprints, but it will not be fixed within the current sprint.

Once a bug is committed, the team creates a task or tasks to fix the bug and assigns the task(s) to the team member(s) who will be fixing it. Each of these new tasks is linked to the bug. Each task can be assigned to a different team member, and each team member is responsible for updating the Remaining Work field.

Entering Bugs

You can enter a bug in Visual Studio, Excel, or SharePoint. Whichever tool you chose, the information is stored in TFS so it is accessible to other tools and reports.

To enter a bug in Visual Studio, you select Team ➪ New Bug. Then you fill in the following fields:

- ➤ Title
- ➤ Iteration
- ➤ Assigned To
- ➤ State
- ➤ Backlog Priority
- ➤ Effort
- ➤ Severity
- ➤ Area

These fields are not all required in Visual Studio, but throughout the flow and life cycle of a bug, they are all used. The following sections describe them in more detail, and Figure 7-3 shows the Visual Studio screen where you enter bugs. You reach this screen by selecting Team ➪ New Bug.

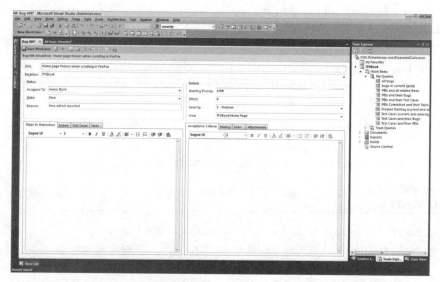

FIGURE 7-3: Bug entry in Visual Studio.

Title

In the Title field you enter a short description of the bug. The title you enter here will appear on lists and reports in Excel, Visual Studio, and SharePoint. Shorter titles are better, as they are more manageable in Excel, where you often print or view many columns. The title should convey distinguishing features of the bug, such as "crashes on low memory systems" or "can enter % over 100 in discount field."

Iteration

In the Iteration field you enter the sprint in which the team committed to fixing the bug. Bugs are very similar to PBIs in that they go onto the product backlog when they are waiting to be scheduled. TFS defaults to the project, indicating that it's on the product backlog. A bug is moved to the sprint backlog during sprint planning when the team sets this field to the current sprint.

It's common for a team to fix bugs as soon as it finds them, within the current sprint. In that case, you set this field to the current sprint and immediately create a task for someone to fix the big.

Assigned To

In the Assigned To field you select the name of the person responsible for prioritizing the bug within the backlog — typically the product owner. It's important to note that bugs are not assigned to team members; tasks are. Each bug should spawn a task, and the task is then assigned to a team member.

State

In the State field you track the current state of the bug. A bug can be in one of five states, starting with new and ending with either removed or done:

➤ **New** — The bug is entered into TFS. As a new bug, it hasn't yet been reviewed by the team or product owner, nor is it scheduled to be fixed.

➤ **Approved** — The bug has been approved by the product owner and team. Collectively, the team has estimated the effort (for example, in story points), classified it into an area path, and assigned a severity.

➤ **Removed** — The bug is no longer tracked. This is useful when you're pruning the bug list to remove duplicates, to consolidate similar bugs, or to simply remove the bugs that were reported erroneously and will not be fixed.

➤ **Committed** — The bug has been assigned to a sprint, and the team has committed to fixing it.

➤ **Done** — The bug is fixed, and the product owner has tested and verified it.

> **BUG AND PBI STATES**
>
> You will notice that the state diagram and transitions defined for a bug are identical to those defined for a PBI. This is because both PBIs and bugs are work items in TFS, and they are treated the same way in Scrum for tracking purposes.

Backlog Priority

In the Backlog Priority field you enter the relative priority of fixing the bug, compared to items in the backlog. Because the backlog is typically sorted by priority in ascending order, a bug or PBI with a lower priority value appears earlier in the list. Bugs default to priority 1,000, which places them at the bottom of the list.

Effort

In the Effort field you enter the relative effort to fix the bug. As with a PBI, this is not expressed in hours or days, but it is a relative value of effort. Sometimes this is estimated as in story points (complexity) or ideal days (which don't exist in nature). It's a best practice to use numbers in the Fibonacci sequence to estimate PBIs, where you have greater resolution with small estimates than you do with large estimates. This works for estimating PBIs because their complexity varies greatly.

 Unlike with PBIs, the effort associated with a bug is generally small. It may be estimated at 1 or 0.5.

Severity

In the Severity field you enter the severity of the bug to the product, from critical to low priority. The team uses this setting to prioritize work and schedule the bug for a sprint.

Area

In the Area field you enter the component of the product in which the bug exists. This field is present on all work items in TFS, but it is especially important for bugs. It's common for the product owner to view the current bug list by area, since the area indicates the readiness or quality of a specific component. It's common for the team to view the current bug list this way as well, since different people typically work on different areas of the product so they can quickly assess how their components are doing.

Viewing the Bug List

Once you have begun capturing bugs using the basic attributes just described, you can easily classify the bugs. By using a simple query in TFS, you can pull all the bugs into Excel to sort, filter, or pivot them for useful aggregations. The following classifications are common:

➤ Open bugs by Area setting

➤ Open bugs by Severity setting

➤ Open bugs by Assigned To setting

You can create a list and chart in Excel of the open bugs by area, indicating how many are approved and how many are committed. To do so, you open Visual Studio and follow these steps:

1. Create a query for listing only the bugs in the current release. To do so, open the sprint backlog query under the Current Sprint folder in the Team Explorer. (You're starting with the sprint backlog query because it has the filter defined almost the way you want it for this list.)

2. Click Edit Query so you can change the query options.

3. Change the Type of Query setting from Tree of Items to Flat List (Default).

4. Next to Work Item Type, set Operator to = and set Value to Bug.

5. Click the Add Columns button and add Area Path and Severity.

6. Select File ➪ Save Sprint Backlog [editor] As to save the query you modified. Name the query Bugs in Current Sprint either in the My Queries folder or the Team Queries folder.

7. Click Run to see the bugs in the current sprint. If you don't have enough bugs entered, you can change the Iteration field to the project rather than the sprint. The resulting list should look similar to the one shown in Figure 7-4.

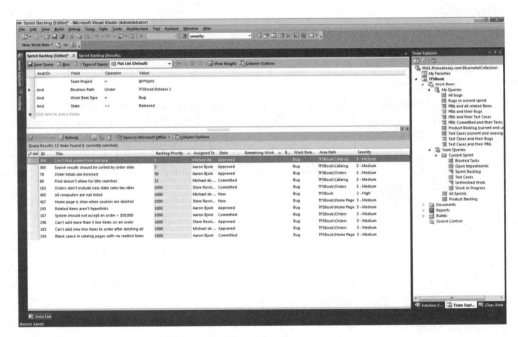

FIGURE 7-4: Bugs in the current sprint in Visual Studio.

8. Select Open in Microsoft Office ➾ Open the Query in Microsoft Excel 2007 or Later. Excel opens, as shown in Figure 7-5.

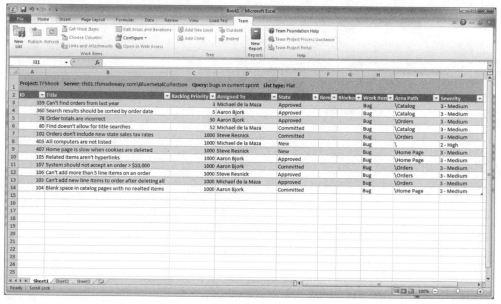

FIGURE 7-5: The Bugs in Current Sprint query in Excel.

9. In Excel, select all the data, including column headers. For example, because there are 13 bugs listed in Figure 7-5, in this example, you would select cells A2 through H14.

10. On the Insert tab in Excel, click PivotChart under the PivotTable button. Excel prompts you for where to place the PivotChart.

11. Choose to place the PivotChart in a new worksheet.

12. From the Design tab in Excel, click Change Chart Type and choose Stacked Column.

13. Drag Area Path from the Choose Fields to Add to Report section to the Axis Fields (Categories) section.

14. Drag State from the Choose Fields to Add to Report section to the Σ Values section. It will default to Count of State.

15. Drag State, for a second time, from the Choose Fields to Add to Report section to the Legend Fields (Series) section.

Excel should now look as shown in Figure 7-6, showing a chart with the number of approved and committed bugs in the current sprint.

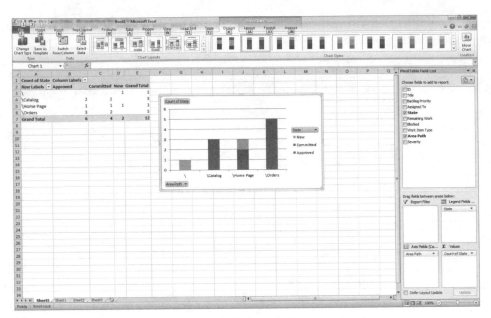

FIGURE 7-6: An Excel PivotChart showing the bugs in the current sprint.

Now that you've seen the workflow for bugs and how to enter and query them, you're ready to learn to do the same for tasks.

The Workflow for Tasks

Tasks are work items that capture the work necessary to fix a bug or to implement a PBI. Individually, they represent the work associated with one component; collectively, they represent the total amount of work in a sprint.

As shown in Figure 7-7, tasks go through a simple workflow. They begin in the new state, move through in progress state, and conclude in the done state.

Entering Tasks

You can enter a task in Visual Studio, Excel, or SharePoint. Whichever tool you chose, the information is stored in TFS and is accessible to other tools and reports. To enter a task in Visual Studio, you select Team ➪ New Task. Figure 7-8 shows the task entry screen that appears.

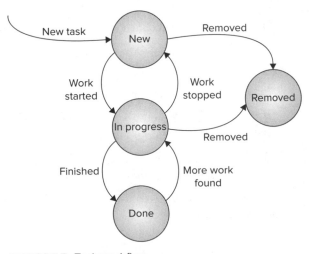

FIGURE 7-7: Task workflow.

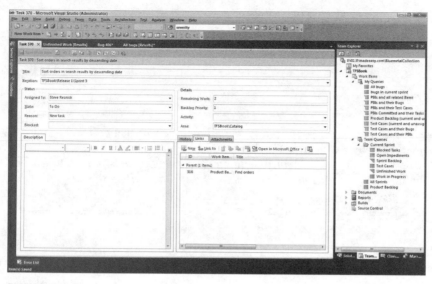

FIGURE 7-8: The task entry screen.

Tasks store similar elements to bugs and PBIs for categorization and prioritization, and they also have a few fields specific to tracking work:

➤ Remaining Work

➤ Activity

➤ Blocked

Remaining Work

In the Remaining Work field you enter the amount of work remaining to complete the task. When estimating remaining work, you should think in terms of time — that is, hours. This is different from PBIs and bugs, where you estimate in story points or some other arbitrary measure.

 Tasks are hours. Hours are time. Time is money.

The minimum amount of time you should allocate for a task is 2 hours. Nothing ever takes less than that. The maximum amount of time for a task should be 40 hours, or 1 week. Greater than that, and you probably don't know how long it will take, so it's better to break the task into subtasks.

Activity

In the Activity field you enter the type of work required for the task. The Scrum template allows the following field values:

➤ Design

➤ Development

➤ Deployment

➤ Documentation

➤ Requirements

➤ Testing

 The Activity field is helpful when you're planning who will be working on what and want to sort the list by activity. It's also helpful for planning. For instance, if you have 180 hours of tasks for deployment activities but only one person who does deployment working for the remaining week of the sprint, you know you need to adjust something.

Blocked

You can leave the Blocked field blank or enter Yes to indicate whether something is blocking the task from being complete.

The Unfinished Work Query

The unfinished work query, shown in Figure 7-9, lists the PBIs, bugs, and tasks in the current sprint. Together, these work items comprise the work remaining in the sprint. The unfinished work query is very useful when you are assessing how much work is remaining and how much of that work deals with quality issues.

You run this query by selecting Unfinished Work under Team Queries in the Team Explorer.

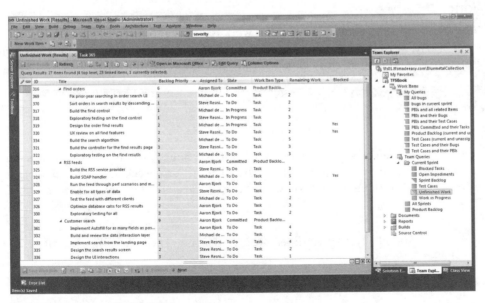

FIGURE 7-9: The unfinished work query.

TEST CASES

Setting quality expectations is crucial for ensuring product acceptance. Expectations can be defined in terms of performance, security, usability, or other attributes. Regardless of how quality expectations are defined, they need to be measured. And for anything that is going to be measured, the team needs to define how, when, and by whom the testing will occur.

Quality is associated with PBIs. For each PBI, you should define its acceptance criteria and create one or more test cases to verify that the PBI meets those criteria. Typically, a product manager defines the acceptance criteria as he or she creates the PBI. Then, when a PBI is allocated to a sprint, the product manager or team member creates test cases.

Acceptance Criteria in a PBI

Acceptance criteria should be at a similar level to the PBI description. More detail is helpful, but with Scrum, the subtle communication of acceptance criteria occurs between the product owner and the team member implementing the feature. Greater detail should be provided in the specific test cases that are used to verify the PBI.

You should enter acceptance criteria in each PBI. These criteria should be specific about how the feature will be tested. If you have performance metrics that must be met or specific data validation requirements, it is helpful to include that information here.

Figure 7-10 shows an example of acceptance criteria in a PBI.

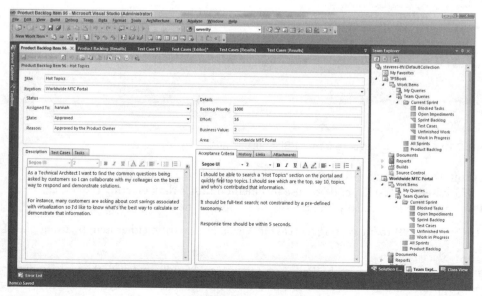

FIGURE 7-10: Acceptance criteria in a PBI.

Defining Test Cases

Each PBI needs test cases to ensure that the software is exercised sufficiently to ensure that it meets its quality expectations. The more complex the feature, the more test cases you need to adequately test it. You should use negative testing, where you test for failure conditions, in addition to positive testing, where you test for success conditions.

Each item in the product backlog needs to be tested after it is scheduled in a sprint and implemented. A project with hundreds of PBIs will have hundreds of test cases. Some of them will be simple, and some will be complex; some will contain automated steps, and others will be automated.

There are a number of ways to create test cases, both from Visual Studio and from Microsoft Test Manager. With either tool, it's important to link the test case back to the PBI. The following are the two methods for creating test cases:

➤ **Visual Studio** — With a PBI open in Visual Studio, go to the Test Cases tab and click the New button. A dialog box appears, as shown in Figure 7-11, asking for very basic information. After you provide this information and click OK, Visual Studio opens the New Test Case window with the PBI linkage already populated.

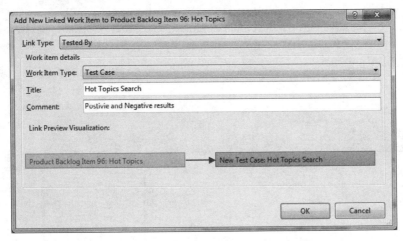

FIGURE 7-11: Creating a test case from a PBI in Visual Studio.

➤ **Microsoft Test Manager** —Right-click Work Items in the Team Explorer and select New Work Item ➪ Test Case. If you use this method rather than creating the test case from the PBI, you have to manually link the two work items (the PBI and the test case).

You can link an existing PBI to an existing test case in Visual Studio from either item by using one of two methods:

➤ **From an existing PBI** — Select the Test Cases tab in Visual Studio and click the Link To button. A dialog appears, and in it you can create or browse queries that will search for test case items.

➤ **From an existing test case** — Select the Tested Backlog Items tab in Visual Studio and click the Link To button. A dialog appears, and in it you can create or browse queries that will search for PBIs.

Regardless of how you create a test case and link it to the PBI, you need to record some basic information about it, as shown in Table 7-1. Figure 7-12 shows the Visual Studio screen for entering a test case.

TABLE 7-1: Essential Test Case Attributes

ATTRIBUTE	DESCRIPTION
Title	The name of the test case that appears on reports and queries.
Iteration	The name of the project, release, or sprint to which this test case applies.
Area	The component of the system to which this test case applies.
Assigned To	The person responsible for defining the test case.
State	The current state of the test case. It defaults to Design, meaning that the test case must be designed. The next State setting in the workflow is Ready, which means that the test is ready to be run. Finally, if the test is no longer valid, it can be set to Closed.
Priority	The relative priority of the test case, ranging from 1 to 4 and defaulting to 2. A lower number indicates a higher priority.
Automation Status	An indication of whether this is a manual or automated test. The default is Not Automated. Another initial value is Planned, meaning that there will be an automated test associated with this test case. Once you associate an automation class with the test case, the status is Automated.
Description (on the Summary tab)	A textual description of the test case.

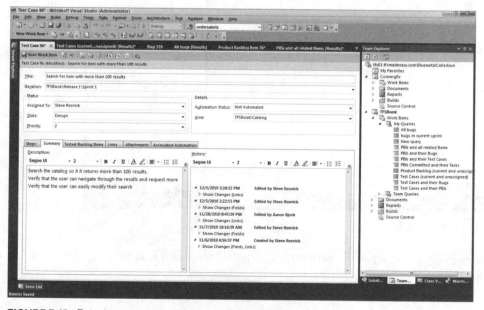

FIGURE 7-12: Entering a test case in Visual Studio.

The Workflow for Test Cases

Figure 7-13 shows the workflow associated with a test case. When a test case is first identified, it is in the design state, meaning that the test must be designed and implemented. After a product owner or team member designs the test, the test case enters the ready state, meaning that the test is ready to be run. It remains in the ready state for the duration of the project, until the test is no longer needed, at which point it is placed in the closed state.

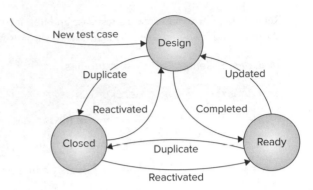

FIGURE 7-13: Test case workflow.

Test cases in the design state represent potential risk to the project. They represent PBIs that need to be tested but for which nobody has completely defined test cases. It may not be a very large risk, because the PBIs may not be built yet, but when they are built and ready for testing, additional work must be done before testing can begin.

To find the list of test cases that are still in the design state, you simply run the predefined test cases query in the Current Sprint folder of Team Queries and then sort on the State field. Figure 7-14 shows this query.

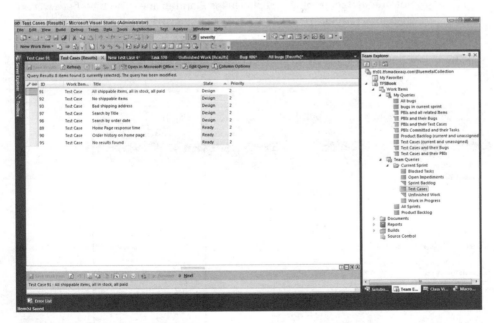

FIGURE 7-14: The test cases query.

It's okay to have many test cases in the design state early in a release. But as the iterations progress, more test cases should be in the ready state. Figure 7-15 illustrates a theoretical project in which test cases are created early and initialized in the design state and then marked as ready when they are fully defined with manual and automated steps.

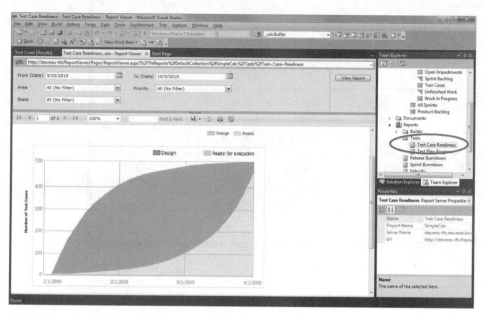

FIGURE 7-15: A test case readiness report.

Defining Manual Steps for a Test Case

In Visual Studio Ultimate Edition and Visual Studio Test Professional Edition, you can define manual steps for a test. In other editions of Visual Studio, you must specify the test steps in the description of the test case. This section applies to Visual Studio Ultimate and Visual Studio Test Professional.

You enter manual steps for a test case into Test Manager. You can access the screen to enter manual steps in one of two ways:

> **From the test case in Visual Studio** — Go to the Steps tab and click the Open for Edit button.

> **From Test Manager** — Launch Test Manager from the Start menu in Windows. Open a test plan and click the Add button in the right side of the window. Test Manager brings up a query for all test cases not associated with the test plan. Choose the test case you want to add and click OK. Then open the test case.

Regardless of the method you use here, the result is the screen shown in Figure 7-16.

In addition to defining the manual steps, you can reference shared steps by clicking the Insert Shared Steps button. TFS launches a window and displays the shared steps, which you can include in this test case.

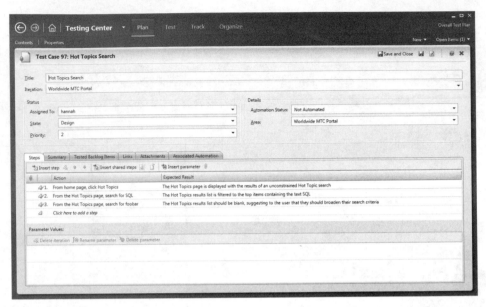

FIGURE 7-16: Adding manual steps to a test case.

Defining Shared Steps for Test Cases

If you have a sequence of steps that is used in many test cases, you can save yourself some time by defining the sequence once and then referencing it from test cases. You store this sequence of steps in TFS as a shared steps work item. Doing this is a convenient way to ensure consistency across test cases.

> *Like manual steps, shared steps are available only in Visual Studio Ultimate and Visual Studio Test Professional, so this section applies only to those versions.*

For example, in a public-facing web application, portions of the site might require authentication. In those parts of the site, the user must answer a challenge, such as providing the correct username and password, and then is granted access. This process might have the following three steps:

1. Click the Sign In link in the upper right of the screen.

2. Enter the username `Shopper` and the password `RichGuy`.

3. Click the Sign In button.

In a shared steps work item, you specify the sequence of steps that a team member will follow as part of validating a test case. For each step, you specify instructions for carrying out the step and the expected result. When the test is run later, the team member will be prompted to run each step and verify that the result is as expected.

You can create a shared steps definition in either Test Manager or Visual Studio, but you can only edit the steps within Test Manager. When using Visual Studio, you follow these steps:

1. Right-click Work Items in the Team Explorer and select New Work Item ⇨ Shared Steps.

2. Fill in the fields. Only Title is required.

3. Click Save Work Item to save the shared step definition. If you don't save the shared step definition, you won't be able to edit it in Test Manager. Figure 7-17 shows the shared step created in Visual Studio before it is edited in Test Manager.

4. From the shared steps work item in Visual Studio (see Figure 7-17), click the Open for Edit button. The Test Manager screen appears, and you can edit the shared steps.

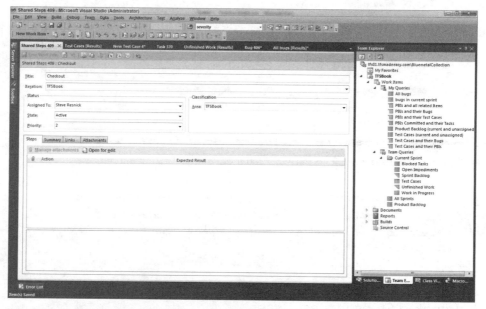

FIGURE 7-17: A shared steps work item in Visual Studio.

 In Figure 7-17, note that there are very few data elements captured. Shared steps are more of a productivity tool than a tracking element for Scrum, so they are not associated with iterations, PBIs, and so on.

To create shared steps from Test Manager, follow these steps:

1. From a test case, select a set of steps by Shift+clicking the steps.

2. Right-click these steps and select Create Shared Step. The Test Manager Shared Steps edit screen appears, as shown in Figure 7-18.

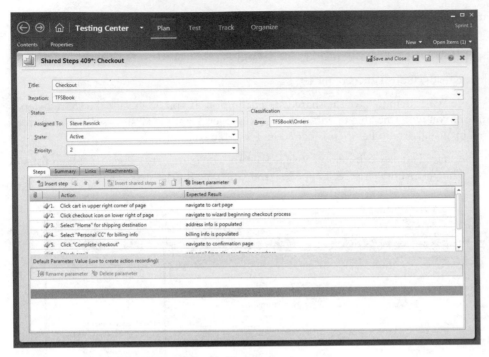

FIGURE 7-18: A shared steps work item in Test Manager.

You can also create a shared steps definition from Visual Studio or Test Manager. Regardless of how you create it, you must edit the actions and results in Test Manager.

Using Automated Steps for Test Cases

Most components you build in Visual Studio will have automated tests. Some will have just a few automated tests, and others will have hundreds or thousands of them. Visual Studio has very sophisticated tools for creating automated tests — from simple unit tests that validate individual components or assemblies to coded user interface tests that verify onscreen data and actions to performance tests.

Component tests in Visual Studio are generally defined in code. They are code artifacts that exercise specific technical features of a system and validate those features against expected results. Visual Studio ships with templates where you replace the stubbed code with your own testing logic. The tests are attributed with [TestMethod] so they can be run as part of the Visual Studio testing infrastructure. The results of the tests are stored in the file system, either on the client if tests are executed there or on the build server if tests are queued and built centrally.

Manual tests, on the other hand, are generally stored in SQL and managed by TFS, not in code. They are accessible from the Team Explorer, from Visual Studio, and from Test Manager. The Test Manager tool that ships with Visual Studio Ultimate and Visual Studio Test Professional deals mostly with manual tests.

Automated steps are the intersection between the component-level testing infrastructure of Visual Studio and the system-level testing infrastructure of TFS. You define component-level tests in Visual Studio and then reference those tests in TFS. When you run test scripts in Test Manager, Lab Manager communicates with System Center Virtual Machine Manager (VMM) to start a virtual machine to run the component-level tests.

Automated testing and Agile testing methodologies are beyond the scope of this book.

USING MICROSOFT TEST MANAGER TO DEFINE TEST PLANS

Now that you've looked at defining test cases in Visual Studio and shared steps across Visual Studio and Test Manager, you can examine Test Manager in more detail. Test Manager has four major sections:

➤ **Plan** — In this section, you define your test plans, test suites, and test cases. It has tools for linking test cases to PBIs and assigning them to testers. This is the main section that you'll use for managing and tracking items for sprints.

➤ **Test** — In this section, you run the tests. It works with Lab Manager to start virtual machines in which the tests are run. It is optimized for running test and verifying bugs.

➤ **Track** — This is an alternate user interface to Visual Studio's query screens and some build-management functions. In this section you can access all the personal and team queries and define new ones.

➤ **Organize** — This section provides an overview of the testing environment and has some reporting for showing the status of tests.

Figure 7-19 shows the startup screen of Microsoft Test Manager, showing a test plan titled Sprint 1. From the top menu, you can navigate to the four primary sections just described.

FIGURE 7-19: Microsoft Test Manager.

Test Manager provides tools for defining, organizing, and reporting on test plans. The goal of test planning is to group specific test cases into larger sets that can then be applied and measured at certain milestones within a project. Rather than track individual test cases, you can track the status of your test plan. Test Manager enables a team to organize test plans based on PBIs.

A *test plan* in Test Manager is a collection of test suites. A *test suite* is a collection of test cases. *Test cases* are used to verify the correctness of PBIs.

 You can define test cases in Test Manager or in Visual Studio.

For a Scrum project, you can align test plans to sprints. At the beginning of a sprint, after the team has committed to PBIs in the sprint planning meeting, you should verify that you have test cases defined for each PBI. Then you can use Test Manager to define a test plan for the sprint.

Figure 7-20 shows the hierarchy of test plans, test suites, and test cases. The following sections discuss test plans and test suites in more detail. For information on creating test cases, see the "Defining Test Cases" section earlier in this chapter.

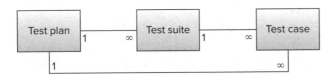

FIGURE 7-20: Test plans, test suites, and test cases.

From a data tracking perspective, Test Manager is a superset of Visual Studio. While Visual Studio enables tracking and reporting at the test case level, Test Manager enables grouping individual test cases or PBIs for sprint-level planning. Another distinction is that whereas Test Manager is more about tracking and running tests, Visual Studio is more focused on the engineering.

A test case lists the specific steps that the product owner or team members will follow to verify that a PBI meets expectations. Your team can define test cases in either Test Manager or Visual Studio. You can link test cases to PBIs so that their status can be tracked together.

Test cases are not unique to Scrum, and most teams are familiar with test cases. Each PBI should have at least one test case, but most PBIs have dozens of them.

In Test Manager, you can group PBIs or test cases into test suites, which are selected via queries. The purpose of a test suite is to group test cases together so they can be tracked as a unit. A test suite is really nothing more than a collection of test cases.

By including test cases in test suites through queries, you can bring the test cases in from TFS automatically. A good starting point for this technique is to query by area path or sprint to create test suites that cover the entire area path or sprint, respectively.

Organizing Test Plans

Test plans provide structure for organizing test cases based on PBIs. Each test plan typically corresponds to a sprint and encompasses all PBIs for the sprint. Alternatively, a test plan can organize test cases based on system function, such as security or performance, rather than correspond to a sprint. In that case, the test plan will span sprints because the PBIs are addressed in different sprints.

At the start of each sprint, a team should create a test plan that will be executed at the end of the sprint. Defining the test plan up front makes it clear exactly what will be tested. The test plan should include all of the tests associated with all the PBIs that are included in the sprint.

You create a test plan in Test Manager from the testing center. When Test Manager is launched, the dialog box shown in Figure 7-21 appears. You can use this dialog to add and delete test plans.

When a team creates a test plan, it defines the properties of the plan. The test plan properties include basic information about the test plan, such as when it starts and ends and its state. These attributes can be helpful in tracking progress with the test plan progress report. For instance, if a test plan is active, then its results in the test plan progress report are important. If the test plan is not active, you can filter out its results in the test plan progress report.

FIGURE 7-21: Creating a test plan in Test Manager.

Figure 7-22 shows the properties of a test plan, which you access by clicking the Properties link at the top left of Test Manager. You can also access test plans from the Test Plan Manager link on the Organize tab.

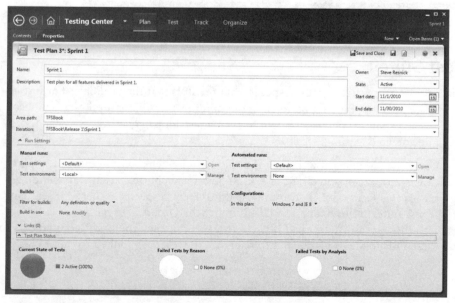

FIGURE 7-22: Test plan properties.

More important than the properties, however, are the actual contents of the test plan. You access the test plan contents by clicking the Contents link in the Plan screen, which is available from the Plan tab in Test Manager. Figure 7-23 shows the Plan screen, which displays the test suites and test cases. Test suites are just a further grouping construct to organize PBIs or test cases.

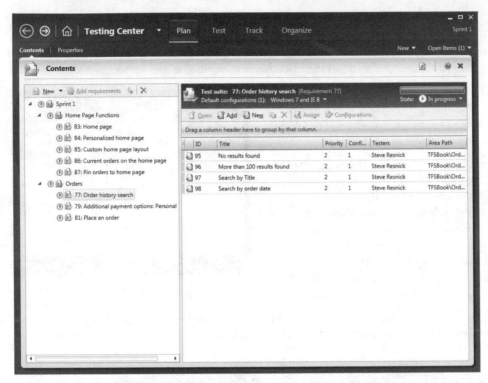

FIGURE 7-23: The test plan Contents screen.

Organizing Test Suites

Using test suites is a convenient way to group test cases and the PBIs that they validate. For instance, using the area path to identify all PBIs that perform a common function is a natural grouping because the PBIs are related in the product. Filtering it down further, a test suite may encompass just those PBIs that are being implemented within a sprint.

You can add test suites in Test Manager by clicking the Add Requirements button on the test plan Contents screen (Figure 7-23). When you click the Add Requirements button, Test Manager opens a screen for selecting PBIs (see Figure 7-24). You can use this screen to specify a query for searching PBIs to include in the test suite. In this example, all PBIs under the Orders area path are being selected for inclusion in the test case. With the PBIs selected, you can click the Add Requirements to Plan button to add these PBIs to the test suite and to reference the test cases linked to those PBIs.

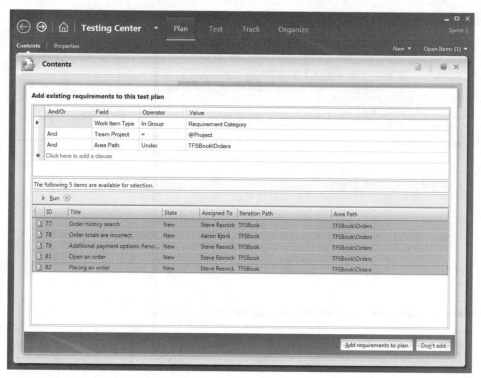

FIGURE 7-24: Selecting items for a test suite.

 The word requirements *in Test Manager may not be the proper term for Scrum. Although its terminology isn't Scrum specific, Test Manager is useful with any methodology, including Scrum.*

In Agile development, requirements are captured as user stories. And in Scrum, user stories are tracked as PBIs. So, to organize a test plan around PBIs, you use the Add Requirements to Plan button. This way, you can add PBIs to the test suite and then add test cases to the test suite.

Figure 7-25 shows a test plan named Sprint 1 with two test suites: Home Page Functions and Orders. To define these test suites, you include each PBI within either the Home Page Functions or Orders area path. In this example, the first PBI in Orders is named Order History Search, and it has four test cases.

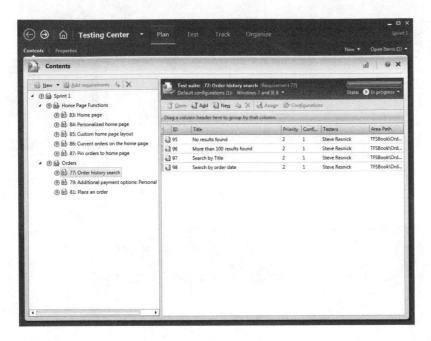

FIGURE 7-25: Test Manager test plan contents.

 In a production environment, there may be hundreds of PBIs and thousands of test cases, so organization is quite important. This is where test suites come in handy.

SUMMARY

Great software has two common elements: usefulness and predictability. Test cases measure usefulness, verifying that the product performs the intended function and meets expectations. Bugs are items that must be fixed within the product so it functions correctly and reliably. By finding and tracking bugs, you can measure predictability.

You count and track bugs in TFS. Your team can fix bugs within the current sprint or defer them to a later sprint. In either case, the bugs are added to the backlog, where they're estimated and classified like other PBIs. After you commit to fixing a bug, you create the task. Tasks track remaining work (in hours or days), as opposed to PBIs, which track relative effort (for example, in story points).

You count and track test cases in TFS by using a combination of Visual Studio and Test Manager. In Visual Studio, there are two built-in reports for tracking test cases: test plan readiness and test case progress. Test Manager enables you to organize test cases into test suites and test plans for greater control when handling thousands of individual tests. Test Manager also includes a sophisticated manual testing tool you can use to script and later automate manual tests. Team members can use this tool to execute manual tests and record whether the system passed or failed each test.

In Chapter 8, you'll see how it all comes together in a release.

Running a Release

WHAT'S IN THIS CHAPTER?

➤   Creating releases.

➤   Developing the product backlog: user stories and tasks.

➤   Entering the product backlog.

➤   Ensuring product backlog and user story success.

➤   Linking PBIs and tasks.

➤   Understanding user story reports.

In Chapter 7, you learned about tracking quality in Team Foundation Server (TFS). In this chapter, you will learn how to create a release in TFS. One of the main activities involved in creating a release is entering product backlog items (PBIs) in the product backlog. The chapter provides detailed examples, with screenshots of how to enter PBIs using TFS, the web portal, and Excel. In addition, this chapter contains a list of success and failure patterns for your product backlog and user stories as well as a description of how to link PBIs and tasks, and a discussion of the PBI reports that are available in TFS.

CREATING A RELEASE

Simply creating a team project creates several releases. However, you sometimes need to create additional releases or modify existing releases; in such cases, you can use the process described here. To create a new release in TFS, follow these steps:

1.   Right-click the project in Visual Studio's Team Explorer and select Team Project Settings ➪ Areas and Iterations, as shown in Figure 8-1. The Areas and Iterations dialog appears.

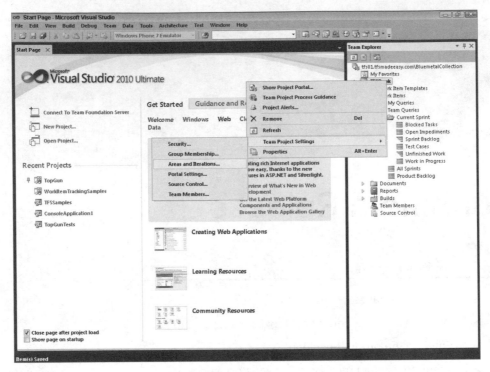

FIGURE 8-1: Creating a new release in Visual Studio.

2. Click the Iteration tab in the Areas and Iterations dialog. This tab should look similar to the one shown in Figure 8-2.

3. Click the green plus sign icon (+) in the upper-left corner of the Iteration tab. Visual Studio adds a new release entry at the end of the list of releases.

4. Type Release 5 or something similar as the name of the new entry. Your screen should now look as shown in Figure 8-3.

5. Select the new release that you just created and click the green + icon again to create a sprint for this release. Each time you do this, TFS adds another new sprint entry for which you should provide a name (see Figure 8-4).

FIGURE 8-2: The Areas and Iterations dialog.

FIGURE 8-3: Adding a new release in TFS.

FIGURE 8-4: Creating a new sprint in TFS.

You have now created a new release. This release will be available in all the reports and items in TFS.

DEVELOPING THE PRODUCT BACKLOG

As discussed throughout this book, one of the key artifacts in Scrum is the product backlog. A high-quality, well-groomed backlog is absolutely critical to the success of a Scrum team. A great team with a bad backlog is a team that will quickly develop the wrong software.

The product backlog usually consists of user stories; it may also include non-functional requirements. Each PBI can have tasks. The product owner develops user stories and prioritizes them based on their business value. The team estimates the effort (typically in story points, as discussed in Chapter 4) required to complete user stories and determines the technical tasks required to finish the PBI. The team estimates how much time each task will take, typically in hours. The following sections discuss user stories and tasks in more detail. There is also a section on verifying that you have created a SharePoint portal that is associated with your team project.

> ### THE IMPORTANCE OF USER STORIES
>
> Using user stories is not the only way to create PBIs, but using them is a recommended practice and a common way to form PBIs. Because most Scrum teams use user stories to organize the backlog, learning what constitutes a good user story and knowing how to create a backlog from user stories is of great importance.

Creating User Stories

User stories typically have a three-part structure that involves a role, a feature, and a benefit. The form of a user story is *"As a <role>, I want to <feature> so that <benefit>."* For example, "As a salesperson, I want to enter my leads so that I remember to contact them."

 Some teams use just the role and the feature in a user story, not the benefit.

Despite the similarity of their names, user stories are very different from use cases. A *use case* specifies the interactions among the actors in a human–machine system. The following is an example of a use case:

1. The user types in a credit card number.

2. The system verifies the credit card number.

3. The system charges the cost of the product to the credit card.

A user story is also quite different from the requirements documents and from specifications created by non-Scrum teams. The Nokia Test, a test a team can use to determine whether it is doing Scrum, makes this clear. One of the statements in the Nokia Test is "The iteration must start before the specification is complete." The Nokia Test originally had eight statements and now has nine:

➤ Iterations must be time-boxed to less than four weeks.

➤ Software features must be tested and working at the end of each iteration.

➤ An iteration must start before specification is complete.

➤ The team must have a product owner.

➤ The product backlog should be prioritized based on business value.

➤ The team should create estimates for the product backlog.

➤ The team should generate burndown charts and know its velocity.

➤ No one (not even project managers) should disrupt the work of the team.

➤ The team should achieve a hyperproductive state.

 The March 25, 2009, version of the Nokia Test is available from Jeff Sutherland at http://jeffsutherland.com/nokiatest.pdf.

The Nokia Test has at least four statements that are relevant to user stories and tasks:

➤ **The team must have a product owner** — The product owner must know Scrum and have a list of stories, prioritized based on business value, at the start of the sprint planning meeting. The product owner should have a road map or release backlog based on the team's velocity.

➤ **The product backlog should be prioritized based on business value** — Ideally, the product owner should check whether the business value is actually achieved when the team delivers a PBI. For example, imagine that the product owner prioritizes the following user story: "As a customer, I want to have an excellent help system so that I can learn how to use the product quickly and easily." The product owner believes that implementing this user story will cause a 10% decline in calls to the customer service center. Once this user story is delivered, the product owner should have a metric that tracks calls to the customer service center, and this person should analyze the impact that this user story has on the number of calls. Based on this data, the product owner should have a better understanding of what creates business value.

➤ **The team should create estimates for the product backlog** — Only the team should create estimates. After all, only the team understands how long a technical task will take. Management should not impose deadlines on the team. Doing so radically increases the amount of dysfunction on the team. The *fudge phenomenon* is an example of such a dysfunction, and it is illustrated in Figure 8-5.

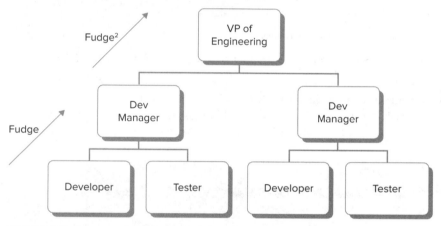

FIGURE 8-5: An example of the fudge phenomenon.

In this example, the development manager on the second level of the organization chart demands that his developer and testers meet a deadline. Because the developer and testers understand that they will be punished if they overshoot the deadline, they "fudge," or pad, the estimate. The development manager in turn fudges the already fudged estimate when presenting a final schedule to the vice president of engineering. Over time, the vice president of engineering learns that he is constantly getting fudged estimates, so he begins to ignore the estimates provided by his own development managers. Consequently, as he generates new deadlines, he reduces the proposed deadlines by what he considers a suitable amount. This leads to a battle in the organization over planning and reduces the transparency and visibility of all actions in the organization.

➤ **The team should generate burndown charts and know its velocity** — The team indicates how many hours are remaining for each task in the sprint backlog. The burndown chart is a daily plot of the total number of hours of work remaining in the sprint.

In Scrum, at no point does the team identify how many hours of work it has done. This is critically important: Keeping track of hours provides a way of controlling and punishing the team, which is inconsistent with the values of Scrum. Note that there is no way to tell how many hours of work a team has done by looking at the burndown chart. For example, suppose the burndown chart shows that the team has 100 hours of work remaining in the sprint on Monday and 80 hours of work remaining in the sprint on Tuesday. Concluding that the team worked 20 hours on Monday is incorrect. The team may have worked 50 hours or 10 hours. For example, if the team discovers that the tasks were more difficult than it originally estimated, it will need to do more than 20 hours of work to reduce the number of hours remaining from 100 hours to 80 hours.

Tasks

Tasks do not conform to any particular structure. The following are some examples of technical tasks:

➤ Investigate bug #XY-1234.

➤ Develop user tests.

➤ Write class `foobar`.

➤ Upgrade the database.

➤ Install a continuous integration server.

The team estimates how much work is remaining on each of these technical tasks.

The team updates the amount of work remaining every day. For example, say that a developer starts to work on the task shown in Figure 8-6. This task shows that there are five hours of work remaining on the task. At the end of his work on that task, the developer believes that he has three hours of work remaining on the task. He updates the hours to reflect this, as shown in Figure 8-7.

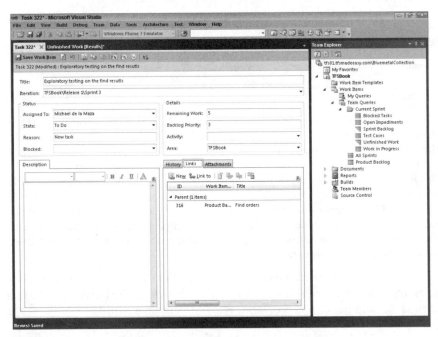

FIGURE 8-6: A task with five hours of work remaining.

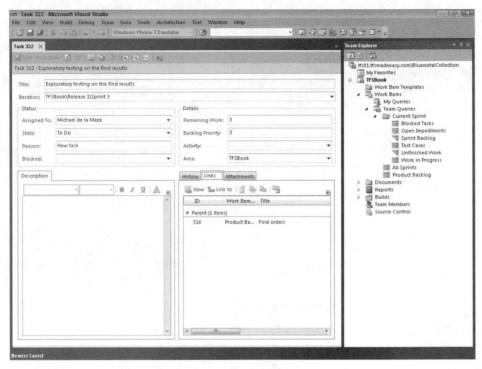

FIGURE 8-7: A task with three hours of work remaining.

Note that the State field of the task in Figures 8-6 and 8-7 is set to To Do. TFS does not require tasks to be set to In Progress in order for time to be updated.

 If a team does not update the State field of every task, all reporting that depends on the state will be incorrect.

Verifying That You Have a SharePoint Portal

As part of the release setup process, you should ensure that you have a SharePoint portal associated with a team project. To ensure that you have a SharePoint portal associated with a team project, follow these steps:

1. In Visual Studio, select Team Project Settings ➪ Portal Settings, as shown in Figure 8-8. The Project Portal Settings dialog appears.

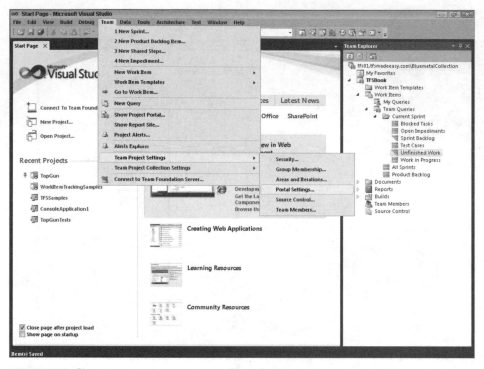

FIGURE 8-8: Checking whether you have a SharePoint portal associated with a project.

2. On the Project Portal tab of the Project Portal Settings dialog, ensure that Enable Team Project Portal is checked, as shown in Figure 8-9.

3. Click the URL link to visit the project portal.

FIGURE 8-9: Enabling the team project portal.

ENTERING PBIS

There are three main ways to enter PBIs: entering PBIs in Excel, entering PBIs using the SharePoint portal, and entering items directly into TFS.

Entering PBIs in Excel

This section explores various ways to use Excel in conjunction with Visual Studio. First, you'll see how to export the backlog from TFS to Excel, edit the backlog in Excel, and then import the edited backlog into TFS. Next, you'll learn how to send the results of a query in Visual Studio to Excel. Then, you'll see how to create items in Excel and export them to TFS. Finally, you'll learn how to use PivotTables to analyze the backlog.

Exporting Items from Excel and Importing Items to Excel

The simplest way to use Excel to add items to TFS is to export the relevant list of items to Excel, modify the items in Excel, and then publish the modifications back to TFS. To illustrate this workflow, follow these steps to work with the sprint backlog shown in Figure 8-10:

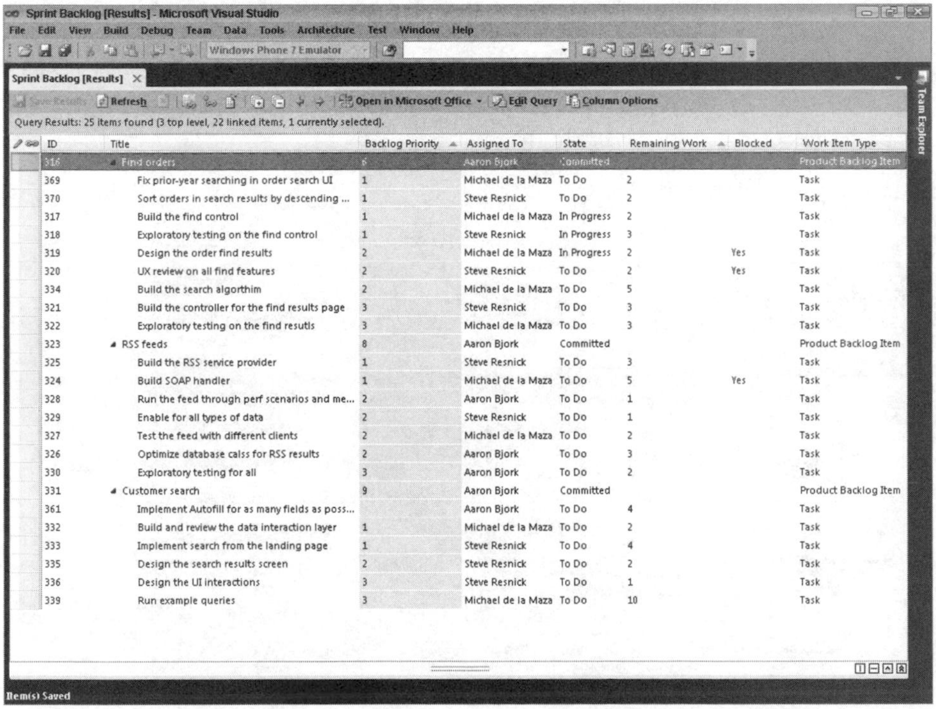

FIGURE 8-10: A sprint backlog with Run Example Queries as the last task on the list.

1. Export the backlog to Excel. To do so, right-click Sprint Backlog in the Team Explorer and then click Open in Microsoft Excel (Tree), as shown in Figure 8-11. TFS opens Excel and creates a table similar to the one shown in Figure 8-12.

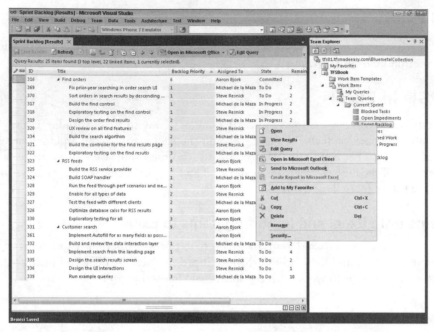

FIGURE 8-11: Exporting a sprint backlog to Excel.

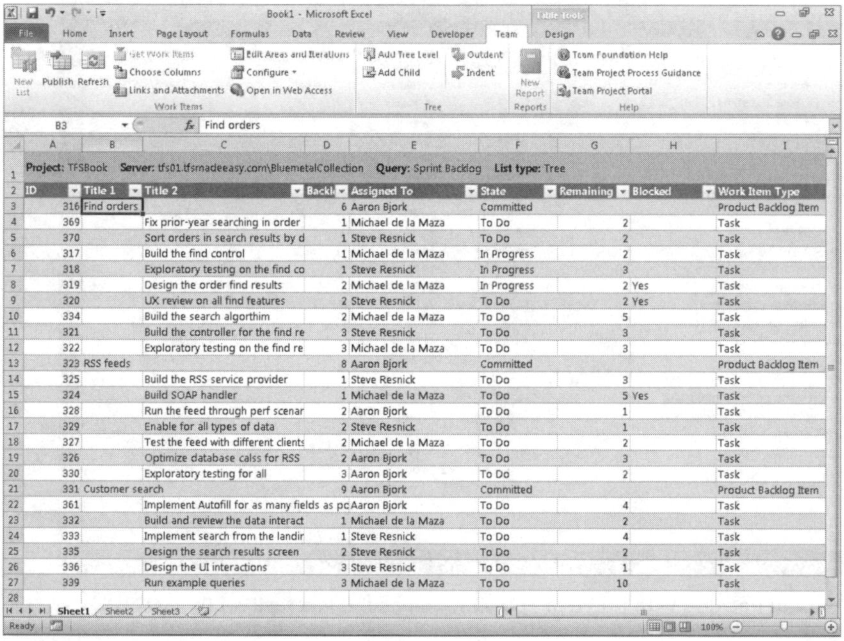

FIGURE 8-12: The sprint backlog in Excel.

2. Click the line below the last item of the Excel table and enter a new task.

 You cannot enter an ID in the Excel table. This is a read-only field that Excel creates.

3. As in the example shown in Figure 8-13, add the following fields on row 28:

➤ Title 2 (column C): Verify page load speed

➤ Backlog Priority (column D): 10

➤ Assigned To (column E): Michael de la Maza (chosen from a pull-down menu)

➤ State (column F): To Do (chosen from a pull-down menu)

➤ Remaining Work (column G): 20

➤ Work Item Type (column I): Task (chosen from a pull-down menu)

ID	Title 1	Title 2	Backl	Assigned To	State	Remaining	Blocked	Work Item Type
316	Find orders		6	Aaron Bjork	Committed			Product Backlog Item
369		Fix prior-year searching in order	1	Michael de la Maza	To Do	2		Task
370		Sort orders in search results by d	1	Steve Resnick	To Do	2		Task
317		Build the find control	1	Michael de la Maza	In Progress	2		Task
318		Exploratory testing on the find co	1	Steve Resnick	In Progress	3		Task
319		Design the order find results	2	Michael de la Maza	In Progress	2	Yes	Task
320		UX review on all find features	2	Steve Resnick	To Do	2	Yes	Task
334		Build the search algorthim	2	Michael de la Maza	To Do	5		Task
321		Build the controller for the find re	3	Steve Resnick	To Do	3		Task
322		Exploratory testing on the find re	3	Michael de la Maza	To Do	3		Task
323	RSS feeds		8	Aaron Bjork	Committed			Product Backlog Item
325		Build the RSS service provider	1	Steve Resnick	To Do	3		Task
324		Build SOAP handler	1	Michael de la Maza	To Do	5	Yes	Task
328		Run the feed through perf scenar	2	Aaron Bjork	To Do	1		Task
329		Enable for all types of data	2	Steve Resnick	To Do	1		Task
327		Test the feed with different clients	2	Michael de la Maza	To Do	2		Task
326		Optimize database calss for RSS	2	Aaron Bjork	To Do	3		Task
330		Exploratory testing for all	3	Aaron Bjork	To Do	2		Task
331	Customer search		9	Aaron Bjork	Committed			Product Backlog Item
361		Implement Autofill for as many fields as po	Aaron Bjork	To Do	4		Task
332		Build and review the data interact	1	Michael de la Maza	To Do	2		Task
333		Implement search from the landir	1	Steve Resnick	To Do	4		Task
335		Design the search results screen	2	Steve Resnick	To Do	2		Task
336		Design the UI interactions	3	Steve Resnick	To Do	1		Task
339		Run example queries	3	Michael de la Maza	To Do	10		Task
		Verify page load speed	10	Michael de la Maza	To Do	20		Task

FIGURE 8-13: Adding a new task to line 28.

4. To publish this new list back to TFS, click the Publish button in the upper-left corner of the Team tab in Excel. TFS automatically refreshes after Excel publishes to it, and you now see an ID for your new task. In Figure 8-14, the ID on line 28 is now 403; it was blank previously.

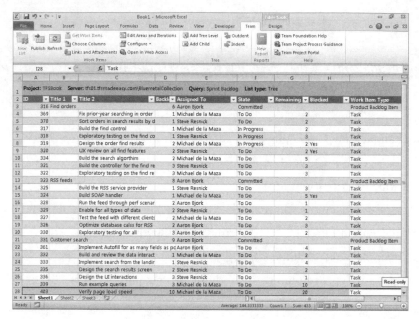

FIGURE 8-14: Excel performs an automatic refresh and causes the ID field on line 28 to update.

5. To verify that Excel has published successfully to TFS, rerun the sprint backlog query in TFS. You see that the new task ("403 Verify page load speed") now appears at the bottom of the sprint backlog, as shown in Figure 8-15.

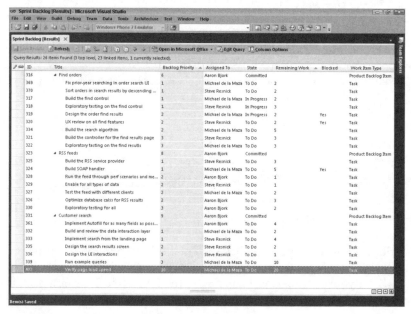

FIGURE 8-15: TFS shows the new task at the bottom of the sprint backlog after you rerun the sprint backlog query.

Sending Query Results to Excel

In addition to working with the product backlog in Excel, you can also send many TFS queries to Excel. For example, to send a work in progress query to Excel, right-click Work in Progress in the Team Explorer and select Open in Microsoft Excel (Flat) from the context menu, as shown in Figure 8-16. Excel opens a table similar to the one in Figure 8-17.

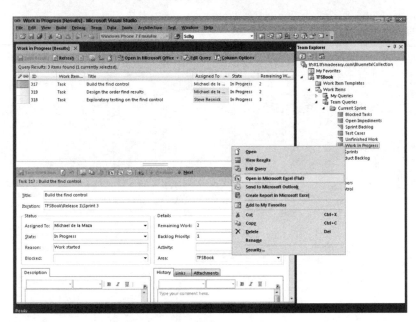

FIGURE 8-16: Exporting a query into Excel.

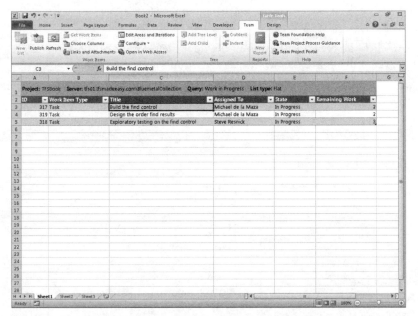

FIGURE 8-17: A table of items in Excel that have been exported from TFS.

Creating Items in Excel

You have just seen how to enter items in TFS by first exporting an existing set of items, such as the sprint backlog or a query, to Excel, editing the list in Excel, and then publishing the list back to TFS. You can also start within Excel and either pull data from TFS and publish the modified data to TFS or, without pulling in data from TFS, you can enter a new item. To enter a new item, follow these steps:

1. Launch Excel and click the Team tab. Figure 8-18 shows the result.

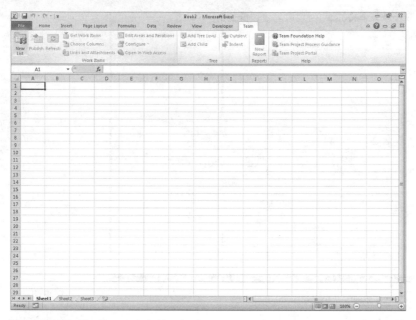

FIGURE 8-18: The Team tab in Excel, when no items have been exported from TFS.

2. To enter a new item, click the New List button in the upper-left corner of the Team tab. Excel asks which server you want to connect to, as shown in Figure 8-19.

3. Choose a server to connect to and click Connect. You then see the New List dialog, as shown in Figure 8-20.

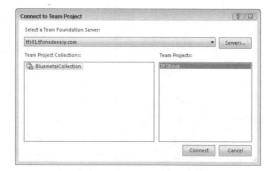

FIGURE 8-19: Connecting to a TFS server from Excel.

FIGURE 8-20: Inputting a new list of items from Excel.

4. To create a new item, click Input List in the New List dialog. Click OK, and the screen shown in Figure 8-21 appears.

 If you select Query List in the New List dialog, Excel will import a list of items from Excel.

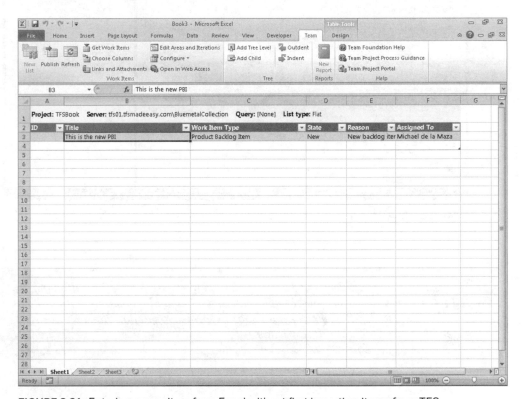

FIGURE 8-21: Entering a new item from Excel without first importing items from TFS.

5. To check that this new PBI has been entered properly, click the Publish button in the Team tab and then run the PBI query in TFS. As you can see in Figure 8-22, the new PBI appears in TFS, with ID number 343.

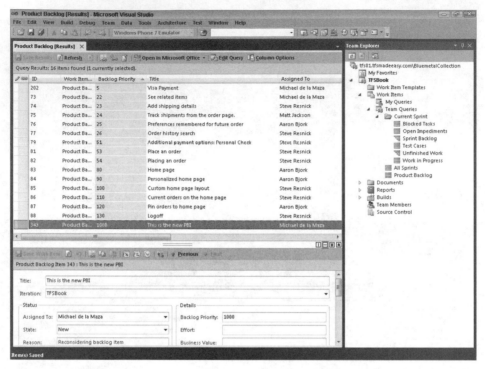

FIGURE 8-22: A new PBI entered in Excel.

 When you enter an item, the State and Reason fields are populated automatically. TFS prevents you from, for example, entering a bug and indicating that work has been completed. All new items must start in the new or to do state, and this Excel functionality enforces this restriction.

Using PivotTables to Analyze the Backlog

One of the advantages of exporting items to Excel is that you can use all of Excel's functionality to explore the data in TFS. One of the most useful functions is the PivotTable. You can, for example, export the sprint backlog into Excel and use a PivotTable to further analyze the data. To do this, follow these steps:

1. Run the sprint backlog query and then click Open in Microsoft Office ⇨ Open Query in Microsoft Excel, as shown in Figure 8-23. TFS exports the data to Excel.

2. Click Table Tools in Excel and then select Summarize with PivotTable from the left end of the Tools tab (see Figure 8-24). Excel prompts you with the Create PivotTable dialog, as shown in Figure 8-25.

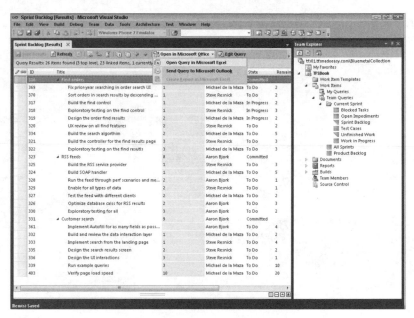

FIGURE 8-23: Exporting a sprint backlog to Excel.

FIGURE 8-24: Converting a table in Excel to a PivotTable.

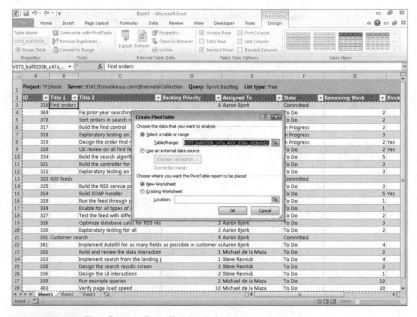

FIGURE 8-25: The Create PivotTable dialog.

3. In the Create PivotTable dialog, accept the defaults by clicking OK. Excel creates a new worksheet with the standard PivotTable options. The worksheet in Figure 8-26 shows the amount of remaining work and the number of items blocked for three people who have been assigned tasks.

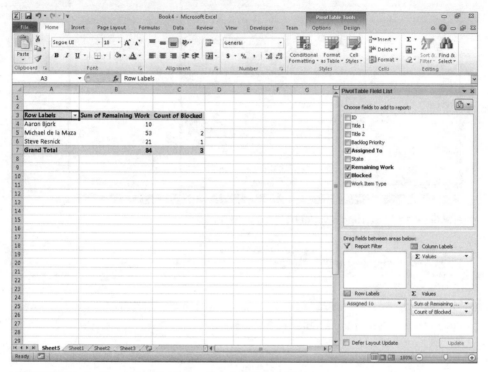

FIGURE 8-26: An Excel PivotTable constructed from TFS data.

Entering PBIs Using the SharePoint Portal

A second way to enter PBIs into TFS is through the SharePoint portal. Your SharePoint portal should look similar to the one shown in Figure 8-27.

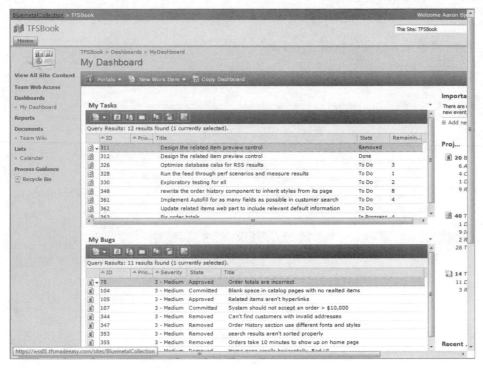

FIGURE 8-27: A team project SharePoint portal.

Before you work through the steps in this section, verify that your project has a SharePoint portal by following the steps listed earlier in this chapter, in the section "Verifying That You Have a SharePoint Portal."

To enter a new PBI using the SharePoint portal, under My Tasks, click the Work Item icon at the upper left and select Product Backlog Item, as shown in Figure 8-28. The New Product Backlog Item screen appears, as shown in Figure 8-29.

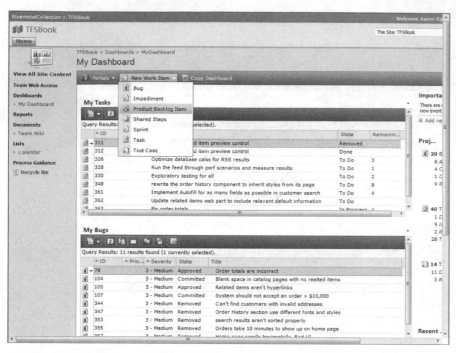

FIGURE 8-28: Beginning to enter a PBI using the SharePoint portal.

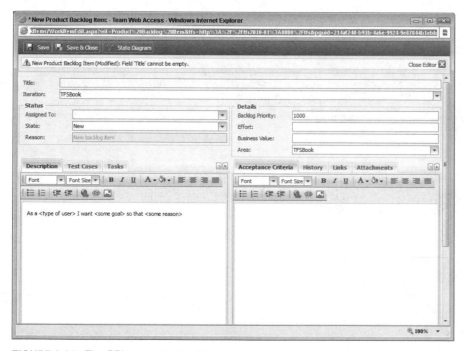

FIGURE 8-29: The PBI screen in the SharePoint portal.

The functionality of the New Product Backlog Item screen is nearly identical to that of the same screen in TFS. Refer to the section "Understanding Releases" in Chapter 4 for information about how to complete the fields in the PBI.

Entering PBIs Using Visual Studio

A third way to enter PBIs is to use Visual Studio. This is discussed extensively in Chapter 4. Figure 8-30 shows the largely self-explanatory PBI screen.

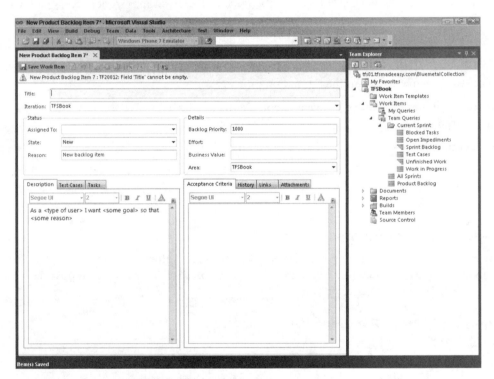

FIGURE 8-30: The PBI screen in TFS.

 The easiest way to enter large numbers of PBIs is to use Excel, and the easiest way to enter a few PBIs is to use Visual Studio. Using the SharePoint portal is the best method for people who do not have Visual Studio installed.

PRODUCT BACKLOG AND USER STORY SUCCESS AND FAILURE PATTERNS

Scrum provides a framework for developing software. Even though the product backlog can take many forms, years of experience across many Scrum teams have led to the development of success patterns for the product backlog and for user stories. Just as there are success patterns for the product backlog and for user stories, there are also failure patterns. The following sections discuss some of the most important success and failure patterns.

Product Backlog and User Story Success Patterns

Over the past decade, the Scrum community has learned what good and bad product backlogs and user stories look like. The following sections describe some of the most important success patterns.

Keeping User Stories a Consistent Size

Keeping user stories roughly the same size provides several benefits to a team:

> ➤ It reduces the time needed in the estimation process.

> ➤ The team will never have the problem of completing small stories successfully but failing to deliver large user stories.

> ➤ Progress throughout the sprint can be more even and steady.

In fact, when all the user stories are the same size, the number of user stories completed in a sprint is an excellent measure of the team's velocity. As discussed in Chapter 1, *velocity* is the speed at which a team can implement items on the product backlog.

Knowing the Definition of *Business Value*

The product owner should prioritize user stories based on business value. Every team member needs to understand how the team is defining *business value*. Therefore, Scrum teams often post their definition of *business value* in their team rooms.

Understanding User Story Personas

Consider the following user story: "As a bank customer, I want an easy-to-use ATM so I do not waste my time." What kind of person is the bank customer? How often does he use the ATMs? How comfortable is he with computers? How valuable is he to the company?

A Scrum team could capture all the questions about the bank customer in the form of a *profile*, or *persona*. Here is an example of the persona the team might come up with for the bank customer:

> ➤ **Name** — Barry the Bank Customer

> ➤ **Income** — $40K–$60K

> ➤ **Location** — Midwest

> ➤ **Use of ATMs** — Once per week

> ➤ **Familiarity with computers** — Minimal. Knows how to use e-mail, a browser, and a word processor.

➤ **Number of customers who fit this profile** — 100,000

➤ **Value** — Significant. Barry is 80% of the bank's customer base in the Midwest.

 A persona helps the team make critical decisions about how much time and effort to invest in various technical options.

Personas have names, such as "Barry the Bank Customer" or "Susan the Salesperson," and they are chock-full of demographic and product-related behavior information. A Scrum team might want to create a collage with pictures that illustrate a customer's lifestyle and product choices for each persona and hang these collages in the team room.

Considering the INVEST Characteristics

INVEST principles are a guide that can help a product owner create a good backlog. INVEST is an acronym that stands for the following:

➤ **Independent** — User stories should not have dependencies. If user story A cannot be started until user story B is finished, this reduces the flexibility the product owner has in prioritizing user stories. It also prevents the team from working on both user stories in parallel, which may reduce the team's velocity.

➤ **Negotiable** — User stories can be changed and modified. More importantly, the product owner elaborates them as needed during the sprint.

➤ **Valuable** — A user story is always written from the perspective of the end user, so when a team completes a user story and the product owner releases it into production, the end user experiences an increase in value. This means that a user story should never be solely about technical tasks. For example, "As a software team, we need to set up continuous integration to improve our velocity" is not a good user story because the end user does not receive any value when this user story is completed. Note, however, that some teams do allow such user stories on their backlog. In addition, some teams may be developing software, such as APIs, that are used by other parts of the company, and so they may have internal users who are not paying customers. User stories that deliver features to these internal users are consistent with INVEST.

➤ **Estimable** — The team needs to understand the user story well enough to create an estimate for it, typically using story points. If the team does not understand the user story enough to create an estimate for it, the team should refuse to accept that story into the sprint. Starting development when a lot of ambiguity remains makes little sense.

➤ **Small** — User stories should be small enough that the team can complete them in one sprint. The usual rule of thumb is that no user story should take more than half a sprint to complete. When user stories take longer than a sprint, the team no longer has a good measure of its progress.

➤ **Testable** — The team should know when it is done with a user story. The product owner often provides clarity on this issue by developing acceptance criteria for a user story. Teams that have advanced to the stage of using behavior-driven tests might work with the product owner to develop behavior-driven tests for each user story.

INVEST is a goal, not a requirement. Often teams and product owners find themselves working with backlogs that do not meet the INVEST criteria.

Product Backlog and User Story Failure Patterns

Just as there are success patterns for the product backlog and for user stories, there are also failure patterns. Many Scrum teams and Scrum coaches have observed these failure patterns over time. The following sections discuss some of the most important failure patterns.

Unavailability of the Product Owner for Discussing User Stories

The product owner should be available to answer questions during a sprint. The team might want to ask the product owner about user stories. The product owner might also need to examine mini demos and provide feedback on the team's progress.

To see the critical importance of a highly available product owner, consider the case of a Scrum team that has fallen behind its sprint goal and needs to stop development on one or more user stories. If the product owner is not available, the team will need to decide which user stories should be dropped from the sprint. This is a less-than-desirable situation.

> **AN EXAMPLE OF PRODUCT OWNER AVAILABILITY**
>
> On one Scrum team, the product owner spent one hour every day in the team's room. During that time, he would be working on grooming the backlog but would accept any interruptions. As a result, he was able to add user stories to the product backlog during the sprint, and he had an excellent understanding of the team's progress throughout the sprint.

If a team finds itself working with a product owner who is not highly available, this issue should be brought to the organization as an impediment.

Team Members Specializing in Certain Types of User Stories

Sometimes team members specialize in certain types of user stories, such as those having to do with one technology layer or persona. This type of specialization creates a bottleneck and reduces collective code ownership.

The number of people who can effectively work with a part of the system is sometimes jokingly called the *truck factor* in Scrum. The truck factor refers to the number of people who have to be hit by a truck before the project will come to a halt. A truck factor of one means that if one person goes on vacation or decides to take a new position, the team's velocity will be severely reduced. When one team member specializes in a certain type of user story to the point that only he can work on those user stories effectively, this creates a truck factor of one for the team. Avoid this situation!

When team members specialize in a type of user story or on a single technical tasks, this also violates the principle of collective code ownership. On a typical non-Scrum software development team, each person specializes in one technology, as illustrated in Table 8-1. This creates a truck factor of one and causes the team to be brittle in the face of change.

TABLE 8-1: A Truck Factor of One

PERSON	DATABASE	USER INTERFACE	BUSINESS LOGIC
Tim	X		
Sally		X	
Mark			X

 Collective code ownership *means that any piece of code can be extended and modified by at least two people.*

In contrast, on a Scrum team that practices collective code ownership, the team members are "generalizing specialists." While each may specialize in a single area, all have some competence in other areas, as illustrated in Table 8-2. As a result, all team members are able to work continuously on multiple areas of the product.

TABLE 8-2: Collective Code Ownership

PERSON	DATABASE	USER INTERFACE	BUSINESS LOGIC
Tim	XXX	X	X
Sally	X	XXX	X
Mark	X	X	XXX

Failure to Groom the Backlog

The product owner should be working on the backlog throughout a sprint. However, product owners sometimes create all the sprint backlogs for a release and then do only minor tuning throughout the release. Given that *agility* means being able to respond to change effectively, working with the backlog in this way is the antithesis of being agile.

A related problem is created by a product owner who copies a similar backlog or inherits a backlog from the previous owner and does not seek to understand it. In both cases, the product owner is acting in a way that causes the product backlog to deteriorate. This is deadly to a Scrum team and will lead it to develop irrelevant, low-priority, and low-business-value user stories.

Changing the Sprint Backlog After the Sprint Has Started

The product owner should typically not change the sprint backlog after a sprint has started except under exceptional circumstances. The product owner has the authority to stop and restart the sprint, but this should happen infrequently.

Both the product owner and the team should guard against adding work to the sprint backlog after the sprint planning meeting. This work should be viewed as an interruption.

Not Having Acceptance Criteria or a Clear Definition of *Done* for User Stories

At sprint demos, sometimes the team presents what it believes to be a finished user story to the product owner, but the product owner rejects the team's work because it fails to meet the acceptance criteria and places the user story back on the backlog. The product owner and the team should have a common understanding of what the team must do for a user story to be accepted by the product owner. Chapter 4 discusses acceptance criteria.

Multiple Product Backlogs

A team should not be working from multiple product backlogs. If it is, the team members will be perpetually confused about what item has the highest priority.

The rule in Scrum is that each person belongs to one and only one team, and each team has one and only one product backlog.

Multiple Product Owners

In many organizations, stakeholders throughout the company are allowed to enter items into the team's work queue. This is a significant boundary violation and is considered unacceptable in most Scrum implementations.

AN EXAMPLE OF MULTIPLE PRODUCT OWNERS

In one company, the following people were allowed to enter items into the product backlog:

➤   Two product owners

➤   The QA manager

➤   The development manager

➤   The VP of engineering

➤   A customer service manager

➤   A program manager

Not surprisingly, the product backlog was in chaos, and no one understood all the items on the backlog.

LINKING USER STORIES AND TASKS

Linking user stories and tasks is critical to maintaining a useful product backlog. Many product backlogs, particularly those managed using bug-tracking tools, contain stand-alone tasks. The top-level items on a backlog should always be user stories. The team should always be working for the customer. The focus on user stories helps to maintain this emphasis.

A team should link stories and tasks by starting with the sprint backlog in Visual Studio. Figure 8-31 shows a backlog as it might appear during the sprint planning meeting. The team then needs to follow these steps:

1. Double-click the first PBI ("Find orders"). The PBI display shown in Figure 8-32 appears.

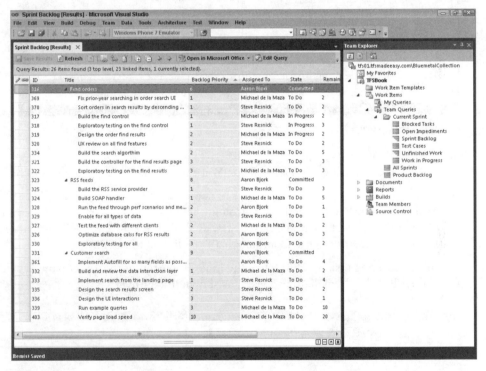

FIGURE 8-31: A sprint backlog.

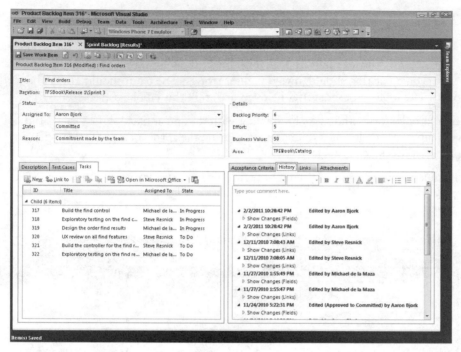

FIGURE 8-32: A PBI.

2. Click the Tasks tab shown in Figure 8-32. You can see that this particular PBI has six linked tasks.

3. To create a new task, click the New button in the upper-left corner of the Tasks tab. The Add New Linked Work Item dialog appears, as shown in Figure 8-33. This dialog allows you to enter a new task that will automatically be linked to the PBI.

4. To link an existing task to a PBI, click the Link To button in the Tasks pane. The Add Link to Product Backlog Item dialog appears, as shown in Figure 8-34.

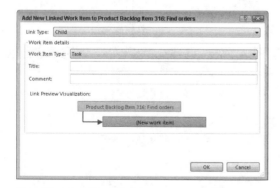

FIGURE 8-33: The Add New Linked Work Item dialog.

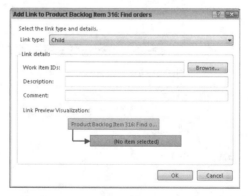

FIGURE 8-34: A dialog that lets you link an existing task to a PBI.

5. To search for a task to link to this PBI, click the Browse button in the Add Link to Product Backlog Item dialog. The Choose Linked Work Items dialog appears, as shown in Figure 8-35. This dialog lets you search for new tasks in a variety of ways.

6. In the Choose Linked Work Items dialog, enter Build in the Title Contains text box to search for tasks that contain the word "Build" in the title. TFS finds a total of six tasks.

7. Select the last task, Build the Search Algorithm. Visual Studio automatically populates the Add Link to Product Backlog Item dialog, as shown in Figure 8-36.

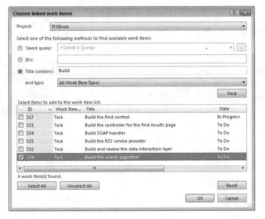

FIGURE 8-35: A dialog that lets you search for an existing task to link to a PBI.

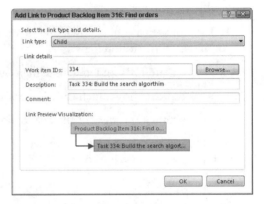

FIGURE 8-36: A dialog that is automatically populated with the task information.

8. Click OK in the Add Link to Product Backlog Item dialog to return to the PBI.

As you can see in Figure 8-37, the PBI now shows the new task.

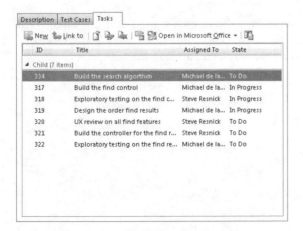

FIGURE 8-37: The PBI after the new task is added.

PBI REPORTS

Three reports in TFS are related to PBIs:

➤ Velocity

➤ Sprint burndown

➤ Release burndown

You can find these reports under Reports in the Team Explorer (see Figure 8-38). You can run each of these reports by simply double-clicking it.

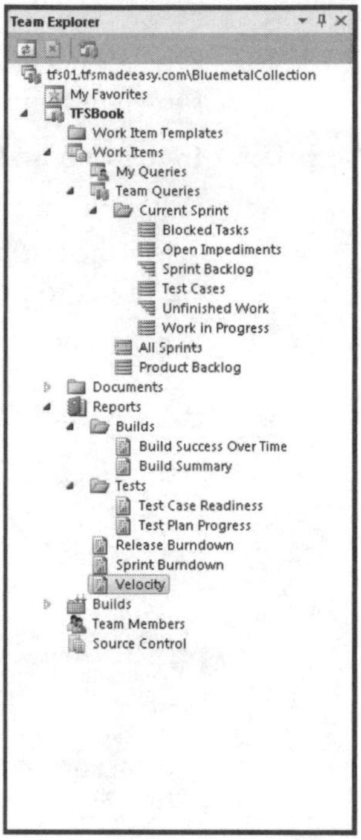

To keep the release burndown and sprint burndown reports up to date, you must do the following:

➤ Create PBIs and associate them with iterations.

➤ Indicate how much time is remaining for each task every day.

➤ Change the state of the task from to do to done.

In addition, completing the Area field for the task gives you the ability to filter the report based on this field.

To keep a velocity report relevant, you must do the following:

➤ Create PBIs and associate them with iterations.

➤ Indicate how much effort is required to complete each PBI. Effort is typically expressed in story points.

➤ Change the state of the PBI from new to done.

If you complete the Area field for the PBI, you can also filter the velocity report based on this field.

FIGURE 8-38: The PBI-related reports are shown under Reports.

SUMMARY

This chapter focuses on creating releases. It covers how to enter PBIs using Excel, the SharePoint portal, and TFS. The chapter also summarizes product backlog, user story success and failure patterns, and user story reports. Chapter 9 describes how to create and manage sprints.

Running a Sprint

WHAT'S IN THIS CHAPTER?

➤ How to create sprints.

➤ Working with PBIs.

➤ Measuring the velocity of a Scrum team.

➤ How to track burndown.

➤ Working with bugs.

This chapter examines how to run a sprint. You'll first explore how to create sprints in TFS and how to prioritize product backlog items. Then you'll learn how to measure the velocity of your Scrum team and how to use burndown charts. Finally, you'll learn about managing bugs on a Scrum project.

CREATING SPRINTS

When a new project is created, Team Foundation Server (TFS) automatically creates releases and sprints. You may need more sprints in a release than TFS creates. Eventually, you will also need more releases.

To add a new sprint, you open TFS and follow these steps:

1. Right-click the project in the Team Explorer window and select Team Project Settings ➪ Areas and Iterations. The Areas and Iterations dialog appears, as shown in Figure 9-1.

2. Click the Iteration tab and click the green plus sign (+) icon in the upper-left corner of the tab.

FIGURE 9-1: The Areas and Iterations dialog.

In Figure 9-1, you see a sprint named Sprint 7; this is a new sprint that the user added.

WORKING WITH PBIS

This section describes a process for working with PBIs. First, you'll learn about the sprint planning meeting, where the product owner presents the prioritized backlog to the team. Then you'll see how the product owner and the team work with PBIs.

The Sprint Planning Meeting

The spring planning meeting has the following essential functions:

➤ **Preparing the sprint backlog** — Prior to the planning meeting, the product owner prepares the proposed sprint backlog. The proposed sprint backlog typically consists of several more PBIs than the team usually accepts into a sprint. The next section describes how Scrum teams use velocity to decide how many stories to accept into a sprint.

➤ **Discussing user stories** — During a sprint, the product owner discusses user stories with the team. A team should spend approximately 10% of its time working with the product owner to elaborate PBIs.

➤ **Estimating PBIs** — At the beginning of the sprint planning meeting, the product owner presents the proposed sprint backlog. The team asks questions about each user story and then estimates PBIs by using Planning Poker. (Planning Poker is discussed in detail in Chapter 3.)

➤ **Creating tasks for the user stories** — During the second part of the meeting, the team creates tasks for each PBI. Examples of tasks include "Create database table," "Modify user interface," and "Write unit tests."

At the end of a sprint planning meeting, the team should be committed to a sprint backlog, and each user story should have a set of tasks associated with it.

How the Product Owner Works with PBIs

The product owner must create the product backlog, the release backlog, and the sprint backlog. This is typically a full-time job.

As the product owner develops PBIs, he or she enters them into TFS, using the procedure described in the section "Entering PBIs" in Chapter 8. The team then uses the sprint planning meeting to prioritize the user stories for the next sprint.

The product owner may use and create many artifacts while preparing and grooming the backlog. For example, if the product owner is engaged in usability studies with end users, the results of these studies might be posted on the SharePoint site associated with the project (see "Verifying That You Have a SharePoint Portal" in Chapter 8).

How a Scrum Team Works with PBIs

A Scrum team develops tasks for each PBI and associates them with the PBI in TFS. On a daily basis, team members update the hours remaining on each task and the status of each task. When every task associated with a PBI is done, the PBI is done. See "Developing the Product Backlog" in Chapter 8 for information about how to create the backlog.

During the sprint demo meeting at the end of the sprint, the team demonstrates all completed PBIs to the product owner. It does this by showing the completed software to the product owner.

> *If at any point the team believes that it will not complete a PBI that it has accepted for the sprint, the team should notify the product owner.*

MEASURING THE VELOCITY OF A SCRUM TEAM

Velocity is a poorly understood concept. Fundamentally, *velocity* is a measure of output divided by input. It is the same concept that economists refer to as *productivity*. Therefore, velocity is a measure of productivity.

> *Remember: Velocity = Output / Input*

To understand this concept, consider a hot dog vendor who runs a hot dog factory. To run the factory, he needs to complete the following tasks:

1. Clean the factory floor.

2. Maintain the machines.

3. Pay the workers.

The vendor assigns hours to each of these tasks and, throughout the week, he updates the number of remaining hours so that he can create a burndown chart. At the end of the week, he has finished his tasks and is happy that he was able to meet his sprint commitment.

How many hot dogs did the factory produce during the week? This information is not available from the data the hot dog vendor has gathered so far. To answer this question, the hot dog vendor must count the number of hot dogs his factory produces.

Similarly, a Scrum team wants to know how much software it produces. After all, the goal of a Scrum team is to increase business value by producing working software. Understanding how much working software a team is producing is a critical measure.

Like the hot dog vendor, the Scrum team needs to measure its output. Unfortunately, there is no simple way to measure the output of a software team. A hot dog vendor counts the number of hot dogs he produces. What does a software team count? One possibility is that the software team could count the number of lines of code it produces. While counting lines of code is easy, this measure suffers from a great number of shortcomings. In particular, lines of code vary widely. Some lines of code are very difficult to write, while others are trivial. Unlike hot dogs, they are not uniform. So giving equal weight to each line of code is a poor measure of productivity. One good method a software team can use to measure its productivity is to use story points, as described in the next section.

Using Story Points to Determine Velocity

In the Agile community, the best-known way to measure the productivity of a software team is to use story points. We discuss story points in detail in the "Understanding Releases" section in Chapter 4.

While using story points is the best-known way to calculate velocity, this method is not without controversy. A post on the Scrum Alliance website asked the question "What exactly is a story point?" (see http://is.gd/IAp3bN). This post points out that there are many different interpretations of story points and that these interpretations are difficult to reconcile with one another. This post generated more than 20 responses, which contained a wide variety of opinions about the interpretation of story points.

Estimating velocity using story points is extremely difficult. Despite the difficulty of estimating a team's velocity, however, there is widespread agreement in the Agile community that the best way for a team to estimate its velocity is by using story points.

If a team uses story points to measure its velocity, it needs to be careful not to artificially inflate the number of story points it assigns to a PBI. One simple way to increase a team's velocity estimate is to simply inflate the story points over time. A user story with a story point value of 8 in sprint 1 may become a user story with a story point value of 13 in sprint 10. In practice, however, if a team achieves an increase in velocity of over 60% (13 / 8 = 1.625), this will be apparent to everyone involved, whether or not story points are used. Likewise, if a team artificially inflates its velocity and achieves an increase of 60%, this will also be apparent.

One reasonable way to measure velocity is to make all the stories approximately the same size. Velocity then becomes the number of user stories completed per sprint. Making all the stories of equal size, however, requires an experienced product owner who is willing to work closely with the team throughout the sprint to develop the backlog.

How to Calculate Velocity Based on Story Points

A team can easily calculate velocity by hand. At the sprint planning meeting, the team assigns story points to each user story by using Planning Poker. (For more information on Planning Poker, see the section "Estimating Product Backlog Items" in Chapter 3.) At the end of the sprint, the team demonstrates the user stories that it completed. The velocity is simply the sum of the points for the completed user stories.

For example, consider the story points in Table 9-1. The team accepts four stories into the sprint. By using Planning Poker, the team determines that the four stories' point estimates add up to 47 (= 8 + 13 + 21 + 5). During the sprint, the team completes only three of the four user stories, so its actual velocity is 34 (= 8 + 21 + 5).

TABLE 9-1: User Stories with Story Points and Completion Information

USER STORY	STORY POINTS	COMPLETED?
1	8	Yes
2	13	No
3	21	Yes
4	5	Yes

The team then keeps track of its velocity over time, using a table similar to the one in Table 9-2. TFS does not keep track of estimated and actual velocity, so we recommend tracking this information in Excel.

TABLE 9-2: Information About Estimated and Actual Velocity

SPRINT	ESTIMATED VELOCITY	ACTUAL VELOCITY
1	110	120
2	114	108
3	108	116
4	148	127

Typically, a team will get better at estimating its velocity over time, so its estimated velocity will be closer and closer to its actual velocity. In addition, a team's actual velocity will increase over time as the team becomes more effective at developing software. This effect can be seen by plotting the estimated velocity and actual velocity figures, as shown in the Excel-created chart in Figure 9-2.

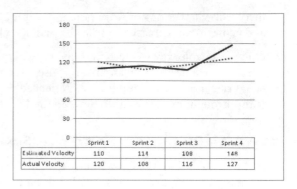

	Sprint 1	Sprint 2	Sprint 3	Sprint 4
Estimated Velocity	110	114	108	148
Actual Velocity	120	108	116	127

FIGURE 9-2: Estimated and actual velocity.

Testing Your Understanding of Velocity

To test your understanding of velocity, consider the following situations:

➤ **Situation 1** — In sprint 1, the team completes user stories with a total story point value of 100. In sprint 2, the team completes user stories with a total story point value of 100 and spends $10,000. Is the velocity of the team the same in sprint 1 and in sprint 2?

➤ **Situation 2** — In sprint 1, the team completes user stories with a total story point value of 100. In sprint 2, the team completes user stories with a total story point value of 100. Sprint 1 lasts two weeks, and sprint 2 lasted one week. Is the velocity of the team the same in sprint 1 and sprint 2?

➤ **Situation 3** — In sprint 1, the team completes user stories with a total story point value of 100. In sprint 2, the team completes user stories with a total story point value of 100. Between sprint 1 and sprint 2, the team adds two team members. Is the velocity of the team the same in sprint 1 and sprint 2?

➤ **Situation 4** — In sprint 1, the team completes user stories with a total story point value of 100. In sprint 2, the team completes user stories with a total story point value of 100 and, in addition, implements a new continuous integration system. Is the velocity of the team the same in sprint 1 and sprint 2?

➤ **Situation 5** — In sprint 1, the team completes user stories with a total story point value of 100. In sprint 2, half the team takes paid vacation time, and the team finishes user stories with a total point value of 50. Is the velocity of the team the same in sprint 1 and sprint 2?

To answer these questions, remember that velocity is output divided by input. In situation 1, the output is the same 100 story points, but the input differs. In sprint 2, the team spends an additional $10,000. As a result, the team's velocity in sprint 2 is less than its velocity in sprint 1.

In situation 2, the input dropped in half between sprint 1 and sprint 2 because the team worked only half as long. So the team's velocity is greater in the second sprint.

In situation 3, the input increased by two team members. So the team's velocity dropped between sprint 1 and sprint 2.

In situation 4, the development of the new continuous integration system is not an output. It is equivalent to installing a new machine at a hot dog factory. The new machine increases the output only if it causes the factory to increase the number of hot dogs it creates. In this situation, the team's velocity in sprint 1 is identical to the team's velocity in sprint 2.

In situation 5, the team spends less time working on the sprint backlog because half the team members are on vacation. Most teams consider time to be the input when calculating velocity because salaries are the most significant cost of running a software development team. Under this definition, the team's velocity is story points per sprint. However, if the goal is to include all inputs, including money spent on rent and software, then all the inputs are typically converted into dollars. Under this definition, the team's velocity is story points divided by dollars. Converting the input into dollars makes it clear that the input has not changed between sprint 1 and sprint 2 because the vacations are paid. As a result, the team's velocity in sprint 2 is less than the velocity in sprint 1.

The Velocity Report

The velocity report is available in the Team Explorer under Reports, as shown in Figure 9-3. Figure 9-4 shows the velocity report.

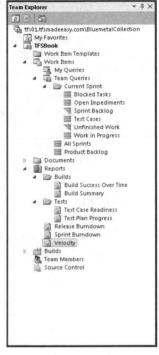

FIGURE 9-3: Selecting the velocity report.

Velocity

Indicates the amount of effort the team is completing in each sprint.

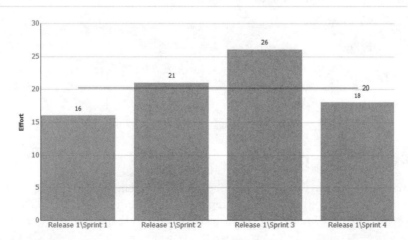

FIGURE 9-4: An example of a velocity report.

TRACKING BURNDOWN

Sprint burndown is typically defined as the number of hours remaining to complete all the tasks in a sprint. However, a team can choose to burn down story points instead of hours.

 While TFS does not directly support story point burndown, a team can implement this type of burndown chart by simply entering story points instead of hours in the Remaining Work field.

The burndown chart does not show how many hours a team has worked on a task. It shows only the amount of work remaining. This is a critical distinction between standard project management techniques and Scrum. Remember that punishing the team for failing to meet deadlines or needing more time than initially expected is verboten in Scrum.

Calculating Burndown by Hand

To generate a burndown chart, each day, team members update the number of hours remaining on every task in the sprint. The sum of the hours remaining on each task appears in the burndown chart.

For example, suppose that there are four tasks, with the remaining work estimates shown in Table 9-3. As described in the next section, the burndown chart will show that a total of 33 hours (= 3 + 5 + 5 + 20) remain to be burned down in the sprint.

TABLE 9-3: Work Estimates for the Tasks in a Sprint

TASK	HOURS REMAINING
1	3
2	5
3	5
4	20

The Sprint Burndown Chart Report

The sprint burndown chart is one of the three charts in the TFS Scrum template. Figure 9-5 (which is not related to the example in Table 9-3) shows an example of a sprint burndown chart. This example shows that the team did not complete all the tasks in the sprint. It still has 20 hours of work remaining.

Sprint Burndown

Indicates the team's progress towards completing its work for a sprint.

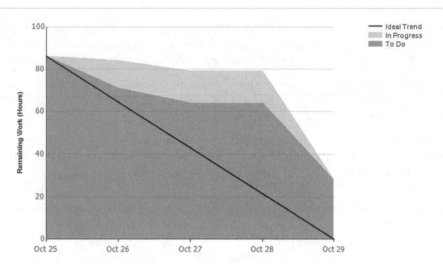

FIGURE 9-5: A sprint burndown chart.

To generate the burndown chart, a team follows these steps:

1. Assign tasks to a sprint.

2. Assign remaining work to tasks.

3. Update the remaining work daily.

4. Update the status of each task.

5. Create the burndown chart by clicking Sprint Burndown in the Team Explorer, as shown in Figure 9-6.

WORKING WITH BUGS

During a sprint, the team will encounter bugs as it develops software. Bugs are different from PBIs because they are not generated by the product owner. As a result, they often cause problems for Scrum teams that have not carefully considered how they are going to manage bugs.

This section describes how to work with bugs in TFS. First, you'll see the high-level bug workflow. This is not the only such workflow, but it is one that many Scrum teams use. Next, you'll see how to create work items from bugs and then how to track bugs.

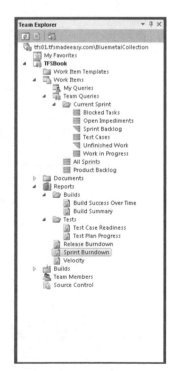

FIGURE 9-6: Generating a burndown chart.

Creating a Bug Workflow

How do Scrum teams handle bugs? The standard workflow involves fixing bugs at different stages, depending on where they occur:

➤ **Bug that pertains to a user story in the sprint** — If a bug pertains to a user story in the sprint, the team fixes it. If a user story has bugs associated with it, the team cannot deliver the user story unless the bugs are removed. This is sometimes called the "bugs first" philosophy.

➤ **Low-priority bug that pertains to a user story outside the sprint** — If a low-priority bug pertains to a user story that is *not* in the sprint, the product owner prioritizes the bug. This prevents the team from getting interrupted by bug-fixing activities.

➤ **High-priority bug that pertains to a user story outside the sprint** — If a high-priority bug pertains to a user story that is *not* in the sprint, the team fixes it. This case occurs infrequently. High-priority, out-of-sprint bugs are almost always in production.

 If the team finds itself addressing critical production bugs every sprint, the team's approach to quality is probably flawed.

The bug workflow is illustrated in Figure 9-7.

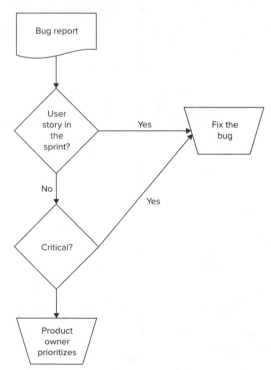

FIGURE 9-7: The typical workflow for bugs on a Scrum team.

Creating Backlog Items from Bugs

To track a bug that will be addressed during the sprint, you follow these steps:

1. In TFS, select Team ➪ New Work Item ➪ Bug, as shown in Figure 9-8.

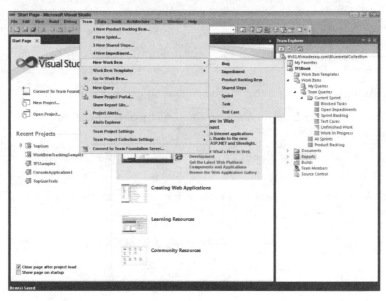

FIGURE 9-8: Creating a new bug work item.

2. Give the bug a title and place the bug into a sprint in the Iteration field, as shown in Figure 9-9.

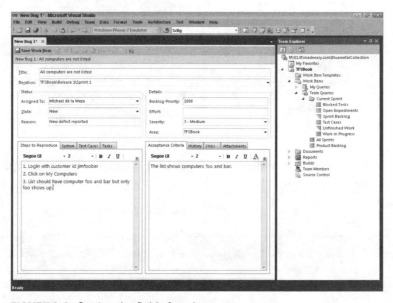

FIGURE 9-9: Setting the fields for a bug.

3. Assign the bug to a team member by using the Assigned To drop-down, as shown in Figure 9-9.

A bug is a task, so each one needs to be assigned to a team member.

4. Fill in the steps to reproduce the bug in the Steps to Reproduce tab for the bug task, as shown in Figure 9-9.

5. Complete the Acceptance Criteria tab for the bug, as shown in Figure 9-9.

6. If your team's workflow for bugs depends on the severity of the bugs, fill in the Severity field, as shown in Figure 9-9.

7. Because it is a good idea to link all bugs to user stories, click the Links tab, as shown in Figure 9-10.

8. Click on the Link To button. The Add Link to New Bug dialog appears, as shown in Figure 9-11.

FIGURE 9-10: Linking the bug to a parent user story.

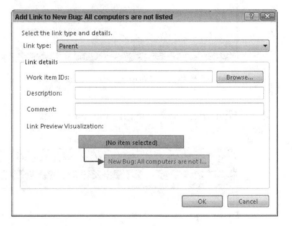

FIGURE 9-11: The Add Link to New Bug dialog.

9. Set a user story to be the parent of the bug by selecting Parent from the Link Type pull-down menu, as shown in Figure 9-11. Click the Browse button. The Choose Linked Work Items dialog appears.

By always linking a bug to a user story, you can ensure that the top-level items on the backlog are always user stories.

10. In the Choose Linked Work Items dialog, select Sprint Backlog from the Saved Query drop-down, as shown in Figure 9-12. The sprint backlog query runs, returning all work items associated with that sprint, as shown in Figure 9-13.

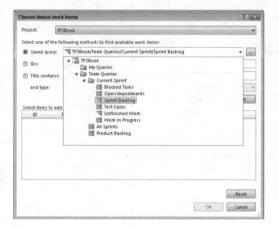

FIGURE 9-12: Running the sprint backlog query.

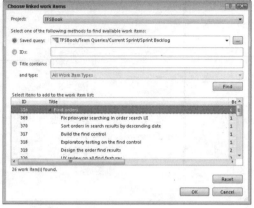

FIGURE 9-13: The sprint backlog query returns all items associated with the sprint backlog.

11. Select the appropriate user story in Figure 9-14. TFS automatically populates the Work Item IDs and Description fields, and it shows a diagram that describes the relationship between the user story and the new bug. Click OK.

12. Finish the bug by completing the Acceptance Criteria tab. TFS saves this information for future reference.

The bug report contains several other components, including a System tab that you use to store information about the build on which the error was found, and an Attachments tab that allows you to attach documents (such as screenshots) to the bug report.

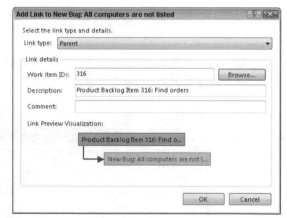

FIGURE 9-14: TFS populating the Work Item IDs and Description fields.

Tracking Bugs

In this section, you will learn how to create a query that allows you to track bugs in TFS. Follow these steps:

1. In Visual Studio, select Team ⇨ New Query, as shown in Figure 9-15. A query definition screen appears.

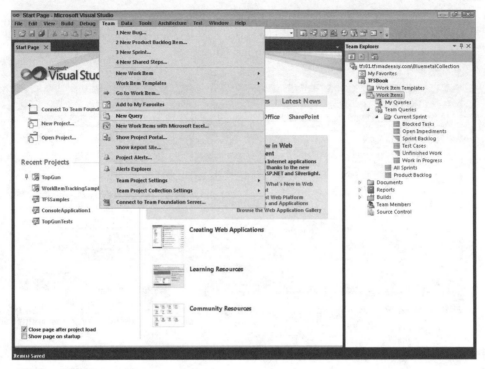

FIGURE 9-15: Creating a new query.

2. Choose Bug from the Work Item Type pull-down, as shown in Figure 9-16, and delete the State clause by selecting the Delete Clauses menu item, as shown in Figure 9-17.

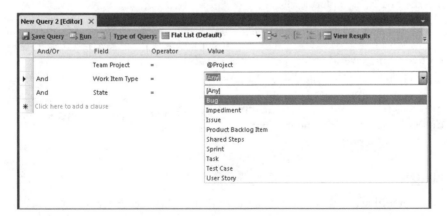

FIGURE 9-16: Choosing Bug under Work Item Type.

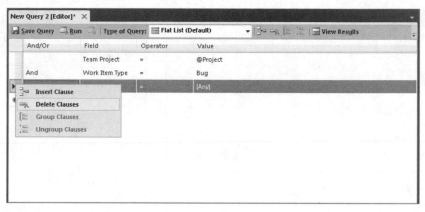

FIGURE 9-17: Deleting the State clause.

3. Run the query by clicking the Run button in the New Query tab. You see all the bugs, as shown in Figure 9-18. You can save this query and rerun it periodically to see how many bugs have been reported.

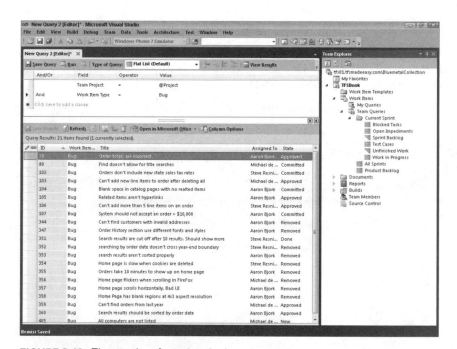

FIGURE 9-18: The results of running the bug query.

4. Click Save Query. When the Save Query As dialog appears, name the query Bugs, as shown in Figure 9-19. Click Save. This query appears under My Queries in the Team Explorer, as shown in Figure 9-20.

You will use the Bugs query in the next section to create a custom bug report in Excel.

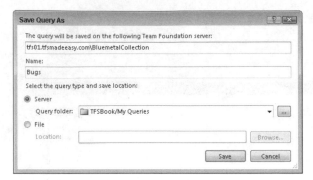

FIGURE 9-19: Saving a custom query.

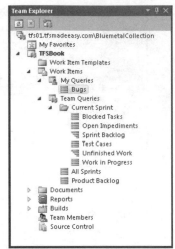

FIGURE 9-20: The new query in the Team Explorer.

Bug Reports

The Scrum template does not ship with any bug-specific reports. However, creating one in Excel takes just a few steps:

1. Connect to the TFS instance by clicking Team ➪ New List. The Connect to Team Project dialog appears, as shown in Figure 9-21.

2. Click the New List button on the upper left of the Team tab. The New List dialog appears.

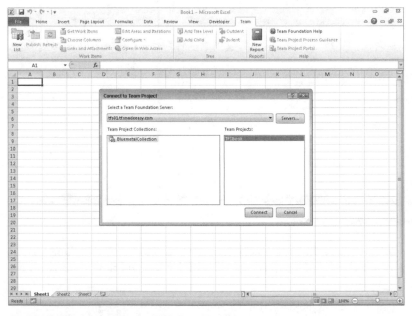

FIGURE 9-21: Connecting to TFS from Excel.

3. Select the Bugs query that you created in the previous section, as shown in Figure 9-22. Excel runs the query and displays a table similar to the one shown in Figure 9-23.

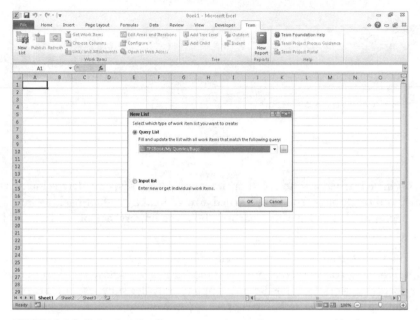

FIGURE 9-22: Selecting the Bugs custom query that you created in the previous section.

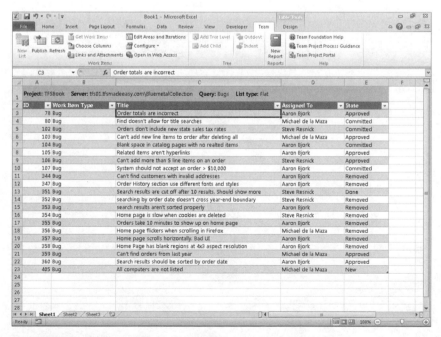

FIGURE 9-23: The result of running the Bugs custom query in Excel.

4. Click on Summarize with PivotTable in Excel's Design tab to create a custom report, as shown in Figure 9-24. Excel now creates and displays the PivotTable.

FIGURE 9-24: Creating a custom report.

SUMMARY

In this chapter, you have learned how to create sprints, prioritize PBIs, calculate velocity, create a burndown chart, and track bugs. You have learned how to load a product backlog into TFS using a variety of techniques. You have also learned about the importance of velocity and how it is calculated and tracked in TFS.

This chapter describes the burndown chart in detail, and you learned that both story points and hours can be burned down. You learned about the standard bug workflow that Scrum teams use and how TFS supports this workflow. The Scrum template provides support for all these key aspects of Scrum. If you want to extend the capabilities of TFS, you can export to Excel.

Chapter 10 delves into the retrospective, one of the most important and valuable activities in Scrum.

10

The Retrospective

WHAT'S IN THIS CHAPTER?

➤ Understanding practices related to retrospectives.

➤ How to use TFS to answer the three retrospective questions.

A retrospective takes place at the end of a sprint. It provides an opportunity for the team to reflect on what has gone well, what has gone poorly, and what the team wants to change. The retrospective is a key component of the inspect-and-adapt Agile framework.

Retrospectives give Scrum teams an opportunity to learn from their mistakes and successes. During a retrospective meeting, which generally lasts three hours, the team asks meta-questions about how effectively it is producing business value, with the intention of implementing changes that increase velocity and team health. A retrospective takes place at the end of a sprint. All members of the team, with the possible exception of the product owner, attend the retrospective.

A team will often generate a prioritized list of impediments and action items during a retrospective. This list typically contains two types of impediments: impediments that can be addressed entirely within the team, such as creating an automated build process, and impediments that must be addressed by the wider company, such as reducing the number of times the team is interrupted. The ScrumMaster takes any changes that require company involvement to the company.

This chapter describes common practices related to retrospectives and how the Team Foundation Server (TFS) Scrum template supports them.

COMMON PRACTICES RELATED TO RETROSPECTIVES

Most retrospectives are structured to answer three questions:

➤ What worked?

➤ What didn't work?

➤ What will we do differently?

This chapter addresses each of these questions separately and discusses some of the practices Scrum teams use to answer them.

Answering "What Worked?"

Teams typically begin a retrospective by focusing on what worked. The purpose of asking "What worked?" is to reinforce good practices and values. After all, if the team spends more of its time doing what works, it will spend less time doing what does not work.

One way for a team to identify what worked is to examine all the user stories that were completed by the team during the sprint and explicitly identify what drove their success. A simple brainstorming technique — such as having each team member write the reasons for success on index cards and then grouping the index cards — is often enough to start a good conversation about the reasons for success.

PRACTICES FOR DETERMINING WHAT WORKED

Here are some other practices a team can use to determine what worked:

➤ Each team member can identify what moment of the sprint was particularly energizing or joyful for him or her.

➤ Each team member can describe the team's greatest success during the sprint.

➤ The team can create a poster that captures the best experiences that the team had during the sprint.

Answering "What Didn't Work?"

To determine what did not go well during a sprint, teams often examine unfinished user stories and the burndown chart. Why were the user stories not completed? Were the estimates for each user story and task accurate?

The shape of the burndown chart often gives clues about what may have gone wrong with a sprint. A burndown chart that is flat or increases during the start of the sprint is often an indication that the user stories were poorly defined. A burndown chart spiking up several times during the sprint suggests that the team was surprised by the technical difficulty of some of the tasks.

Another technique is to have each team member list as many problems as possible on index cards, using one index card per problem. The team members then briefly consolidate the cards and eliminate duplicates. Finally, the team sorts the problems and thinks about how to eliminate the most harmful problems.

Answering "What Will We Do Differently?"

After the team has explored what went well and what did not, it creates a list of action items or changes that it plans to implement. One way to identify the most fruitful changes is to use the *5 Whys* technique, which Toyota Corporation developed to uncover the root cause of a problem.

The goal of the 5 Whys technique is to identify the root cause of a problem. To use it, a team states the problem and then asks *why* five times. For example, say that a team's server is slow. The team might come up with the following answers in the 5 Whys process:

➤ **Why?** — Because it is running out of memory.

➤ **Why?** — Because there is a memory leak.

➤ **Why?** — Because there is a bug in the code.

➤ **Why?** — Because we did not test it properly.

➤ **Why?** — Because we have yet to implement automated testing.

The team can then decide at what level of abstraction to address the problem. The changes that the team chooses to implement to address problems in the sprint become part of the product backlog. The product owner prioritizes these changes. For the slow server example, the team might choose to begin using some of the testing features in Visual Studio to automate testing. If a team wants to simply record the existence of an impediment, without committing to taking any action to remove it, the team should create a new impediment in Visual Studio so that it will appear in the open impediments list.

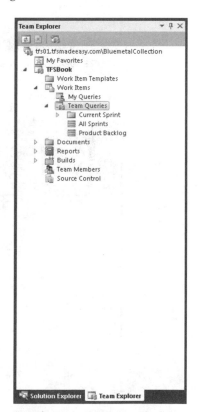

FIGURE 10-1: The Team Explorer window.

In determining what to do differently next time, teams often consider improvements in engineering practices, changes in how they interact with the product owner during the sprint, and changes in the team's charter.

SCRUM TEMPLATE SUPPORT FOR THE THREE RETROSPECTIVE QUESTIONS

A sprint work item directly supports the three key retrospective questions with prompts in the Retrospective tab in Visual Studio. To locate the Retrospective tab, follow these steps:

1. Find the project in Visual Studio's Team Explorer.

2. Expand Team Queries. The Team Explorer window should look similar to Figure 10-1.

3. Click All Sprints. You should see a window similar to that shown in Figure 10-2.

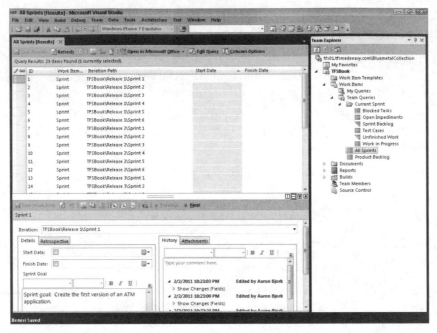

FIGURE 10-2: Query results.

4. Click on one of the sprint work items. The screen should look similar to Figure 10-3.

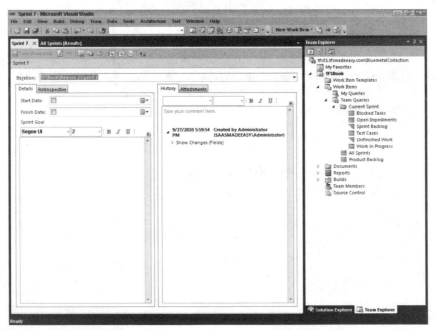

FIGURE 10-3: A sprint work item.

5. Click the Retrospective tab. The screen should look similar to Figure 10-4. As you can see, the Scrum template prompts the team to answer the three key retrospective questions.

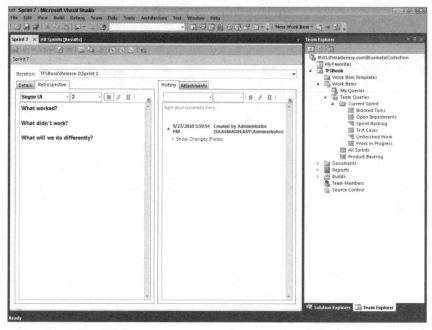

FIGURE 10-4: The Retrospective tab.

When the team has answered these three questions (by using the 5 Whys technique, for example) and the retrospective is complete, the results of the team's findings are permanently stored in the Retrospective tab.

The following sections describe how the team should go about answering the three questions.

To record the results of a retrospective, try projecting Visual Studio on the wall in the room in which you're holding the retrospective. This way, everyone on the team can see the work within Visual Studio.

How to Answer the "What Worked?" Question

The "What worked?" question is, surprisingly, often the most difficult to answer. Teams tend to focus on failures instead of successes, but the Scrum method focuses on successes.

To answer the "What worked?" question, a team should look at finished backlog and bug items as well as the burndown chart. You can easily access this information by using TFS. During the retrospective, consider projecting TFS on the screen so that everyone can see these items.

For each product backlog item (PBI) successfully completed, identify what engineering practices and team practices contributed to the success. The engineering practices and artifacts might include the following:

➤ An automated build

➤ Unit testing

➤ User interface testing

➤ Scripts to automatically create test environments

➤ Automated deployment

➤ Continuous integration

➤ Source control

➤ Dependency management

➤ Pair programming

➤ Code reviews

➤ Refactoring

This list contains only a small sample of engineering practices that a team might implement.

 Consider creating a standard list that you can work through for each successfully completed PBI.

The team might choose to reinforce practices such as the following:

➤ Agreeing on the definition of *done*

➤ Clearly identifying the product owner and ensuring that this person is highly available

➤ Ensuring excellent team communication

➤ Holding effective daily standup meetings

➤ Using big, visible charts

Once the team has worked through all the completed PBIs, it should reflect on which engineering and team practices have contributed most. It should list these practices in the "What worked?" section of the Retrospective tab. For example, the team might enter the following:

➤ Helpful acceptance tests developed by the product owner and presented at the sprint planning meeting

➤ One-touch deployment

➤ Automated suite of end-user functionality tests

When the team has looked at the completed PBIs and bug items, it might turn to the burndown chart. The burndown chart is likely to move up and down at varying rates. The team should examine the times when a lot of work is being burned down and use that data to spur discussion about what went well during those periods.

Many factors can contribute to a favorable burndown chart. Here are some of them:

➤ Effective team collaboration

➤ A build process that ensures that no one can break the build

➤ An excellent discussion during the sprint planning meeting

➤ Constant refactoring

It is important to use the burndown chart to prompt discussion but be careful not to rely too heavily on it. There is a lot of variance in software development. The team should take care not to assign too much meaning to short-term successes. In addition, an over-emphasis on any particular metric will lead to incorrect conclusions. For example, if the team believes that its goal is to create good-looking burndown charts, this could lead to dysfunctional behavior such as overestimating the effort required to complete a story.

Finally, the team should examine the sprint goal in the Details tab for a sprint work item (see Figure 10-5).

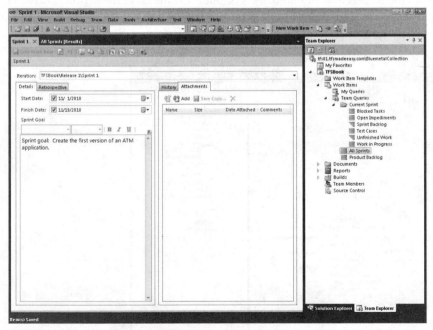

FIGURE 10-5: A sprint work item.

If, during the review meeting with the product owner, the team reported that the sprint goal had been met, this should be noted in the "What worked?" section of the Retrospective tab. The team might also want to address any reasons for success that have not already been covered by examining the backlog and bug items, as well as the burndown chart.

How to Answer the "What Didn't Work?" Question

Three queries are particularly helpful in answering the "What didn't work?" question:

- ➤ The blocked tasks query
- ➤ The unfinished work query
- ➤ The work in progress query

For each of these queries, the team should ask "Why?": "Why are there blocked tasks?" "Why is there unfinished work?" and "Why is there work in progress?" If the answer to any of these questions is not immediately apparent, you might promote discussion by using a facilitation technique such as the 5 Whys process described earlier.

For blocked tasks, the team should ask why the tasks have been blocked and what can be done to unblock them. Sometimes the team is able to unblock tasks, but for some tasks the ScrumMaster may need to ask other people in the company for support. Figure 10-6 shows an example of a blocked task.

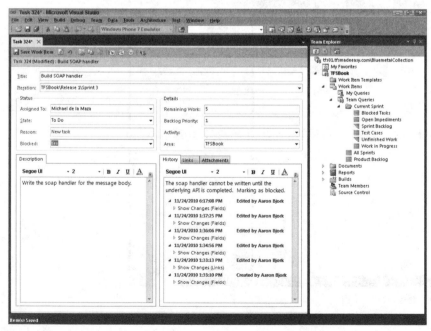

FIGURE 10-6: A blocked task.

The team may want to consider why it was unable to complete unfinished work and work in progress. Here are some possibilities:

➤ The team underestimated the effort needed to complete the task.

➤ The team was interrupted.

➤ The team underestimated the effort required for another task, which prevented the team from completing this task.

➤ The team did not reorganize itself effectively during the sprint.

➤ The team did not know that there was unfinished work.

Figure 10-7 shows an example of an unfinished work query.

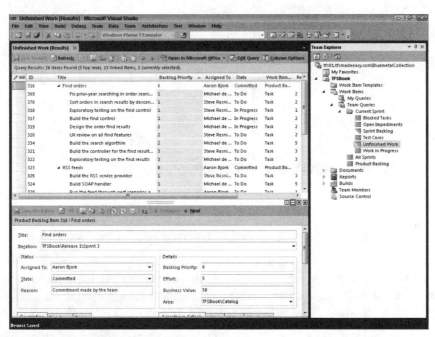

FIGURE 10-7: An unfinished work query.

The goal in examining unfinished work and work in progress is to spark a wide-ranging discussion about the effectiveness of the team. The goal is not to blame or judge any particular team member; rather, it is to improve the business value generated by the team.

As when it answered the "What worked?" question, the team may also want to examine the burndown chart when answering the "What didn't work?" question. Regions of the chart which show that work is not being burned will focus the team's attention on periods of reduced velocity and will prompt discussion about what caused this reduction.

If the team reported to the product owner that the sprint goal was not met, this should be noted in the "What didn't work?" section of the Retrospective tab. This will spur further discussion if the team has not already fully explored why it failed to meet the sprint goal.

The team should use the impediments list to capture all the impediments it identifies during the retrospective. Figure 10-8 shows an example of an impediments list.

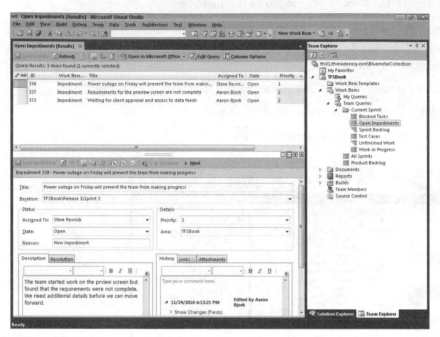

FIGURE 10-8: An impediments list.

How to Answer the "What Will We Do Differently?" Question

Once the team has fully explored what went well and what did not go well during the sprint, it works together to determine what it will do differently during the next sprint. Agile teams "inspect and adapt." In answering the first two key retrospective questions, the team inspects its work system. In answering this third question, the team addresses how to best adapt its work system.

As the team considers how to adapt, many of the changes it chooses to make will fall into the following categories:

➤ **Improvements in engineering practices** — The team might choose to adopt an engineering practice such as test-driven development.

➤ **Adjustments to the team's charter** — Enhancing the definition of *done* is an example of such a change.

➤ **Changes to the organization** — Changing the number of people in a software development group is an example of an organizational change.

➤ **Adoption of new cultural norms** — An example of a new cultural norm might be choosing not to make cutting remarks, even in jest.

Changes in engineering practices often involve learning about new features in TFS and Visual Studio. If the team chooses to improve its testing procedures, it may choose to explore the functionality of Visual Studio's Test Manager and Lab Manager. A team using TFS and Visual Studio should stay within the tool to take advantage of the tightly integrated development, build, test, and source control environment.

Adjustments to the team's charter and changes to the organization may change the way the team works with TFS. For example, if the team is geographically distributed across time zones, managing the build may be especially complicated, and this organization may force changes in engineering practices. In order to maintain shared understanding across space and time, a team might also choose to create new queries or reports.

New cultural norms are typically beyond the scope of the Scrum template. However, if you find a creative way to support a cultural change using the Scrum template, Visual Studio, or TFS, please write a short note about it to us, at michael@hearthealthyscrum.com.

SUMMARY

The retrospective is a key component of a team's practice. During this meeting, the team learns from its successes and failures and figures out how to adapt.

Through its preconfigured queries, charts, and reports, the Scrum template supports the retrospective in a variety of ways. In particular, a team should consider using the following features in the Scrum template during a retrospective:

➤ The Details tab for a sprint work item

➤ The Retrospective tab for a sprint work item

➤ The blocked tasks, open impediments, unfinished work, and work in progress queries under Team Queries

➤ The burndown chart

The team might also want to access other features, such as the product backlog and the sprint backlog.

11

Improving Scrum by Using Spikes

WHAT'S IN THIS CHAPTER?

➤ Understanding spikes.

➤ Understanding the two types of spikes.

➤ How to execute a spike on your team.

Estimating new work from your product backlog is often a difficult and daunting task. At any stage of the project, your team may find itself unclear about how to design or implement a piece of functionality. The new functionality might be a particularly complex problem, or it might have multiple dependencies that make the design more complicated than other parts of the product.

When your team finds itself facing significant unknowns, continuing with traditional sprints as described in the previous chapters of this book can lead to bigger problems. Sprints are successful when a team has clear goals and clear requirements. When one or both of these two things are not clear, the team needs to find a new way to work until both are back in focus. Scrum deals with this lack of clarity with a time-boxed exercise known as a *spike*. In this chapter, you will learn how to use and run spikes with Team Foundation Server (TFS) and the Microsoft Visual Studio Scrum 1.0 process template.

WHAT IS A SPIKE?

A *spike* is a time-boxed technical investigation that is meant to produce the answer to a problem that is blocking a team. As with any other iteration of work in Scrum, the goal of a spike is to produce value. However, a spike is different from a sprint in that the goal is not to produce value for customers. Instead, a spike produces value for the team. A spike provides the team with information needed to help make good decisions.

THE ORIGINS OF SPIKES

Ward Cunningham is a pioneer in design patterns and Extreme Programming (XP), and Kent Beck is creator of XP and one of the original signatories of the Agile Manifesto. Together, Cunningham and Beck coined the term *spike* on the C2.com wiki (see http://c2.com/cgi/wiki?SpikeSolution). The term emerged from their efforts to find a simple indicator of whether they were on the right track to solving a problem.

Spikes are useful when a team does not have enough information to move forward in a predictable manner. Scrum is about predictability and cadence. As you saw in Chapter 3, the Scrum framework aims to reduce and minimize risk by time-boxing events and breaking down work into smaller, manageable pieces.

It is common for items further down the product backlog to have higher risk and less detail than items at the top of the backlog. Your team learns new information as it progresses through sprints. New requirements emerge, and existing requirements evolve. Figure 11-1 illustrates this situation. Product backlog items (PBIs) lower on the backlog have a higher degree of uncertainty than PBIs at the top of the backlog

By using a spike, your team can avoid spending weeks studying, documenting, and researching areas of high risk or high uncertainty on the product backlog. A spike allows your team to dig into the details of the problem and learn quickly so it can return to producing value for its customers.

Priority	Product Backlog	Level of Certainty
1	PBI	High
2	PBI	High
3	PBI	High
4	PBI	High
5	PBI	Medium
6	PBI	Medium
7	PBI	Low
8	PBI	Medium
9	PBI	Low
10	PBI	Low

FIGURE 11-1: Requirements from a product backlog.

When a PBI contains unknown elements that prevent the team from producing a usable estimate, the team should delay the PBI until it has time to execute a spike to investigate the unknown elements. This approach enables the product owner to prioritize the research of the product backlog separately from the implementation.

A team should prioritize spikes ahead of related PBIs because spikes allow the team to create a more reliable estimate for the implementation of the item. That is, a team's chances of success increase greatly when the team has time to execute a spike.

SPIKE GOALS

What your team produces at the end of a spike can take many different forms. If a spike is about researching performance issues in the product, the result of the spike may be a set of performance benchmarks collected from different layers of the product. If the spike is about gaining clarity on vague requirements or customer scenarios, the result of the spike might be a storyboard of the scenario coupled with customer feedback. Whatever form the result takes, the goal of the spike is to unblock the team so it can continue to make progress against the product backlog. Common spike goals include the following:

➤ An architectural document

➤ A detailed design document

➤ A prototype for a specific piece of functionality

➤ Customer feedback on a prototype or storyboard

Make sure your team sets clear and achievable goals before starting a spike. Just as acceptance criteria define the finish line for each PBI, a spike goal defines what a team will set out to achieve. Without a clearly defined goal, a team can easily lose focus and lose track of the problem and solution. Remember, the reason for having a spike in the first place is to unblock the team. You want to get your team back to delivering tangible customer value from the product backlog as soon as possible.

TYPES OF SPIKES

Two types of spikes are common in Scrum: spikes between sprints and spikes during a sprint. Figure 11-2 illustrates a spike between sprints. Figure 11-3 illustrates a spike during a sprint. The following sections discuss these two types of spikes in more detail.

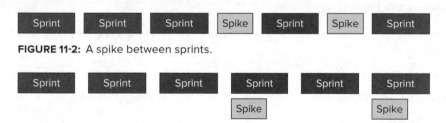

FIGURE 11-2: A spike between sprints.

FIGURE 11-3: A spike during a sprint.

Spikes Between Sprints

A spike planned between sprints is time-boxed just like a sprint. However, spikes are usually shorter than sprints. You want your team to return to producing value for customers through sprints as soon as possible. Long spikes can distract the team and take focus away from producing value.

A good rule of thumb when deciding on the length of a spike is that a spike should be half the length of a sprint — or less. If your team operates on four-week sprints, a one- to two-week spike is probably appropriate. If your team operates on two-week sprints, a spike length of one week or less makes more sense. The one exception to this rule is if your team is operating on one-week sprints. In this case, a one-week spike is appropriate. Anything shorter than one week likely does not give your team the time it needs to dig into the problem it is trying to solve. Ultimately, your team must decide what is best in each situation.

A spike planned between sprints should involve all members of your team. You want the entire team to learn from the spike, and the best way for team members to learn is to be involved. Depending on the size of your team, this can often be difficult to achieve, but it is a good principle to keep in mind.

If you do not have work for the entire team during the spike, it might be appropriate to switch to using a spike during a sprint rather than running a spike between sprints.

It is good practice to continue with the standard sprint meetings and cadence during a spike. Each meeting should be condensed and shortened to accommodate the length of the spike, but the intent of each meeting is the same as in a sprint. Your team holds an abbreviated sprint planning meeting (now called a spike planning meeting) to establish the goal of the spike. Daily standups continue throughout the spike so your team can share progress and achievements. You use the regular standup format, with each team member contributing what he or she has accomplished, what he or she has planned next, and anything that might be impeding progress. Finally, your team holds an abbreviated sprint review meeting (now called a spike review meeting) in which the team reviews what it accomplished and learned.

Guidelines for Spikes Between Sprints

Keep in mind the following guidelines when running a spike between sprints:

- ➤ Establish clear start and end dates.
- ➤ Ensure that the spike is no longer than half the length of your sprints (except in the case of one-week sprints).
- ➤ Establish a clear goal and set of deliverables.
- ➤ Involve all members of your team.
- ➤ Hold daily standups during the spike.

Creating a Spike Between Sprints

To create a spike between sprints, follow these steps:

1. From within the Team Explorer, right-click your team project and select Team Project Settings ⇨ Areas and Iterations. The Areas and Iterations dialog appears, as shown in Figure 11-4.

FIGURE 11-4: Adding a spike between sprints.

2. In the Iteration tab of the Areas and Iterations dialog, select the Release 1 node to add a spike within this release. Then click the Add a Child Node button in the toolbar at the top of the dialog. TFS adds a new node for your spike under Release 1.

3. Add a name for the spike, prefixing the iteration name with the word *Spike*. Figure 11-5 shows a new spike named Spike - Drag and Drop.

FIGURE 11-5: A new spike.

4. Use the arrow buttons at the top of the dialog to move the spike to the correct location. Figure 11-6 shows the new spike occurring between sprint 4 and sprint 5.

5. Click Close to close the Areas and Iterations dialog.

6. Right-click the Work Items node in the Team Explorer and select New Work Item ⇨ Sprint, as shown in Figure 11-7. TFS opens a new work item form, as shown in Figure 11-8.

7. In the Iteration text box on the new work item form, select the spike iteration you just created.

FIGURE 11-6: A spike between sprints 4 and 5.

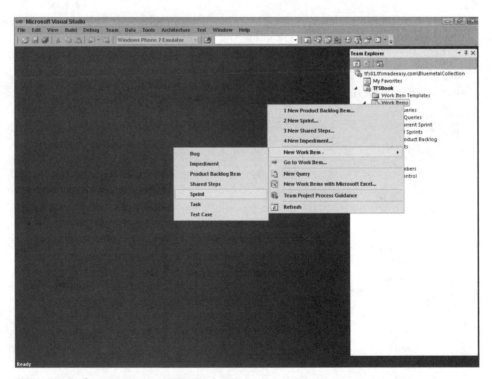

FIGURE 11-7: Creating a new sprint work item.

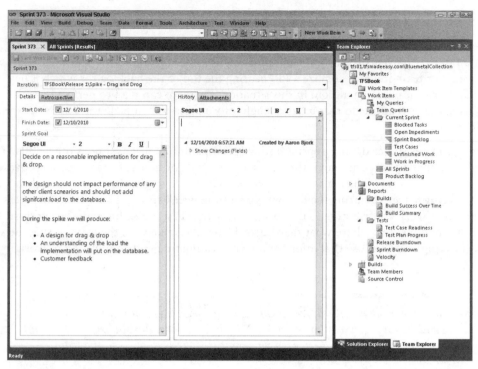

FIGURE 11-8: Spike details.

8. Enter start and end dates for the spike in the Start Date and Finish Date drop-downs.

9. Enter a goal for the spike into the Sprint Goal field.

10. Save the sprint work item.

11. Adjust any existing sprint work item dates to ensure that none of them overlap the boundaries of the new spike. You do this by running the all sprints work item query and editing sprint work items that overlap.

STARTING A PROJECT WITH SPIKES

A team decided to start a project with a series of one-week spikes rather than a traditional sprint. This project had a level of uncertainty, and the team wanted clarity before starting. The first three weeks of the project were dedicated to one-week spikes. The team built prototypes, wrote design documents, and uncovered key details on high-risk PBIs. At the end of the spikes, the team was ready to begin work on the first sprint, and it had a higher level of confidence about the implementation and strategy. Some teams refer to a spike before the first sprint as *sprint 0*.

Spikes During a Sprint

Spikes during a sprint are appropriate when a team needs to learn something specific about a PBI that prevents the team from estimating that PBI during sprint planning. For example, your team might recognize a PBI nearing the top of the backlog for which it has uncertainty about implementation. In this situation, the team can plan to perform a spike on the PBI during the next sprint so that it has enough information to complete the PBI in the sprint that follows.

A team estimates spikes during a sprint during sprint planning, just as it does other PBIs. The difference is that a team does not estimate a spike in effort or hours; instead, it time-boxes a spike to a specific period during the sprint. For example, you might choose two members of your team to perform a spike during the first week of a three-week sprint. Those team members should have no other work contributing to the sprint during that first week. Instead, they perform a spike. When they're done, they share what they learned from the spike with the team during the sprint review meeting and then use that information when estimating and committing to work in the next sprint.

> *When executing a spike during a sprint, be sure other sprint work is not dependent on the results of the spike. You need to commit to work in the sprint during sprint planning. Any learning from the spike is applied to the team's next sprint.*

Guidelines for Spikes During a Sprint

Keep in mind the following guidelines for spikes during a sprint:

➤ Time-box a spike for a period of time during the sprint.

➤ Ensure that your team is clear on who is participating in the spike.

➤ Ensure that the spike has a clear goal and a clear set of deliverables.

➤ Ensure that team members participating in the spike continue to attend and participate in daily standups.

Creating a Spike During a Sprint

To create a spike for completion during a sprint, follow these steps:

1. In the Team Explorer, right-click the Work Items node and select New Work Item ⇨ Product Backlog Item, as shown in Figure 11-9. TFS opens a new PBI form, as shown in Figure 11-10.

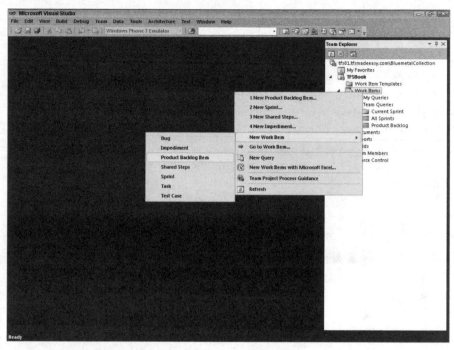

FIGURE 11-9: Creating a new PBI.

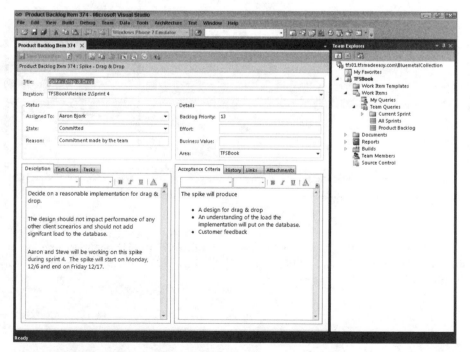

FIGURE 11-10: A spike during a sprint.

2. In the Title field of the new PBI form, enter a title for the spike, prefixed with the word *Spike*. Figure 11-10 shows a new spike named Spike - Drag & Drop that the team has committed to complete in sprint 4.

3. Enter a goal for the spike in the Description field.

4. During sprint planning, decide the duration of the spike and who from your team will work on it. Set the Assigned To field to the team member leading the spike and note the length of the spike in the Description field.

5. Link the spike to any related PBIs by selecting the Links tab and clicking the Link To button on the links toolbar. The Add Link to Product Backlog Item dialog appears, as shown in Figure 11-11.

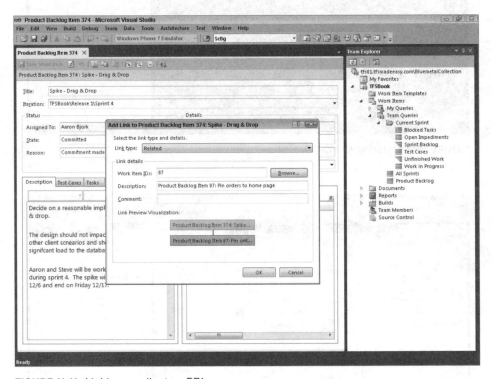

FIGURE 11-11: Linking a spike to a PBI.

6. Select Related from the Link Type drop-down and enter the ID of the PBI being linked, as shown in Figure 11-11. Click OK. Figure 11-12 shows the result: a spike linked to a PBI during a sprint.

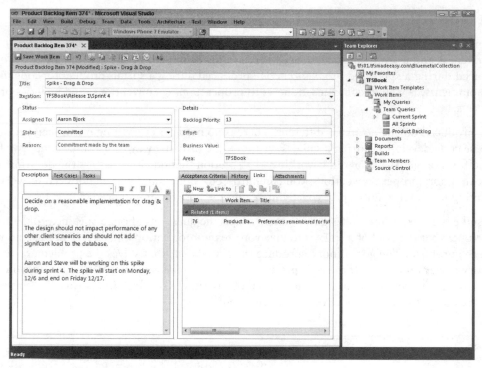

FIGURE 11-12: A spike linked to a PBI.

EXECUTING A SPIKE

The most common way to execute a spike is to create a small prototype, or program that demonstrates the functionality in question. You can read and study different approaches, but most people find that nothing helps them understand a problem more than writing working code.

BUILDING PROTOTYPES AS PART OF A SPRINT

On a recent project, a team came across a PBI that it was unsure how to implement. The scenario involved customers dragging and dropping items in order on a list. Solving this problem seemed simple at first. However, the team was conflicted about the correct approach to implement. It wanted to ensure that it did not affect performance in other areas of the product.

To gain clarity, the team added to its next sprint a spike that aimed to build three different prototypes of the drag-and-drop functionality. After the prototypes were completed, the team presented them to customers for feedback on the design and user experience of each. The learning gained from building the prototypes and the feedback provided by customers made the correct implementation obvious. In the next sprint, the team implemented the drag-and-drop PBI and delivered the functionality desired.

Code Quality

When writing code for a spike, you obviously want the code to work so you can evaluate its effectiveness and learn from it. However, there is a big difference between *throwaway code* produced during a spike and *production code* produced during a sprint. Production code includes rich comments, is well documented, adheres to proper naming conventions, and includes proper unit tests.

Code produced during a spike is different. There is no need for everything mentioned previously because code developed during a spike is written to be thrown away. With spike code, you focus your efforts on getting something working — a solution that quickly answers the question at hand. You can ignore proper conventions, you can hard-code values, and you do not need to worry about validating user input. With spike code, you can do the bare minimum needed to achieve the goal.

The spike is an experiment, designed to answer specific questions about a specific problem. Remember that the goal of a spike is to give your team information and experience to know how to solve the problem. The goal is not to produce the actual code that solves the problem, or to produce an ivory-tower prototype. If the code produced during a spike is particularly valuable, you can share it with the team, check it in as documentation, or save it to a research folder. Just remember not to treat the code as anything more than an experiment.

 Be careful not to use spikes as an excuse to avoid disciplined development practices common to all high-performing software teams.

Architectural Slices

Layers are a common architectural design pattern for structuring applications. Each layer in the architecture has a different responsibility. For example, a common layer in all software is the presentation layer. This layer is responsible for presenting the user interface to the user of the software. When possible, you want your spikes to slice through all the architectural layers in your product. The more layers your spikes slice through, the more your team will learn.

It is easy to design or prototype a solution in a single architectural layer; success is usually very high. However, when that solution begins to interact with a new layer in the product, flaws often appear in what before appeared to be a sound design or implementation.

A spike is meant to provide as much information to the team as possible. By crossing architectural layers, you can be assured that the solution your team chooses will not crumble when it is integrated into the full product. For this reason, spikes are designed to be thin end-to-end slices that run through the entire product. Conducting a spike in Scrum is akin to driving an actual spike through a set of boards. Figure 11-13 illustrates this concept.

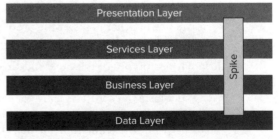

FIGURE 11-13: A spike cutting across architectural layers.

SUMMARY

There are times in every software project when the team needs to step back from the product and think deeply about a problem it is facing. The team needs time to experiment and test various approaches. It needs time to try, fail, and try again. Sprints are not appropriate for this type of activity because a sprint is based on a commitment to a set of known activities. A team cannot commit to something it does not understand.

In this chapter, you have seen how you can use spikes to gain clarity and understanding when faced with uncertainty about items on your product backlog. Throughout this book, you have learned how to implement Scrum using TFS and the Microsoft Visual Studio Scrum 1.0 process template.

As stated in Chapter 1, the Agile Manifesto is the starting point for understanding the principles on which Scrum is based. The four high-level values from the manifesto frame the methodology:

➤ Individuals and interactions over processes and tools

➤ Working software over comprehensive documentation

➤ Customer collaboration over contract negotiation

➤ Responding to change over following a plan

The first value statement of the manifesto states clearly that people are more valuable than tools. The tools described in this book will not bring success to a software project unless they are used by a committed team of people who value each other and customers. Tools do not build great software; teams do. We hope you enjoy and have fun implementing Scrum on your team and are able to delight your customers along the way.

Working with Scrum Assessments

WHAT'S IN THIS CHAPTER?

➤ Using assessment templates.

➤ Looking at a sample assessment.

➤ Using checklists for the product owner and ScrumMaster.

Continuous assessment is a key part of doing Scrum successfully. Creating checklists of desired behavior is an excellent way to achieve shared understanding about what is working and what is not working. This appendix provides assessment worksheets for the daily Scrum, the demo meeting, the retrospective meeting, and the planning meeting. The appendix also includes a sample assessment that is based on an actual assessment provided to a client who was just starting to implement Scrum.

USING ASSESSMENT TEMPLATES

This section provides assessments for the daily Scrum, the demo, the retrospective, and the planning meeting. You should print out these assessments and fill in each one during the appropriate meeting. At the end of the meeting, you can post the assessment on the SharePoint portal. The ScrumMaster, product owner, and technical team can all learn from these assessments.

Assessing the Daily Scrum

Table A-1 shows a template for assessing the daily Scrum. The first column consists of a list of questions. Any member of the team can answer these questions, but, in practice, the ScrumMaster is often the one who completes the checklist.

The second column indicates the ideal answer. All questions are either Yes/No (Y/N) questions or rating questions (A–F). The third column indicates how many points each answer should be given. For rating questions, the scores of the intermediate letters decline by equal increments. For example, if the third column indicates "A = 20; F = 0," then B = 16, C = 12, D = 8, and E = 4.

The fourth column contains coaching notes. The fifth column stores the answers to the questions. You should add new date columns as needed.

 You should post this template on the SharePoint site and complete it every day. Your team can discuss the results during the retrospective meeting.

TABLE A-1: The Daily Scrum Assessment Template

	IDEAL ANSWER	SCORE	COACHING NOTES	2/7/2011
Is the meeting held? (Y/N)	Y	Y = 20; N = 0		
Does the meeting start on time? (Y/N)	Y	Y = 10; N = 0		
Does the meeting end on time? (Y/N)	Y	Y = 10; N = 0		
Does the team follow its charter? (A–F)	A	A = 20; F = 0	F = The team does not have a charter	
Do the team members stand up? (Y/N)	Y	Y = 10; N = 0		
Do all team members speak? (Y/N)	Y	Y = 20; N = 0		
Do all team members show up on time? (Y/N)	Y	Y = 20; N = 0		
Do the team members self-organize? (A–F)	A	A = 20; F = 0	F = The ScrumMaster has to prompt people to speak	
Do the team members answer the three questions? (A–F)	A	A = 20; F = 0	A = Every team member answers the three questions and does nothing else	
Are all team members prepared to answer the three questions? (A–F)	A	A = 20; F = 0		
Do the team members problem solve? (A–F)	A	A = 20; F = 0	A = Team does not problem solve	

	IDEAL ANSWER	SCORE	COACHING NOTES	2/7/2011
Does the team use the task board? (Y/N)	Y	Y = 20; N = 0		
Are all communication methods (Skype, videoconference, etc.) working? (A–F)	A	A = 20; F = 0		
Do people who are not on the team participate? (Y/N)	N	Y = 0; N = 10		

Assessing the Demo

Table A-2 shows a template for assessing demos. The first column consists of a list of questions. Any member of the team can answer these questions, but, in practice, the ScrumMaster is often the one who completes the checklist.

The second column indicates the ideal answer. All questions are either Yes/No (Y/N) questions or rating questions (A–F). The third column indicates how many points each answer should be given. For rating questions, the scores of the intermediate letters decline by equal increments. For example, if the third column indicates "A = 20; F = 0," then B = 16, C = 12, D = 8, and E = 4. The fourth column contains coaching notes.

TABLE A-2: The Demo Meeting Assessment Template

	IDEAL ANSWER	SCORE	COACHING NOTES
Is the meeting held? (Y/N)	Y	Y = 20; N = 0	
Does the meeting start on time? (Y/N)	Y	Y = 10; N = 0	
Does the meeting end on time? (Y/N)	Y	Y = 10; N = 0	
Does the team follow its charter? (A–F)	A	A = 30; F = 0	
Does the team demo only completed user stories? (A–F)	A	A = 50; F = 0	
Does everyone agree on the definition of *done*? (Y/N)	Y	A = 30; F = 0	
Are finished user stories shippable? (Y/N)	Y	Y = 50; N = 0	In special cases, a story may not be shippable.
Do people who are not on the team speak? (Y/N)	N	Y = 0; N = 20	

Assessing the Retrospective

Table A-3 shows a template for assessing the retrospective. The first column consists of a list of questions. Any member of the team can answer these questions, but, in practice, the ScrumMaster is often the one who completes the checklist.

The second column indicates the ideal answer. All questions are either Yes/No (Y/N) questions or rating questions (A–F). The third column indicates how many points each answer should be given. For rating questions, the scores of the intermediate letters decline by equal increments. For example, if the third column indicates "A = 20; F = 0," then B = 16, C = 12, D = 8, and E = 4. The fourth column contains coaching notes.

TABLE A-3: The Retrospective Meeting Assessment Template

	IDEAL ANSWER	SCORE	COACHING NOTES
Is the meeting held? (Y/N)	Y	Y = 20; N = 0	
Does the meeting start on time? (Y/N)	Y	Y = 10; N = 0	
Does the meeting end on time? (Y/N)	Y	Y = 10; N = 0	
Does the team follow its charter? (A–F)	A	A = 30; F = 0	
Do all team members attend the meeting? (Y/N)	Y	Y = 20; N = 0	
Does the team create action plans to remove impediments? (Y/N)	Y	Y = 50; N = 0	
Does the team only answer the what went well/what went poorly/what do we want to improve questions? (Y/N)	N	Y = 0; N = 30	An elite team will dig deep to understand the root causes of specific problems.
Do people who are not on the team attend the meeting? (Y/N)	N	Y = 0; N = 30	

Assessing the Planning Meeting

Table A-4 shows a template for assessing the planning meeting. The first column consists of a list of questions. Any member of the team can answer these questions but, in practice, the ScrumMaster is often the one who completes the checklist.

The second column indicates the ideal answer. All questions are either Yes/No (Y/N) questions or rating questions (A–F). The third column indicates how many points each answer should be given. For rating questions, the scores of the intermediate letters decline by equal increments. For example, if the third column indicates "A = 20; F = 0," then B = 16, C = 12, D = 8, and E = 4.

TABLE A-4: The Planning Meeting Assessment Template

	IDEAL ANSWER	SCORE
Is the meeting held? (Y/N)	Y	Y = 50; N = 0
Does the meeting start on time? (Y/N)	Y	Y = 10; N = 0
Does the meeting end on time? (Y/N)	Y	Y = 10; N = 0
Does the team follow its charter? (A–F)	A	A = 20; F = 0
Does the product owner attend the meeting? (Y/N)	Y	Y = 50; N = 0
Does every team member attend the meeting? (Y/N)	Y	Y = 50; N = 0
Are the user stories prioritized? (Y/N)	Y	Y = 30; N = 0
Does each user story have acceptance tests? (Y/N)	Y	Y = 30; N = 0
Does everyone involved understand the definition of *done*? (Y/N)	Y	Y = 30; N = 0
Does everyone know the start date of the sprint? (Y/N)	Y	Y = 30; N = 0
Does everyone know the end date of the sprint? (Y/N)	Y	Y = 30; N = 0

A SAMPLE ASSESSMENT

This section contains a sample assessment that is based on an actual assessment provided to a client. Note that client assessments are not just copies of the assessments provided in the previous section. They contain analysis and suggestions.

Planning Meeting Assessment

The planning meeting took place on February 1, 2011, from 10 A.M. to 1 P.M., in the Sodium conference room. The meeting was attended by:

➤ **Product owner** — Ben Bitdiddle

➤ **ScrumMaster** — Alex Agile

➤ **Technical team** — Chris Code, Bill Bug, Sally Subversion, and Mary Map

➤ **Attendees who are not on the team** — Rick Rooster, Ed Executive

Problems:

➤ The meeting started seven minutes late.

➤ Breaks were not clearly identified.

➤ The team did not create a sprint goal.

➤   The ScrumMaster failed to effectively facilitate the meeting.

➤   Team members repeatedly entered into side conversations.

➤   All the team members did not participate in estimating every story.

➤   The team members in India were not included in the discussion.

➤   Leftover user stories from the previous sprint were not prioritized.

➤   The team did not use its velocity to determine how many stories to accept into the sprint.

➤   The team didn't use the Team Foundation Server Scrum template effectively.

Suggestions:

➤   The ScrumMaster should prepare a planning meeting checklist and follow that checklist.

➤   The product owner must attend the planning meeting, with an appropriately groomed backlog.

➤   All leftover stories from the previous sprint must be prioritized before the planning meeting.

➤   The team should agree to a sprint goal and publish it.

➤   The team should videotape the meeting.

➤   Every team member should estimate every user story.

➤   The team should use its velocity to cap the amount of work it takes into the sprint.

➤   Every member of the team should buy this book and study it.

Daily Scrum Assessment

The daily Scrum took place on February 2, 2011, from 10:00 A.M. to 10:15 A.M. in the Potassium conference room. The meeting was attended by:

➤   **Product owner** — Ben Bitdiddle

➤   **ScrumMaster** — Alex Agile

➤   **Technical team** — Chris Code, Bill Bug, Sally Subversion, and Mary Map

➤   **Attendees who are not on the team** — Rick Rooster, Ed Executive

Problems:

➤   Attendees who are not on the team spoke repeatedly.

➤   Impediments were not recorded.

➤   Team members tried to solve problems.

➤   The meeting started eight minutes late.

➤   The meeting ended four minutes late.

➤   The team did not use the task board.

Suggestions:

> ➤ The daily Scrum should begin and end on time.
>
> ➤ The team members should answer the three questions and only the three questions.
>
> ➤ The team should clearly identify that the meeting is over.

Demo Meeting Assessment

The demo meeting took place on January 31, 2011, from 10 A.M. to 11 A.M. in the Mercury conference room. The meeting was attended by:

> ➤ **Product owner** — Ben Bitdiddle
>
> ➤ **ScrumMaster** — Alex Agile
>
> ➤ **Technical team** — Chris Code, Bill Bug, Sally Subversion, and Mary Map
>
> ➤ **Attendees who are not on the team** — Rick Rooster, Ed Executive

Problems:

> ➤ The team was not prepared to demo.
>
> ➤ The projector was not set up before the meeting.
>
> ➤ The product owner arrived late.
>
> ➤ The team demonstrated partially completed work.

Suggestions:

> ➤ The ScrumMaster should set up the room 15 minutes before the meeting.
>
> ➤ The ScrumMaster should provide the team with a template for the demo. Here is a suggested template:
>
>> ➤ Slide 1: Start and end times of meeting
>>
>> ➤ Slide 2: Meeting participants: Identify team members
>>
>> ➤ Slide 3: The team's demo charter
>>
>> ➤ Slide 4: User story 1: Include the story points assigned to this story and the business value, if available
>>
>> ➤ Slide 5: User story 2
>>
>> ➤ Slide 6: User story 3
>
> ➤ The ScrumMaster should coach the team through the demo.
>
> ➤ The product owner will be required to wear a pink hat at the next planning meeting as a reminder not to be late.

Retrospective Meeting Assessment

The retrospective meeting took place on January 31, 2011, from 11 A.M. to 2 P.M. in the Mercury conference room. The meeting was attended by:

➤ **Product owner** — Ben Bitdiddle

➤ **ScrumMaster** — Alex Agile

➤ **Technical team** — Chris Code, Bill Bug, Sally Subversion, and Mary Map

➤ **Attendees who are not on the team** — Rick Rooster, Ed Executive

Problems:

➤ The comments were superficial.

➤ The team did not create action plans.

➤ The meeting started late.

➤ Lunch was not provided.

Suggestions:

➤ The team should consider using the 5 Whys technique to uncover the root cause of a problem.

➤ The ScrumMaster should prepare a list of detailed questions prior to the meeting and step the team through the questions. Here are some examples:

  ➤ What user stories were not estimated well? Why were the estimates too high or too low?

  ➤ Why did the release not go as planned? Should we assign a release master?

  ➤ Who is on the team? Why do we have people who participate in our meetings but do not work on our backlog?

➤ Lunch should be provided. If that is not possible, have a 12-pack of Jolt cola in all meeting rooms.

➤ Because the meeting started late, everyone should wear pink hats during all of the next sprint.

WORKING WITH CHECKLISTS

For beginning product owners and ScrumMasters, knowing what to prioritize is critical. A checklist can help focus attention on the highest-value objectives. The following sections provide checklists for product owners and ScrumMasters. You can use these checklists as a basis for creating your own checklists.

A Checklist for the Product Owner

The product owner is critical to a team's success. The team might be able to create software quickly, but if it is the wrong software, the organization will fail.

Table A-5 provides a checklist for a product owner to use throughout a sprint. The questions in the Question column help a product owner determine whether he or she is focusing on the correct objectives. The suggestions listed in the Techniques column can help drive the answers to the questions in the right direction.

A Checklist for the ScrumMaster

A ScrumMaster is a coach and leader servant. The ScrumMaster assists a team in becoming better and better at Scrum. Table A-6 provides a checklist for a ScrumMaster to use throughout a sprint. The questions in the Question column help a ScrumMaster determine whether he or she is focusing on the correct objectives. The suggestions listed in the Techniques column can help drive the ScrumMaster and the team in the right direction.

Some of the questions and techniques in Table A-5 and Table A-6 may not apply in your situation. Simply delete any such items from the checklist and create your own.

TABLE A-5: The Product Owner's Checklist

QUESTION	ANSWER	TECHNIQUES
Does the team understand each story in the sprint backlog?		Visit each team member once a week, ask what he or she is working on, and ask for a quick demo.
Do you hold office hours every day?		
Do you get the team's input on the backlog?		Pair with an architect or a senior developer on critical backlog items.
Does each backlog item meet the Independent, Negotiable, Valuable, Estimable, Small, and Testable (INVEST) standards?		Track how many user stories the team rejects or modifies during the planning meeting.
How does the team think you performed during the last sprint?		
Do you exchange information with other product owners in the company?		Work with another product owner on creating a backlog at least once per release.
Do you examine the burndown chart?		Suggest to the team members that they look at the burndown chart during the daily Scrum.
Do you introduce new user stories during the sprint?		Track how many user stories you add during a sprint and see how this influences velocity.
Are you adjusting the release backlog based on the team's velocity?		Create a well-oiled technique for calculating how many story points the release backlog should have.
Is the team excited about building the product?		Ask the team members if they would be willing to recommend the product to their friends.
Are you relentlessly focused on creating a backlog that defines the minimum viable, usable, and feasible product?		Constantly ask yourself what you would cut if the team's velocity dropped by 10%. If you can live with what you cut, then cut it and ship earlier.
Do you validate the business value when the product ships?		For every user story, calculate the actual business value received when the product ships and compare it to your estimated business value.

TABLE A-6: The ScrumMaster's Checklist

QUESTION	ANSWER	TECHNIQUES
Have all team members agreed wholeheartedly to do Scrum?		Have the team sign a large poster that reads "I want to do Scrum." Hang this poster in a highly visible location.
Does the team have a charter for the daily Scrum, the demo, the retrospective, and the planning meeting?		List the key points in the charter, using short phrases (e.g., "No side conversations") and place this list in the meeting room.
Does the team have a great programming environment?		If the team is having a problem performing any basic task (e.g., building the system or running automated tests), realize that you must remove this impediment.
Do you have an impediments list?		At each daily Scrum, require each team member to share at least one impediment. Keep a prioritized list of all impediments.
Are you always removing impediments?		Make a commitment to the team to remove at least one impediment per sprint.
Does the team stay on the sprint backlog?		Calculate a "focus" metric that shows what percentage of a team's effort is on backlog items.
Are team members constantly improving their skills?		Keep track of how many technical breakthroughs the team experiences per sprint.
Is the team's truck factor greater than one?		Create a chart that shows how many team members can work in each area.

B

References

There are many good books and helpful websites on Agile development and Scrum. These texts and sites transcend the tools, covering what to do, when to do it, how to do it, and with whom. In writing *Professional Scrum with Team Foundation Server 2010*, we used a number of sources to compare our ideas with those of others. You can find many good approaches and solutions in the following sources:

Berkun, Scott. *Making Things Happen: Mastering Project Management*. O'Reilly, 2008.

Cohn, Mike. *Agile Estimating and Planning*. Prentice Hall, 2006.

Cohn, Mike. *Succeeding with Agile: Software Development Using Scrum*. Addison-Wesley, 2010.

Cohn, Mike. *User Stories Applied for Agile Software Development*. Addison-Wesley, 2004.

Gousset, Mickey, Brian Keller, Ajoy Krishnamoorthy, and Martin Woodward. *Professional Application Lifecycle Management with Visual Studio 2010*. Wiley, 2010.

Krishnamoorthy, Ajoy. *Agile Planning Tools in Visual Studio Team System 2010*. http://msdn.microsoft.com/en-us/magazine/dd347827.aspx.

McCarthy, Jim. *Dynamics of Software Development*. Microsoft Press, 1995.

McCarthy, Jim, and Michele McCarthy. *Software for Your Head: Core Protocols for Creating and Maintaining Shared Vision*. Addison-Wesley, 2002.

Pichler, Roman. *Agile Product Management with Scrum: Creating Products That Customers Love*. Addison-Wesley, 2010.

Schwaber, Ken. *Agile Project Management with Scrum*. Microsoft Press, 2004.

Schwaber, Ken. *The Enterprise and Scrum*. Microsoft Press, 2007.

Smith, Greg, and Ahmed Sidky. *Becoming Agile in an Imperfect World*. Manning Publications Co., 2009.

Sutherland, Jeff. *Agile Principles and Values*. http://msdn.microsoft.com/library/dd997578.aspx.

INDEX